INDIA'S BILLION PLUS PE

2001 CENSUS HIGHLIGHTS, METHODOLOGY AND MEDIA COVERAGE

INDIA'S BILLION PLUS PEOPLE

2001 CENSUS HIGHLIGHTS, METHODOLOGY AND MEDIA COVERAGE

ASHISH BOSE

Assisted by

Anita Haldar
Mohan Singh Bist
Ajay Pandey

B.R. Publishing Corporation
[A Division of BRPC (India) Ltd.]
Delhi-110035

Distributed by :

BRPC (India) Ltd.

4222/1, Ansari Road, Darya Ganj,
New Delhi-110002
Ph. : 3259196, 3259648
Fax : 3201571
E-Mail : *info@brpcltd.com*

© 2001 Ashish Bose (b 1930—)

ISBN 81-7646-227-6

Published by :

B. R. Publishing Corporation

[A Division of BRPC (India) Ltd.]
3779, 1st Floor, Kanhaiya Nagar,
Tri Nagar, Delhi-110035
Phone: 7152140
E-Mail: *info@brpcltd.com*

Laser Typeset by :

Raj Kumar

Delhi-110 035

Printed at: Unique Color Carton, New Delhi-110064.

PRINTED IN INDIA

Dedicated to

The people of India whose
resilience keeps the
country going

Summary of Contents

Preface

Acknowledgements

Organisation of the Book

Overview

PART ONE
>> About Census of India 2001

PART TWO
Demographic Profile of India/States/ UTs, 2001

PART THREE
Implications: First Thoughts on the Provisional Results of Census of India, 2001

PART FOUR
2001 Census Methodology: Definitions & Classifications

PART FIVE
Media and the 2001 Census

Preface

This is not a research monograph but a handbook for users of Indian census data and the general public. I had produced a much smaller volume in April 1991 soon after the first results of the 1991 census were released by the Census Commissioner on 25 March 1991. To quote the Preface to this book (*Population of India: 1991 Census Results and Methodology*): "The provocation for bringing out this book so hastily lies in my inability to cope with requests for exclusive interviews and popular articles for the press, commenting on the first results of the 1991 census...." The situation remains the same after a decade: the demands of the electronic and print media have increased and so also the questions posed to me on phone. There were several reprints of my little book on the 1991 census. With the increase in the literate population of India (in fact, there has been a sharp jump in the literacy rate during the last decade), a book like this is very much needed. There is, however, one major improvement this time in the dissemination of census data. The Census Commissioner for the 2001 census has, with lightning speed, brought out the first results in the form of a monograph and made it a priced publication. The user of census data has, therefore, immediate access to the provisional results of the census of 2001. The Census Commissioner (J K Banthia) deserves the gratitude of all users of census data. Even then I felt that I should go ahead with my publication which processes the 2001 census data in a user-friendly manner and gives the census methodology. Frankly, I do not find the formating of data in *Paper 1 of 2001* – very convenient : each table starts with Jammu and Kashmir and ends with Andaman and Nicobar Islands (28 states and 7 union territories). The 1991 census and earlier census practice was to put the states in *alphabetical order* followed by union territories in alphabetical order. In *Paper 1 of 2001*, there is only one table which puts the 35 states and UTs in alphabetical order (the states and UTs are not shown separately). There is however, a code for each state and UT and the code number is also the serial number in the tables. I find this as cumbersome as consulting a railway time table! I have processed and repackaged the statistical material in *Census Paper No.1 of 2001* in my own way, the details of which are discussed in the note on 'Organisation of this book'.

The practice of conducting an Economic Census along with the Population Census which was in vogue in 1991 and in earlier censuses was abandoned in 2001. The focus, therefore, is on the economic questions in the census of 2001.

One of the major issues concerns the definition of 'workers'. Time and again, women's organisations, in particular, have expressed their misgivings about the reliability of census data which record a low participation rate for women in the workforce. This has largely to do with the actual operation of the census enumeration, the way the questions are asked and the perception (including gender bias) of the census enumerator as well as the respondent. This in turn depends on the training given to the enumerators and the specific instructions recording women's work. I have, therefore, taken the liberty of reproducing at length the relevant portions dealing with economic questions from the *Instruction Manual for Enumerators* prepared by the Census Commission for the 2001 census. The user of census data must have a clear idea of the concepts, definitions and classifications adopted by the census.

In 1991, I was associated with a TV film on the census which was shown on Delhi Doordarshan. Glimpses of enumeration work all over India were shown on this film. This time the census organisation produced its own video films for training enumerators and also used radio, TV and the print media in a big way to popularise the census and inform the citizens about their responsibility in co-operating with this national endeavour. The media (print as well electronic) did not give much importance to the first results of the census of 2001 when these were released to the press by the Census Commissioner on 26 April, 2001. Unfortunately, this coincided with the Oscar Award and the national film awards which stole the limelight. Census is regarded as a dull subject by the media. Nevertheless, most newspapers and magazines did show considerable interest in the census of 2001. I have taken the liberty of putting some excerpts from news items, articles and editorials in India's leading newspapers and magazines, together after classifying the material into several sections. This will give the reader a fairly good idea about the media coverage of census. Needless to say, in view of the gravity of the population problem, constant media focus is essential for the success of our population control programmes. The electronic media, in particular, can make a dramatic impact on the minds of people. Scientific advocacy and informed public opionion can contribute greatly to the success of our population policy announced in February 2000.

Much before the 2001 census was actually conducted I had occasion to speak on census methodology on several occasions all over India, notably at the Indian Statistical Institute, Calcutta, International Institute for Population Sciences, Bombay, and at the last annual conference of the Indian Association for the Study of Population, Vishakhapatnam (22 February, 2001) where I delivered the George Simmons Memorial Lecture, and other forums like the International Conference on Statistics organised by the International Indian Statistical Association where I spoke on 'Census of India, 2001, Vision and Strategy' (New Delhi 1st January, 2001). I also wrote on census of 2001 for *Economic and Political Weekly* and *Yojana*. I have included in this book articles from these journals but not my other papers on Census which would have made this book bulky. This book is directed at the general reader and not to researchers.

I wish to express my gratitude to the Census Commissioner, Mr. J K Banthia, IAS, for his unfailing help and co-operation, all through my work on this book.

My research and computer associates, Anita Haldar, Mohan Singh Bist and Ajay Pandey have worked sincerely and put in their best efforts to bring out this book speedily. Anita took the responsibility of scanning the newspapers and magazines and preparing Part V of this book (Media and the 2001 Census), apart from preparing graphs and charts. The bulk of computational work was done by Mohan Singh and Anita. Ajay joined me recently and was associated mostly with processing the material for publication. All of them deserve my special thanks.

Without the help of my wife, Manjula, and her constant logistical support, I could not have completed this book within three weeks after the release of the first results of the census. This meant added strain on her. She deserves full credit for her *sthitadhi* stance and ungrudging support. Much to our delight, our sons Joydeep and Pradeep came from the USA on a very short visit to cheer us up. My task of compiling census statistics became less tedious. The computer floppy and my dog Loppy gave me constant company, much to my joy.

New Delhi
21 April, 2001

Ashish Bose

Acknowledgements

My earlier book on *1991 Census Results and Methodology* (1991) was dedicated to Asok Mitra, "whose outstanding contribution to Indian census inspired me in my research career". He passed way two years back and I am deprived of the opportunity of giving the first copy of this book to him. I pay homage to his memory. As the Census Commissioner for 1961 Census, he had thrown open his doors to scholars and researchers. Since then, his successors have continued this tradition.

My constant interaction with leading scholars and experts in the field of population has been of great help to me in my academic activities. In particular, I wish to thank the following:

Mr. A. R. Nanda, Secretary, Department of Family Welfare, Government of India (who was the Census Commissioner in 1991).

Mr. J. K. Banthia, Registrar General and Census Commissioner (for 2001 Census). Also the staff of the Office of Registrar General with some of whom I have interacted for the last four decades, in particular :

Dr. Minati Ghosh, Deputy Registrar General, Mr. S. K. Sinha, Deputy Registrar General, Mr. R. G. Mitra, Deputy Registrar General.

Professor B. K. Roy Burman (formerly Deputy Registrar General).

Dr. S. P. Gupta, Member, Planning Commission, New Delhi.

Professor J. K. Ghosh, Jawaharlal Nehru Professor, Indian Statistical Institute, Calcutta.

Professor Samir Guha Roy, ISI, Calcutta.

Dr. K. Srinivasan, Executive Director, Population Foundation of India.

Professor M. K. Premi (formerly with JNU).

Professor Sudesh Nangia, JNU, New Delhi.

Professor Murali Dhar Vemuri, JNU, New Delhi.

Dr. B. Zutshi, JNU.

Mr. R. P. Tyagi, Institute of Economic Growth, Delhi, and other colleagues at the Population Research Centre, Institute of Economic Growth.

Dr. T. K Roy, Director, International Institute for Population Sciences, Bombay.

Professor Sharit Bhowmik, Department of Sociology, Bombay University, Bombay.

Mr. Krishna Raj, Editor, *Economic and Political Weekly*, Bombay.

Professor Ramprasad Sengupta, Indian Institute of Management, Calcutta.

Professor K. B. Sahay, IIT, New Delhi.

Dr. K. C. Seal, formerly, Director General, Central Statistical Organisation, New Delhi.

Dr. Vina Mazumdar, Chairperson, Central for Women's Development Studies, New Delhi.

Ms. Usha Rai, Press Institute of India, New Delhi.

Mr. Alok Mukhopadhyaya, Executive Director, Voluntary Health Association of India, New Delhi.

Mr. Mahadeb Pakrasi, Editor, *Yojana.*

Dr. O.P Vig, Society for Applied Research in Humanities, New Delhi.

Dr. Rafiqual Huda Choudhury, UNFPA, Kathmandu.

Dr. Almas Ali, UNFPA, Consultant in Ministry of Health and Family Welfare, New Delhi.

Mr. Deepak Gupta, UNFPA, New Delhi.

Mr. Ashit Mitra, Kassar Trust, Pondicherry and Mankote (Uttaranchal).

Mr. R. S. Tolia, Principal Secretary, Dehra Dun (Uttaranchal).

Mr. Nisheeth Kumar, Deputy Director, UP Academy of Administration, Nainital.

Thanks are due to Mr. Rashpal Malhotra, Founder Director, Centre for Research in Rural and Industrial Development (CRRID), Chandigarh for making available to me computer facilities at my home during my tenure as visiting professor with CRRID.

Finally, I wish to record my appreciation of the keen interest of several outstanding media persons (both print and electronic) who gave me the opportunity of expressing my views on population issues. It was a delight to interact with persons like Mark Tully, Daniel Lac, Dileep Padgaonkar, Usha Rai, Lalita Panicker, Soma Wadhwa, Rajdeep Sardesai, to mention just a few media personalities.

Ashish Bose

Organisation of the Book

The main object of this book is to present in a user-friendly manner, the first results of the Census of 2001, released by the Census Commissioner, discusses briefly the methodological aspects of the census, in particular, the definition of 'worker', and give a quick analysis of the data to bring out the implications for planners and policymakers.

The Overview gives the highlights of the 2001 census operation as well as the highlights of the first results of the census and then proceeds to point out the most dismal finding, namely, a sharp decline in the sex ratio of the child population (0-6 years) in states like Punjab, Haryana, Himachal Pradesh and Gujarat which we call DEMARU (daughter-killer) states.

Part one is about the 2001 Census and gives details about the houselisting operation in 2000 and the questionnaire canvassed in February 2001 during the enumeration. The questionnaires are reproduced in full in the Appendixes to Part I. The new features of the 2001 census are also briefly mentioned.

Part two presents the data culled out from the Provisional Totals (*Paper 1 of 2001*) published by the Registrar General which we shall call the 'Blue Book'. The data presented in the Blue Book are not user-friendly, nor the graphs and charts. The states and UTs are put in some sort of geographical order, starting from Jammu & Kashmir and ending with Andaman & Nicobar Islands. We have processed and re-arranged the data. Since we consider population size as the most important variable in demographic analysis, we have grouped the 28 states and 7 UTs in the following three categories:

A. Mega States (9)

(population : Over 50 million and more than 5 per cent of India's total population)

Uttar Pradesh, Maharashtra, Bihar, West Bengal, Andhra Pradesh, Tamil Nadu, Madhya Pradesh, Rajasthan, Karnataka

B. Bigger States/UTs (10)

(population : Over 10 million and more than 1 per cent of India's total population)

Gujarat, Orissa, Kerala, Jharkhand, Assam, Punjab, Haryana, Chhatisgarh, Delhi NCT, Jammu & Kashmir

C. Smaller States/UTs (16)

(population : Less than 10 million and less than 1 per cent of India's total population)

Uttaranchal , Himachal Pradesh, Tripura, Manipur, Meghalaya, Nagaland, Goa, Pondicherry UT, Chandigarh UT, Mizoram, Arunachal Pradesh, Sikkim, Andaman & Nicobar Islands, Dadra & Nagar Haveli UT, Daman & Diu UT, Lakshadweep UT.

At the second stage, we have classified the states and UTs in 11 categories, depending on the unique characteristics of these states. While doing this, we have taken note of the latest vital statistics based on SRS data released by the Registrar General. The groupings are as follows:

I.   Demographic Profile of India
II.   BIMARU States
III.   Offshoots of BIMARU States (three new states)
IV.   Southern States
V.   Jammu & Kashmir
VI.   North Western States
VII.   Western India/UTs
VIII. North-Eastern States
IX.   West Bengal
X.   Orissa
XI.   Islands

The Census papers giving the provisional totals in each state are not yet available. These papers give districtwise data. We had access to such data for all the DEMARU states and we have included these data in Part two. We must await the publication of all the State/UT Census Papers for the 2001 Census giving provisional tables, districtwise figures.

Part Three presents in brief some implications of the census data presented in Part two. In particular, we have discussed the dominant role of BIMARU states and the perverse role of DEMARU states.

Part four gives detailed excerpts from the manual of instructions for enumerators for the 2001 census. Our focus is on the concept of 'workers' in Indian census methodology. The gross underestimation of the number of women workers and the low participation rate of women workers in the labour force in states like Punjab are issues which merit discussion on the methodology of census taking, concepts and definitions, the way the questions are asked by the enumerators, the perception of women's work on the part of respondents and enumerators and so on. After the 1991 census results were published in detail, at the instance of UNIFEM several surveys and studies were initiated and reports prepared by scholars commissioned by the Indian Association of the Study of Population and Society for Applied Research in Humanities. In the absence of 2001 census data on workers, it is too early to comment on women's economic activity as reflected in this census. The 2001 Census Commissioner did take several steps to ensure a better quality of enumeration of women workers. The data should reveal to what extent he succeeded in doing this.

Part five is a special feature of this book: it gives an idea of coverage of census by the print media. It will take years before detailed tables are available to scholars and experts and a few more years before books are written on the dynamics of population based on 2001 census. Scholarly articles in journals also take years before these are published. On the other hand, newspapers, magazines, and semi-technical journals publish quick responses from scholars and experts as well as interviews with them. The electronic media does it even faster. As we have pointed out, the most dismal aspect of the 2001 census results is the decline in the sex ratio of child population (0-6 age group) all over India (except in Kerala and some smaller states). The widespread recourse to foeticide must be the most important factor which can explain this phenomenon. Demographers no matter how good they are in Statistics, cannot throw much light on this unless they do field work and this takes time and money Journalists are in a better position to go to the field and report on grassroots reality. We have, therefore, a whole section in Part five devoted to reports of field investigations and articles and editorials on this subject. The Akal Takht has taken the lead in condemning female foeticide, particularly among the Sikhs. This is a step in the right direction and we hope that other religious organisations and social reformers will come forward to check the perverse practice of foeticide.

Overview

The decennial census of 2001 is in the 21st century and deserves special attention. India is poised to emerge as a world political and economic power and has the potential to be a world leader in information technology. The census is the most important signle source of information on the life of the people of India. To give an idea of the census operation which is a gigantic administrative exercise, comparable to the conduct of general elections in India, we highlight a few facts below about the 2001 census.

➢ Most comprehensive census operation in the world

➢ Second largest census. enumeration in the history of census-taking in the world

➢ House numbering and houselisting operation carried out from April to September, 2000

➢ Population enumeration undertaken between 9 to 28 February 2001 (both days inclusive); revisional round from 1 to 5 March 2001

➢ 2 million enumerators

➢ 220 million households covered

➢ 1027 million persons counted in

➢ 28 States

➢ 7 Union Territories

➢ 5564 tahsils/talukas

➢ 640,000 villages

➢ 5161 towns and cities

➢ In Jammu & Kashmir, unlike in 1991 when the census enumeration did not take place, in 2001, Jammu & Kashmir was covered and the actual census figures included in the all India total (in 1991 the estimated population of Jammu & Kashmir was considered)

➢ Reference date : 00.00 hours on 1st March 2001

> Provisional Tables released with lightning speed on 26 March 2001 by Jayanta Kumar Banthia, IAS, Registrar General & Census Commissioner, in the form of *Census of India 2001, Series - I INDIA, Provisional Population Totals, Paper 1 of 2001* (Price Rs. 115)

We may also highlight a few other administrative details about this Census :

> Census schedules were printed in 16 languages and the Manual in 18 languages.

> About 7,000 metric tonnes of paper were consumed in printing various Census schedules.

> Training of Census officers in the Directorate of Census Operations in each state started in October 1999.

> District Collector/Municipal Commissioner was the principal Census Officer in each district. The charge officers were Tahsildars, Block Development Officers and Executive Officers of municipalities.

> A team of trainers called 'Master Trainers' was created to give training to enumerators and supervisors. These Master Trainers were selected from principals, lecturers and government officers.

> Video films, audio-cassettes, overhead projectors and power point presentations were used for imparting training.

> Census Help Centres abd Census Help Lines/Telephone Help Lines were established for the first time to give assistance to enumerators and also register complaints from the public. In rural areas, Help Centres were opened at Tahsil/Taluka/Block headquarters.

> Slum Enumeration Blocks were identified for the first time at this Census, in each town or city having a population of 50,000 and above.

> A system of Permanent Location Code Number (PLCN) was intoduced for the first time and each village/ward of town or city was assigned an eight digit code. Thus each administrative area in any geographical region was uniquely identified. This will help in ensuring comparability of data in future censuses and help in tracking jurisdictional changes in villages/towns.

> A special postage stamp was released to commemorate the Census of 2001.

> Newspapers, radio and TV networks as well as postal and other public uitility stationeries were used in seeking co-operation for the Census enumeration.

> A census logo with the motto 'people-oriented' was introduced by the Census organisation.

Census Paper 1 of 2001 : Provisional Population Totals

Census Paper 1 of 2001 : PROVISIONAL POPULATION TOTALS, issued by the Registrar General and Census Commissioner in the series CENSUS OF INDIA 2001 SERIES -1 : INDIA, New Delhi, March 26, 2001. Pages 184, Price Rs. 115.

A new feature of the 2001 Census is access to provisional census data through a priced publication. In earlier censuses, provisional figures were available only to a restricted number of persons.

The provisional tables relate to the following characteristics of the population:

➢ Size and distribution of population between States/UT

➢ Density

➢ Sex ratio

➢ Literacy rate

➢ Growth rate

➢ Comparision with population projections

The following may also be noted :

➢ No rural/urban breakdown available

➢ No age distribution: except for 0-6 & 7+ age groups

➢ No data on workforce

➢ Adjusted data (for 1991) for the truncated states of Bihar, Madhya Pradesh & Uttar Pradesh and for the new States Jharkhand, Chhatisgarh and Uttaranchal are given

➢ Data for states/UTs presented according to geographical regions and not in an alphabetical order, as was the practice in earlier censuses.

The most remarkable aspect of *Paper I of 2001* is the speed with which this publication was brought out: the census enumeration took place from 9 February to 28 February, with 00.00 hours of 1st March as the reference date, and the revisional round was over on 5 March, 2001. Thus the provisional figures were published in just three weeks. No developed country can match this performance. In India this is possible because of a combination of manual tabulation and use of computers, fax and e-mail. The two million census enumerators added up the number of males and females, literates and illiterates and population in the age group 0-6 years every night and on the last day, conveyed the figures to the supervisors who in turn passed on the figures to the charge officers and so on till the chain ended in the Registrar General's Office in New Delhi. For conducting this gigantic census, the second biggest operation in the world, full credit must be given to the Census Commissioner and his staff in New Delhi and all states and union territories and above all, to the two million enumerators who conducted the census successfully. It is inevitable that in such a massive headcount some persons are missed out. To get an estimate of underenumeration, a separate post census enumeration sample survey is conducted. This reveals extent of underenumeration. In Part three, we have discussed, the question of accuracy of the Indian Census and presented the relevant material from the post census enumeration survey conducted after the 1991 census enumeration was over. The results of such a survey for the 2001 census will be known in due time.

Census coverage

As already noted, the 2001 census covered the whole of India : 28 States, 7 Union Territories, 5,564 tahsils/talukas, 640,000 villages and 5,161 towns and cities.

It may be noted that in 1991 the census enumeration could not take place in Jammu & Kashmir. In 2001 the census enumeration did take place in Jammu & Kashmir in spite of the threat from militants. Another important aspect to be noted is that 2001 census data are available for the three newly formed states of Jharkhand, Chhatisgarh and Uttaranchal. The data are adjusted for previous census years (1991, 1981 etc) in order to enable the user to study past trends.

Highlights of the first results

➢ The population of India on the 1st March 2001 was 1027 million (102.7 crores). This includes the population of Jammu & Kashmir where the 1991 census could not be conducted while the enumeration was done in 2001.

➢ In the last decade (1991-2001) the population of India increased by 181 million.

➢ In percentage terms, the decadal growth rate was 21.3 per cent compared to 23.9 per cent during the previous decade (1981-91).

➢ The decline in the decadal growth rate was 2.5 per cent points during 1991-2001 decade.

➢ Bihar recorded the highest decadal growth rate, which in fact increased from 23.4 per cent to 28.4 per cent.

➢ Andhra Pradesh recorded the sharpest decline in the decadal growth rate : 13.9 per cent during 1991-2001 compared to 24.2 per cent during 1981-1991 or a decline of 10.3 per cent points.

➢ The lowest growth rate was recorded by Kerala (9.4 per cent) followed by Tamil Nadu (11.2 per cent) and Andhra Pradesh (13.9 per cent).

➢ Uttar Pradesh even after the new state of Uttaranchal was carved out in 2000, continues to be the most populous state in India with a population of 166 million (Uttaranchal population is 8.5 million). Thus Uttar Pradesh as of 1991 has a population of 175 million in 2001.

➢ Uttar Pradesh has 16.2 per cent of India's population followed by Maharashtra (9.4 per cent) and Bihar 8.0 per cent.

➢ The density of India is 324 per sq km. in 2001 compared to 267 in 1991 or an increase of 57 during the last ten years.

➢ West Bengal has the highest density (904) followed by Bihar (880).

➢ The sex ratio (females per 1000 males) is 933 in 2001 compared to 927 in 1991, or an increase by 6 points during the last decade.

➢ Kerala has the highest sex ratio (1058) and Haryana the lowest (861).

➢ The child sex ratio (0-6 age group) was 927 in 2001 compared to 945 in 1991 or a decline by 18 points.

➢ The sharpest decline in the sex ratio of the child population was in Punjab, Haryana, Himachal Pradesh, Uttaranchal, Gujarat and Maharashtra.

➢ The literacy rate (for population 7 years and over) was 65.4 per cent in 2001. The male literacy rate was 75.9 per cent and the female literacy rate was 54.2 per cent.

➢ Compared to 1991 the overall literacy rate increased by 13.2 percentage points (52.2 in 1991 to 65.4 in 2001). The increase in the male and female literacy rate were 11.7 and 14.9 percentage points respectively.

➢ The gap between male and female literacy rates has decreased from 28.8 percentage points in 1991 to 21.7 in 2001.

➢ For the first time since independence there has been an absolute decline in the number of illiterate persons : the number of illiterates declined by 32 million during the last decade. Among males the number declined by 21.5 million and among females by 10.5 million.

➢ The literacy rate was highest in Kerala (90.9 per cent) and lowest in Bihar (47.5 per cent)

India is the second most populous country in the world, with a population of 1027 million (on 1st March 2001) compared to China which had a population of 1,278 million (on 1st February 2000).

Dismal aspects of census results: Sharp fall in sex ratio of children (0-6 age group)

We shall confine our comments to the most alarming finding, namely, the sharp decline in the female/male ratio (called sex ratio in the census to denote the number of females per thousand males), among the children in the 0 to 6 age group, in the face of an increase in the sex ratio of the total population. Let us quote a few figures. In 1991 the sex ratio for the total population was 927 (females per thousand males); it increased to 933 in 2001, an increase of 6 points. In contrast, the sex ratio of the child population (0-6 age group) which was 945 in 1991 *decreased* to 927, a decrease of 18 points. One more figure will give a clue to the increase in the overall sex ratio. If we consider the population aged 7 years and over, the sex ratio works out to 923 in 1991, and it increased to 935 in 2001, an increase of 12 points. In short, the girl child (below 6 years) has lost out badly in spite of numerous projects and programmes, seminars and conferences focusing attention on the girl child for over a decade. It would be wrong to think that the 2001 figure is a freak. In fact, the decline in the sex ratio of the child population is a secular trend. In 1961, the sex ratio in the 0-6 age group was 976, it declined to 964 in 1971, 962 in 1981 and 945 in 1991. But the sharpest decline has been during 1991-2001: But what is alarming about the 2001 census data is the drastic decline in Punjab, Haryana, Himachal Pradesh, Gujarat and also in Chandigarh and Delhi. Let us look at the figures.

In Punjab, the sex ratio (0-6 age group) declined from 875 to 793 (a decrease of 82 points), in Haryana from 879 to 820 (-59 points) in Himachal Pradesh from 951 to 897 (-54 points), in Gujarat from 928 to 878 (-50 points), in Chandigarh from 899 to 845 (-54 points) and in Delhi from 915 to 865 (-50 points).

Migration cannot explain this phenomenon which must be the consequence of female foeticide on a massive scale if not female infanticide and higher female child mortality rates. The Census Commissioner rightly observes in his report: "One thing is clear - the imbalance that has set in at this early age group is difficult to be removed and would remain to haunt the population for a long time to come. To say the least, demographically the sex ratio of 927 of the population in the age group 0-6 does not appear to augur well for the future of the country" (p 96).

In 1980s we had classified the demographically backward states as BIMARU states (Bihar, Madhya Pradesh, Rajasthan and Uttar Pradesh), an acronym which is now generally accepted. The 2001 census results fully validate our diagnosis of India's population problem in terms of the adverse role of these four BIMARU states. In fact, the situation has worsened. In Bihar, for example, the decadal growth rate of population has *increased* from 23.4 per cent during 1981-91 to 28.4 per cent during 1991-2001.

To take note of the alarming data from 2001 census , we would like to coin another acronym - DEMARU where D stands for daughters and 'MARU' stands for killing. In English 'E' will denote 'elimination'. On the basis of a statistical cutoff point of 50 points decline in the juvenile sex ratio, we would classify Punjab, Haryana, Himachal Pradesh and Gujarat as DEMARU states.

According to a UNI report (April 18) 'Akal Takht Jathedar Joginder Singh Vedanti' has notified the Sikh community that "acts of female foeticide were violative of Sikh principles and that offenders would be excommunicated". This is a good move. But what will Gujarat and Maharashtra do? And the hill people of Himachal Pradesh and Uttaranchal!

Persons who are conversant with the field situation in Punjab and Haryana are aware of the misuse of medical technology (which started with amniocentesis but now it is the widespread use of simpler techniques like ultrasound and imaging) to determine the sex of the unborn child culminating in female foeticide. In spite of the law which prohibits such misuse, it is more than clear that the law cannot be enforced unless the Government hires thousands of private detectives.

The doctors know how to dodge this law. For example, they will never put down anything on paper. A 'V' sign shows it is a boy. Blurting out the word 'negative' is enough to convey that it is a girl. For historical reasons, the son complex is very strong in North-West India but what is shocking about the 2001 census results that the decline in sex ratio of the child population is in every state of India with the exception of Kerala, Mizoram and Tripura where the sex ratio has increased slightly and Sikkim and Lakshadweep where there is a big jump which is difficult to explain at this stage.

States like Gujarat and Maharashtra have also joined the ranks of Punjab and Haryana in the perverse practice of foeticide. Even in Uttaranchal, an off-shoot of the erstwhile Uttar Pradesh which is advanced in terms of the literacy rate (72 per cent) the sex ratio has decreased by 42 points. In Maharashtra it has decreased by 29 points.

Let us give even more shocking figures for districts.

During the last decade, in Punjab, the sex ratio (0-6 age group) declined from 874 to 754 (-120 points) in Fatehgarh Sahib district, followed by Kapurthala (-104 points), Gurdaspur (-103 points), and Patiala (-101 points). In Ambala district of Haryana, the sex ratio (0-6) decreased from 888 to 784 (-104 points). In Kangra district of Himachal Pradesh, the sex ratio came down from 939 to 836 (-103 points). The perverse impact of Punjab is evident in all the districts of Himachal Pradesh neighbouring Punjab. In the remote Lahul and Spiti district, the sex ratio (0-6) *increased* from 951 to 986 (an increase of 35 points). In Mehesana district of Gujarat, the sex ratio (0-6) decreased from 897 to 798 (-99 points). In Maharashtra, every single district showed a decline in the sex ratio (0-6) except Akola where it increased by only 2 points between 1991 and 2001.

The unholy alliance between tradition (son complex) and technology (ultrasound etc.) is playing havoc with Indian society. The mindless consumerism which is being propagated for 24 hours on TV channels is helping this process. Increasing greed goes with increasing dowry. The message for the would be parents is clear: "If you produce girls you will be financially crippled....Better to spend a few thousand rupees now on pre-birth sex determination tests and sex selective abortions rather than spend lakhs of rupees on dowry after years of frustrated saving." Who will lament for the unborn daughters?

Dominant Role of BIMARU states and their offshoots

The results of the 2001 census fully validate our diagnosis of India's population problem in terms of the dominance of the BIMARU states (Bihar, Madhya Pradesh, Rajasthan and Uttar Pradesh) done in the early 1980s. Our logic was as follows: The much trumpeted Kerala model was, to our mind, not replicable in the BIMARU states. This is not to deny the importance of social investment on health and education but the fact remains that the human settlement pattern in Kerala is quite unique in India: it is a rural-urban continuum and the average size of a 'village' is very large. One hundred per cent of the villages are connected by road or waterways which makes access to health and education easy in Kerala. The situation is totally different in BIMARU states: the two largest states in terms of area, Madhya Pradesh and Rajasthan have a poor transportation network. The situation is no better in the two most populous states of Uttar Pradesh and Bihar. In our opinion, the sheer size of land area and the sheer size of population of the BIMARU states, which form a contiguous geographical and to some extent, socio-cultural region cannot be compared to the small state of Kerala (both in size and population). There is no point in adding Orissa to this list, no matter how miserable this state is. The birth rate of Orissa is not high but the death rate and the infant mortality rate are the highest in India. The focus, therefore, has to be on health and not on family planning in Orissa. Fortunately, the ICPD (Cairo, 1994) focussed on **Reproductive Health**, which includes health and family planning. The Government of India rightly added 'child' to this package making it clear that the focus should be on reproductive and child health (RCH).

The 2001 census tables which we have presented in Part Two and Three clearly bring out the dominant role of BIMARU states (with or without the three newly formed states of Jharkhand, Chhatisgarh and Uttaranchal). We have also mentioned that truncated Bihar and also Orissa deserve the category of *ATI-BIMARU* states (intensely sick states).

In Part Five (Media and the Census of 2001), we have reproduced an article which argues that Madhya Pradesh should be taken out of the BIMARU states and Karnataka in South India should be included in BIMARU states. We totally disagree with this view. When we consider the birth rate, death rate and infant mortality rate (from SRS data) and the decadal growth rate and the gap between male and female literacy rates (as revealed by 2001 census data), there is no reason why Madhya Pradesh should be removed from the list of BIMARU states, merely because the population growth rate has slowed down and literacy has increased rapidly. The fact remains that Madhya Pradesh has unacceptable levels of high birth, death and infant mortality rates; 50 per cent of the females are illiterate. Are these not signs of demographic sickness? Taking a lenient view, all that can be said about Madhya Pradesh is that this state is the least BIMARU among the four states. As for Karnataka, the figures presented in Part Three and Four, make it clear that it continues to be a demographically progressive state, though among the four southern states, Karnataka is the least progressive. The arguments given by the author (Vyasulu) to include Karnataka in our list of BIMARU states are political, rather than demographic. Our concept is not based on perceived political considerations or advocacy of certain states nor on downgrading certain states. To recall, the acronym was coined by us when the then Prime Minister (Rajiv Gandhi) wanted some concrete advice about the stagnating family welfare programme. At that time, nobody talked of the Tamil Nadu model or the Andhra Pradesh model. It was only the Kerala model which was nationally and internationally acclaimed and recommended. The assessment which we gave to the Prime Minister played down the Kerala model as irrelevant in the then demographic context (and this is true even today) and we highlighted the role of BIMARU states on **statistical** grounds: These states accounted for 39 per cent of India's population, 42 per cent of growth rate (during 1981-91) and 48 per cent of the total illiterate population . We had also indicated that in future, the dominance of the BIMARU states would increase. The results of 2001 census confirm this. We must hasten to add that we did not challenge the philosophy behind the Kerala model of substantial investment in health and education. The celebrated state of Kerala has only 3.1 per cent of India's population and contributed only 2.2 per cent to the total increase in population of India during 1991-2001. Statistically speaking Kerala is not important nor is Goa where the birth rate is the lowest in India.

It is worth noting that the state which has emerged as the best state from the point of view of decrease in the decadal growth rate of population is Andhra Pradesh. From the point of view of the literacy level, it may be classified as a BIMARU state in South India.

Whether we like it or not, India's family planning programme is dominated by sterilisation, and that too, female sterilisation. Even in the enlightened state of Kerala, this is true. It is also a fact that illiterate masses can be more easily persuaded (or pressurised?) to take to sterilisation. A well-thoughtout programme of sterilisation (as was true in Tamil Nadu, thanks to administrators like T. V. Anthony, who made a success of the vasectomy programme), can certainly succced. In Andhra Pradesh, because of political will and bureaucratic push to the family welfare programme, women have taken to sterilisation. Unfortunately, during the emergency (1975-77), an immature politician (an extra-constitutional authority) in combination with a servile bureaucracy derailed the family planning programme. In fact, it did a permanent damage to the programme. The people of India punished the politicians in the general elections.

Even today, it cannot be said that India's family planning programme is a thundering success. Things have worsened in Bihar, as the 2001 census statistics reveal. Things are no better in Uttar Pradesh. It is unlikely that given the state of parliamentary democracy today, population issues will get *priority* attention from our political leaders. But we have great hope in the resilience of the people of India to whom this book is dedicated.

Contents

Summary of Contents — vii

Preface — ix

Acknowledgements — xiii

Organisation of the Book — xv

Overview — xix

List of Tables — xxxi

List of Figures — xxxiii

PART ONE

About Census of India 2001 — **1-24**

   I.   Houselisting Operation, 2000 — 3

   II. Beyond a Headcount of One Billion — 7

   III. New Features of 2001 Census — 12

Appendix to Part One

   I.   Houselist Schedule (canvassed in 2000) — 16

   II. Household Schedule (canvassed in 2001) — 18

PART TWO

Demographic Profile of India/States/UTs, 2001 — **25-99**

   1. Demographic Profile of India — 27

   2. BIMARU States — 50

   3. Offshoots of BIMARU States (three new states) — 56

   4. Southern States/UTs — 60

   5. Jammu & Kashmir — 68

   6. North-Western States/UTs — 70

   7. Western States/UTs — 77

   8. North-Eastern States — 83

   9. West Bengal — 93

  10. Orissa — 95

  11. Islands — 97

PART THREE

Implications : First Thoughts on the Provisional Results of Census of India 2001   **101-132**

1. Demographic Astrology : How good were the population projections?   103
2. DEMARU states : Decline in the sex ratio of child population (0-6 years)   107
3. Role of BIMARU States   118
4. Increase in literacy rates in 2001   125
5. Vital Statistics, 1999   128

PART FOUR

2001 Census Methodology : Definitions & Classifications   **133-184**

I. Economic Questions : characteristics of workers and non-workers   135
II. Migration Characteristics   166
III. Houseless Population   174
IV. How Accurate is the Census?   176

PART FIVE

Media and the 2001 Census : Excerpts from Print Media   **185-252**

I. Census publicity   189
II. General   195
III. Census enumeration   200
IV. Caste   209
V. Sex workers?   215
VI. Reporting the first results of the 2001 census   218
VII. Unborn Daughters : declining sex ratio of the child population (0-6 years)   236

Sources of Data   253

List of Tables

Table 2.1 :   Demographic Profile of India, 2001   29
Table 2.2 :   Demographic Diversity of India, 2001   37
Table 2.3 :   Size, Distribution and Density of States and UTs, 2001   38
Table 2.4:   Increase in Density of States/UTs, 1991-2001
               (States/UTs ranked according to increase in density
               between 1991-2001)   39
Table 2.5 :   Percentage Decadal Growth Rate of Population 1951-2001   40
Table 2.6 :   Percentage Decadal Growth Rate of States and UTs Ranked
               According to Growth Rate during 1991-2001   41
Table 2.7 :   State/UTs Ranked According to Decline in Annual Growth
               Rate, 1981-2001 and SRS Data 2001   42
Table 2.8 :   Sex Ratio (females per 1,000 males), 1951-2001   43
Table 2.9 :   Child Population (0-6 years), 2001   44
Table 2.10:   Proportion of Child Population in the Age Group 0-6 to
               Total Population, 2001   45
Table 2.11 :   Sex Ratio (females per 1,000 males), of Child Population,
               (0-6 and 7+ age group), 2001   46
Table 2.12 :   Literacy Rate by Sex, 2001   47
Table 2.13 :   Distribution of Illiterate Population, 2001   48
Table 2.14 :   Per cent Distribution of Illiterate Population, 2001   49

Table 3.1 :   Projected Population of India in 2000/2001 by Different
               Individuals and Organisations in the Last Fifty Years   103
Table 3.2 :   Projected and Provisional Population of India, States and
               UTs as on March 1, 2001   104
Table 3.3 :   Difference Between Projected and Provisional Population
               in Selected States, 2001 (in '000)   105
Table 3.4 :   Sex Ratio in 0-6 Age Group, 1961-2001   109
Table 3.5 :   Sex Ratio in States/UTs Ranked According to Variation
               during 1991-2001   110
Table 3.6 :   Child Sex Ratio (0-6 age and 7+ age group) State/UTs
               Ranked According to Decline in Sex Ratio of 0-6 Population 111
Table 3.7 :   Percentage of Population in the Age Aroup 0-6 Ranked
               According to the Decrease in the Female Percentage in 2001 113
Table 3.8 :   District Level Data on Sex Ratio, Selected States/UTs   114

Table 3.9 :   Population Growth Rates in BIMARU States, 1981-91 &
              1991-2001   118
Table 3.10 : Population of Three New States Added to BIMARU States
              1981-91 & 1991-2001   121
Table 3.11 : Share of Population and Increase in Population   121
Table 3.12 : Share of Population of Three New States added to BIMARU
              States and Increase in Population   123
Table 3.13 : Increase in Absolute Population (in million)   123
Table 3.14 : Increase in Absolute Population of Three New States and
              BIMARU States (in million)   124
Table 3.15 : Literacy Rate in States/UTs by Sex, 2001, Ranked
              According to Female Literacy Rate   126
Table 3.16 : Literacy Rate in States/UTs by Sex, 1991-2001, Ranked
              According to Variation in Female Literacy Rate (per cent)   127
Table 3.17 : Birth, Death and Infant Mortality Rates, 1999   129
Table 3.18 : Distribution of Illiterate Population in BIMARU States, 2001 131

Table 4.1 :   Net Omission Rates (per thousand) by Sex and Residence,
              India and Zones   181
Table 4.2 :   Rates of Gross Omission, Duplication and Net Omission   181
Table 4.3 :   Net Omission Rates by Sex and Residence 1981-1991   181
Table 4.4 :   Net Omission Rates by Type of Error, Sex and Residence,
              India   182
Table 4.5 :   Net Omission Rates by Age and Sex, India   182
Table 4.6 :   Net Omission Rates for those Aged 7 Years and above by
              Literacy and Sex, India   182
Table 4.7 :   Net Omission Rates by Marital Status and Sex, India   182
Table 4.8 :   Net Omission Rates by Sex and Relationship to Head   183
Table 4.9 :   Net Omission Rates (Type II) and Distribution of
              Persons Enumerated in PEC by Residential Status   183
Table 4.10 : Distribution of Persons Counted in Census by their
              Enumeration Status   183
Table 4.11 : Age Distribution of Population Adjustment for Omission   184

Table 5.1 :   Crude Death Rates by Sex and Sex Ratio (males per 100
              females) among Total Deaths, India, 1983-1993   238
Table 5.2 :   SRS based Estimates of Sex Ratio at Birth for the Major
              States, 1981-90   238

List of Figures

Fig 2.1	Population of India, 2001 (in million)	30
Fig 2.2	Decadal Growth, Absolute Increase, 1951 to 2001 (in million)	30
Fig 2.3	Decadal Population Growth, 1951 to 2001 (per cent)	31
Fig 2.4	Density of India, (persons per sq. km.) 1951 to 2001	32
Fig 2.5	Sex Ratio (females per 1000 males), India 1951 to 2001	32
Fig 2.6	Sex Ratio of 0-6 and 7+ age groups, India 1991 and 2001	33
Fig 2.7	Literacy Rate in India, 1951-2001 (per cent)	34
Fig 2.8	Birth, Death, Natural Growth Rate, Infant Mortality Rate, SRS, 1999, (per thousand)	35
Fig 2.9	Most Populous Countries of the World	36
Fig 3.1	North-South Demographic Divide : Population (in million), 1991 & 2001	119
Fig 3.2	North-South Demographic Divide : Decadal Growth Rate (per cent)	119
Fig 3.3	North-South Demographic Divide : Average Annual Exponential Growth Rate (per cent)	120
Fig 3.4	North-South Demographic Divide : Decline in Growth Rates, 1991-2001 compared to 1981-91	120
Fig 3.5	North-South Demographic Divide : Share of Total Population of India (per cent)	122
Fig 3.6	North-South Demographic Divide : Per cent Contribution to total population growth of India 1981-91 & 1991-2001	122
Fig 3.7	North-South Demographic Divide : Increase in Absolute Population (in million)	124

PART ONE

ABOUT CENSUS OF INDIA 2001

INDIA'S GIGANTIC CENSUS OF 2001

I. Houselisting Operation, 2000*

In April 2000, the first major step in decennial Census taking was taken by the newly appointed Census Commissioner (J. K. Banthia) by launching the houselisting operation in a phased manner all over the country (lasting up to the end of September 2000). The Indian Census tradition, right from 1872 (when the first all-India Census was conducted on a non-synchronous basis) and 1881 (when the first synchronous Census was conducted) has centred round a vast army of 'volunteers' – primary school teachers and petty revenue officials who are given quick training and entrusted with the task of data collection in two stages: first, a houselisting operation with several questions asked regarding the household as a whole, a process which starts one year prior to the actual Census enumeration, and second, the actual enumeration which involves collection of data regarding **every** man, woman and child in India. The Indian Census conducted every ten years is a gigantic national administrative exercise. It must be noted that there are very few countries in the world with a history of **uninterrupted** decennial Censuses going back to 1881. We should be truly proud of our Census.

We shall confine our comments to the houselisting operation. First, my disturbing thoughts. As a researcher in Census methodology, I am having increasing doubts about the **quality** of Census data. The days are gone when the mighty British Government could strike terror in the hearts of primary school teachers and get voluntary work done by them and occasionally pat their backs by giving them certificates for doing a great national duty. The present breed of our political masters have an all time low level of respect and credibility and are most unlikely to inspire over 2 million Census enumerators who have just been drafted on a so-called voluntary basis to do Census work. I asked a school teacher in Chandigarh about her work in the houselisting operation. She replied: "We had 4 days' training and we have to be in the field for 16 days. All we will get is seven hundred rupees (Rs. 700/-) . Of course, there will be no school duty but we have to start work early in the morning and put in long hours. People are not co-operative. They ask me how will they benefit

---

* Originally published in *Economic and Political Weekly*, April 22, 2000.

by answering numerous questions. I have no answer. I cannot promise the slum dwellers - my respondents - that they will get drinking water after the Census is over". She asks me a counter question: "Why does the government not employ the growing numbers of educated unemployed to do Census work? They will get Rs. 700 for the houselisting and another Rs. 1,500 for the Census enumeration next year. I can do without this petty amount - I get more than Rs. 10,000 per month". I asked her "What about national duty?" She laughs and says: "Are our corrupt ministers and bureaucrats doing national duty? Why ask me to do national duty? I can donate Rs. 700/- to the Government".

This is also what happened to the Pakistani Census. School teachers said that they not only did not want to do Census work but were willing to donate the equivalent amount of honorarium to the Government. Pakistan had to call the army to help in Census enumeration work. Of course, Pakistan calls the army for running the government also! I hope India will not follow the Pakistan model of Census enumeration.

Initially, I also thought that involvement of students in Census work was a good idea but I had to change my views when I talked to a veteran Census administrator – H. L. Kalla from Srinagar. He was associated with the Census of 1961, 1971, 1981 and 1991 and also with the ad hoc Census in Ladakh region of Jammu and Kashmir state in 1986. It may be recalled that the 1991 Census enumeration could not take place in Jammu and Kashmir because of disturbed conditions. Mr. Kalla opposed the induction of senior students and unemployed graduates in Census work because the government will have no control over them. As he put it, they may leave half way and make a mess of the Census. The primary school teachers and revenue officials will always dread the prospect of punishment or adverse confidential report. Another serious problem which the previous Census Commissioners and Directors of State Censuses were confronted with was the demand by the temporary Census staff to be absorbed in permanent government (Central) service. I have witnessed gheraos and angry demonstrations of such workers in state capitals. Imagine the 2001 Census Commissioner being asked by a trade union of 2 million Census enumerators (assuming that they are specially recruited to do the Census enumeration work) to regularise their services and absorb them in the government! It would be an impossible situation and no government will walk into such a trap to conduct the forthcoming Census of India. On the other hand, I would like to ask: "Is it possible to conduct a **good** Census (by this I mean, collect reliable data) through an army of unmotivated, disinterested and even hostile school teachers and petty bureaucrats in these days of individualism, consumerism and the universal tendency of quick money-making?" What should we do to ensure minimum levels of accuracy of Census data?

I had a long discussion with the new Census Commissioner who is working 12 hours a day for 7 days a week to get organised for the second largest headcount in the world. In terms of scope, coverage and comprehensiveness of data, I rate the Indian Census higher than the Chinese Census and I would venture to say that if we succeed in conducting the 2001 Census, our Census operation will be largest in the history of Census-taking in the whole world, notwithstanding the fact that purely in terms of a headcount, the forthcoming Chinese Census will be the largest operation. Mr. Banthia informed me that he does hope to conduct the Census of 2001 in Jammu and Kashmir state and the Census machinery has already been set up.

"What is unique about the 2001 Census?" I asked Mr. Banthia. He gave a detailed reply: "The individual slip which will be canvassed from 9th February to 1st March, 2001 will be more or less the same as before because there is very little scope for expanding the questionnaire which involves over a billion individuals. We therefore, introduced new questions in the Houselist schedule. This will be the first Census in the 21st century and for posterity, we would like a bench mark type of survey of **how people of India live,** and not merely **how many** Indians there are (the head count) and **where** they live (in villages, towns and cities)".

For the benefit of readers, let me summarise Census of India 2001 Houselist Schedule canvassed in 2000.

There are 34 columns in the questionnaire. The data relate to the household as a whole. A household is not necessarily a family (nuclear/joint/extended); the Census defines it as a group of individuals living together and sharing a common kitchen. The houselist schedule is more than a housing Census. The first 8 columns seek to collect data about the predominant material of the floor, wall and roof of the house, the use of the Census house (residence, residence-cum-other use, shop/office, school/college … factory/workshop/workshed, place of worship, etc.) A new question introduced in the 2001 Census refers to "the condition of the Census house: Good, livable, dilapidated". This assessment is to be done by the respondent and not by the Census enumerator.

The next 7 columns refer to the population of the household: number of males and females (and the total), name and sex of the head of the household, whether SC (Scheduled Caste), ST (Scheduled Tribe) or Other (Caste). Q16 refers to the ownership status of the house owned/rented/anyother. Col 17 records the number of dwelling rooms in the household, Col 18 the number of married couples living in the household and Col 19 the number of married couples having "independent room for sleeping". This question does look very western-oriented in the Indian context of extreme housing shortage and the social custom of young children sleeping with their parents. The Census Commissioner's comment was: "At the end of the 21st century, things might improve but we must have the baseline data."

Cols 20 to 25 seek to collect valuable data about what the Census calls basic amenities: drinking water source, where this source is located (within the premises, near the premises and away, all statistically defined), source of lighting (electricity, kerosene, solar, other oil, any other, no lighting), latrine within the house (with type specified), waste water outlet (connected to closed drainage, open drainage, no drainage), and bathroom within the house.

The Census tilts to gender issues by asking about kitchen within the house (Col 26) and fuel used for cooking (Col 27). Cols 28 to 33 refer to consumer durables, namely, ownership of radio/transistor, television, telephone, bicycle, scooter/jeep/van. I would plead for including tractors in this category. It is a common sight in Punjab and Haryana to see tractors used as cars for social visits to the town, recreational activities, apart from their use for agricultural and commercial purposes. It certainly is an important omission in the houselist questionnaire and can be rectified even now. The last question (Col 34) refers to "availing Banking Services" (including postal banking but not chit funds).

All in all, the 2001 Census Houselist Schedule has introduced several new and useful questions as well as modifications in earlier questionnaires and certainly marks a bold step in taking the Census way beyond a headcount. Modern technology will be used. All the questions are self-coded. Though the questionnaires will be canvassed in all the major languages of India, the codes will be only in Arabic numerals which will be scanned and image based on the computers. Short of the modern system of OMR or OCR, this image based scanning technology will be tried for the first time by the Census Commission. This should greatly speed up processing and tabulation of 2001 Census data on households.

But the lingering doubts about the quality of Census data still persist in my mind. A modern technology applied to data which are less than reliable will not guarantee a good Census. Most probably the long Census 'tradition' will somehow see us through in 2001 also.

II. Beyond a Headcount of One Billion*

The Indian Census conducted every ten years is a gigantic national administrative exercise. There are very few countries in the world with a history of **uninterrupted** decennial Censuses going back to 1881. We should be truly proud of our Census.

The Census of India, 2001 will be a landmark Census as we enter the 21st century of Information Technology. It must match the Indian Census tradition dating back to 1872 with the new technology of the 21st century. The Census may fade out in Western countries in view of their annual sample surveys and an efficient registration system of births and deaths on an annual basis but in India, the Census is still the most reliable largest single source of information on the life of the people, in spite of the growing member of sample surveys conducted all over the country in recent decades. At the same time, we must not forget that a Census is more than a headcount – it is a vital tool for policymaking and planning.

The political importance of the Indian Census must not be ignored. The basis of partition for India in 1947 was Census data on religious distribution of population. The linguistic re-organisation of the States in 1956 and in subsequent years was based on the Census data on mother tongue. The reservation for Scheduled Caste, (SC) and Scheduled Tribe (ST) population is based on the Census data on SCs and STs. The Census has far-reaching political , economic and social implications which go far beyond demographic data.

In April 2000, the first major step in decennial Census taking was taken by the newly appointed Census Commissioner (J. K. Banthia) by launching the houselisting operation in a phased manner all over the country (lasting up to the end of September 2000). The Indian Census tradition, right from 1872 (when the first all-India Census was conducted on a non-synchronous basis) and 1881 (when the first synchronous Census was conducted) has centred round a vast army of 'volunteers' – primary school teachers and petty revenue officials who are given quick training and entrusted with the task of data collection in two stages: first, a houselisting operation with several questions asked regarding the household as a whole, a process which starts one year prior to the actual Census enumeration, and second, the actual enumeration which involves collection of data regarding **every** man, woman and child in India.

To give an idea about the wealth of information collected through the houselisting operation in 2000, we will briefly refer to all the questions asked.

There are 34 columns in the questionnaire. The data relate to the household as a whole. A household is not necessarily a family (nuclear/joint/extended); the Census defines it as a group of individuals living together and sharing a common kitchen. The houselist schedule is more than a housing Census. The first 8

---

* Originally published in *Yojana*, February, 2001.

columns seek to collect data about the predominant material of the floor, wall and roof of the house, use of the Census house (residence, residence-cum-other use, shop/office, school/college, factory/workshop/workshed, place of worship etc.) A new question introduced in the 2001 Census refers to "the condition of the Census house: Good, livable, dilapidated". This assessment is to be done by the respondent and not by the Census enumerator.

The next 7 columns refer to the population of the household: number of males and females (and the total), name and sex of the head of the household, whether SC (Scheduled Caste), ST (Scheduled Tribe) or Other (Caste). Q16 refers to the ownership status of the house owned/rented/any other. Col 17 records the number of dwelling rooms in the household, Col 18 the number of married couples living in the household and Col 19 the number of married couples having "independent room for sleeping". This question does look very western-oriented in the Indian context of extreme housing shortage and the social custom of young children sleeping with their parents. The Census Commissioner's comment was: "At the end of the 21st century, things might improve but we must have the baseline data".

Cols 20 to 25 seek to collect valuable data about what the Census calls basic amenities: drinking water source, where this source is located (within the premises, near the premises, and away, all statistically defined), source of lighting (electricity, kerosene, solar, other oil, any other, no lighting), latrine within the house (with type specified), waste water outlet (connected to closed drainage, open drainage, no drainage), and bathroom within the house.

The Census tilts to gender issues by asking about kitchen within the house (Col 26) and fuel used for cooking (Col 27). Cols 28 to 33 refer to consumer durables, namely, ownership of radio/transistor, television, telephone, bicycle, scooter/jeep/van. An important omission in the houselist questionnaire is information about tractor which is being increasingly used for agricultural, commercial and recreational purposes in rural areas in several regions of India, notably in Punjab and Haryana. The last question (Col 34) refers to "availing Banking Services" (including postal banking but not chit funds).

All in all, the 2001 Census Houselist Schedule has introduced several new and useful questions as well as modifications in earlier questionnaires and certainly marks a bold step in taking the Census way beyond a headcount. Modern technology will be used. All the questions are self-coded. Though the questionnaires will be canvassed in all the major languages of India, the codes will be only in Arabic numerals which will be scanned and image based on the computers. Short of the modern system of OMR or OCR, this image based scanning technology will be tried for the first time by the Census Commission.

A vast army of over 2 million (20 lakh) enumerators will do the actual enumeration from 9 February to 28 February 2001. The sunrise on 1st March 2001 will be regarded as the reference date to which the population count will relate.

Let us now briefly describe the household schedule which will be canvassed in February 2001.

Part I of the Household schedule gives the location particulars: State/UT, Tahsil/Taluk/P.S./Dev. Block/Circle/Mandal, Number and/or Name of Ward, District, Town/Village, enumeration Block, Number, Serial number of household. Then information will be collected about the type of household: Normal/Institutional/Houseless.

Part II of the questionnaire refers to **individual** particulars as follows:

Q. 1. Name of the person

Q. 2. Relationship to the head of the household

Q. 3. Sex

Q. 4. Age in completed years

Q. 5. Current marital status: never married, currently married, widowed, divorced or separated.

Q. 6. Age at marriage (in completed years)

Q. 7. Religion: Hindu, Muslim, Christian, Sikh, Buddhist, Jain or other religion.

Q. 8. If Scheduled Caste, name of the caste (Scheduled Castes can be only among Hindus, Sikhs and Buddhists).

Q. 9. If Scheduled Tribe, name of the tribe (Scheduled Tribes can be from any religion)

Q. 10. Mother tongue

Q. 11. Other languages known (enter upto two languages in order of proficiency).

Q. 12. Literacy status: Literate/Illiterate

Q. 13. Highest educational level attained

Q. 14. If attending educational institution: school/college/vocational Institute/other Institute/Literacy Centre or not attending any school, etc.

Q. 15. If the person is physically, mentally disabled. *Type of disability*: in seeing, in speech, in hearing, in movement or mental.

There is a spearate block for workers as follows:

Five questions will be asked to get detailed characteristics of workers:

Q. 16. **Workers:** Did the person work any time last year? **Main worker**: if worked for 6 months or more, **Marginal worker**: if worked for less than 6 months, **Non-worker**: if not worked at all.

Q. 17. (i) Economic activity of the main or marginal worker: cultivator, agricultural labourer, worker in household industry, other worker. (ii) occupation of the person (actual work of the person) (iii) nature of industry: trade or service. where the person works/worked   or of self employment. (iv) class of worker: employer/employee/single worker, family worker.

Q. 18. Marginal worker or Non worker: student/household duties/ dependent/pensioner/beggar/other.

Q. 19. Marginal or Non-working person seeking/available for work.

Q. 20. Travel to place of work: (i) Distance from residence to place of work in kilometres, (ii) Mode of travel of place of work: on foot/bicycle, moped/scooter/ motor cycle, car/jeep/van, tempo/autorickshaw/taxi, bus, train, water transport, any other or no travel. (This is a new question at this census)

Migration: The following questions will be asked to find out the extent and pattern of migration:

Q. 21. Birth Place: if born in the place of enumeration. If not:

(i) State Country, (if birth place within India or outside India)

(ii) District, (if birth place within India or outside India)

Q. 22. Place of last residence, Has the person come to this village/town from elsewhere?

(i) State/Country (if place of last residence within India or outside India)

(ii) District, (if place of last residence within India or outside India)

(iii) At the time of migration, was the place of last residence **rural/urban**

(iv) Reason for migration from place of last residence: work, employment, business, education, marriage, moved after birth, moved with household, any other reason.

(v) Duration of stay since migration (in completed years).

Fertility Particulars: To ascertain the fertility pattern a detailed question will be asked about each ever married (currently married, widowed, divorced or separated) woman as follows:

Q. 23. (i) Number of children surviving at present, (ii) Total number of children ever born alive, (iii) Number of children born alive during last one year (daughter/son).

Part III of the questionnaire seeks to collect valuable data about households engaged in cultivation/plantation as follows:

(i) Total net area of land under cultivation/plantation, (ii) Net area of irrigated land (iii) Tenure status of land under cultivation/plantation, (owned/rented/ owned and rented).

·It may be noted that the 2001 Census will not collect data on OBCs (other Backward Castes) though there was a demand for such data in many circles. I think it was a good decision on the part of Census authorities. We should not rake up caste in the 21st century. Our goal should be a casteless society. Data on SCs and STs are collected because it is a constitutional requirement but here again it is nobody's claim that such reservation should be a permanent feature of Indian society. Genuine efforts must be speedily made for the uplift of the downtrodden but at the same time, nobody should be allowed to take unfair advantage of such reservation. For example, there is a move that income tax payers should not be given benefits which accrue to SCs and STs. Our concern should be with the population below the poverty line, regardless of caste.

The success of this gigantic Census – the second largest in the history of Census operations, in the world, will to a large extent depend on the co-operation of the people, without which no Census can be conducted. Under the Census Act of 1948, persons can be punished for not furnishing Census data but there are limits to what the law can do.

A scientific Census which collects reliable data can be of immense use to the general public as well as to specialised persons, policymakers and planners. To sustain our democracy, we do need a good Census.

III. New Features of 2001 Census

*(Adopted from Census Paper-1 of 2001 :
Provisional Population Totals with excerpts)*

Houselist Schedule

The new features of the Houselisting Schedule are as follows:

➢   For the first time, different uses of census houses have been standardized and grouped into ten main uses and assigned code numbers.

➢   Plastic has been added in the list of material of wall and roof of a census house, as it is often used for shelter in slums and shanties.

➢   In the previous census, the location of drinking water source was categorized into two locations viz. 'within premises' and 'outside premises'. In the Census of India, 2001, the source 'outside premises' was split into two categories namely 'near the premises' and 'away from the premises'.

➢   The scope of question on availability of electricity was expanded to include six sources of lighting. Besides no lighting, this included sources like electricity, kerosene, solar, other oil and any other source.

➢   In 1991 Census, a question on availability of toilet facilities to the household was canvassed while in Census of India, 2001, specific information on availability of latrine within the house by the type of latrine was sought.

The following new questions were added in the Houselist Schedule:

➢   If the Census house was used for residential or party residential purposes, the condition of the census house was categorized as good, livable or dilapidated based on the perception and response of the respondent.

➢   A question on number of married couple(s) living in the household was canvassed.

➢   Information was sought on the number of married couple(s) having independent room for sleeping.

➢   Information as to whether the waste water outlet of the house is connected to 'closed drainage' or has no drainage was collected.

➢   A question on availability of bathroom within the house was included.

➢   Information on availability of kitchen within the house was also sought.

➢   Availability of certain assets to the households namely radio/transistor, television, telephone, bicycle, scooter/motor cycle/moped, car/jeep/van were also included.

➢   It was also enquired whether any banking service was being availed by the household.

Household Schedule

The following new questions were canvassed at the 2001 Census:

➢ A question on total disability was canvassed in the 1981 Census. In the 1991 Census, no question on disability was included. At the Census of India, 2001, a question to elicit information on total or partial disability was canvassed. The five types of disability on which information is collected are – in seeing, in hearing, in speech, in movement and mental.

➢ A new question on 'Travel to place of work' is canvassed mainly for workers engaged in non-agricultural activities. Information on distance from the residence to place of work and mode of travel to place of work is collected under this section.

➢ The Household Schedule has a new set of questions for Household engaged in cultivation/plantation – (i) Net area of land under cultivation/plantation, (ii) Net area of land irrigated and (iii) Tenure status. This question was not canvassed at the 1991 Census but was canvassed in the 1981 Census in a slightly different form.

➢ The signature or thumb impression of the respondent has been taken on the Household Schedule for the first time in the history of census. This was not only aimed at obtaining correct and complete information but for giving an opportunity to the respondents to authenticate the information provided by them. The relationship of the respondent with the head of the household was also obtained.

Modifications in the 1991 Questionnaire adopted in 2001 Census:

➢ Age at marriage was collected for males also, while it was collected for only ever-married females until the 1991 Census.

➢ The type of educational institution attended by a person was enlarged to include school, college, vocational institute, other institute and literacy centre.

The scope of the definition of 'work' was expanded in the Census of India, 2001 to include production of milk for domestic consumption. In the 1981 Census, cultivation of certain crops even for self-consumption was treated as economic activity. The scope of the term 'Cultivation' was expanded in this Census to include certain other crops such as tobacco, fruits, all types of flowers, roots and tubers, potatoes, chillies and turmeric, pepper, cardamom, all types of vegetables and fodder crops etc. This meant that activities related to production of all the abovementioned crops for domestic consumption has been treated as work. Only five crops viz. tea, coffee, rubber, coconut and betel-nuts have been classified under 'Plantation' in the Census of India, 2001.

➤   At the 1991 Census, the question on seeking/available for work was canvassed for only non-workers. At the Census of India, 2001, this question is asked from the Marginal Workers also. A question to elicit information on secondary work canvassed at the 1991 Census, is dropped.

➤   From among the categories of non-workers adopted at the 1991 Census, the category 'Inmates of institutions' has been dropped and 'Retired Persons and Rentiers' has been replaced by the category 'Pensioners'.

➤   A new response category 'Moved after birth' was included in the question on 'reasons for migration' to bring out additional migration patterns. Natural calamities or distress migration as a reason for migration for last residence migrants included in the 1991 Census, is covered under category of 'Other'.

➤   Number of children born alive to currently married women during last one year was collected for male and female children separately.

Slum Enumeration Block

Slum Enumeration Blocks were identified for the first time in census, in each Municipal town having a population of 50,000. Instructions were issued that these Enumeration Blocks do not cut across ward boundaries or non-slum area. It will thus be possible to compile and tabulate special tables for 'slums'.

APPENDIX TO PART ONE

I. Houselist Schedule (canvassed in 2000)

II. Household Schedule (canvassed in 2001)

CENSUS OF INDIA 2001 - HOUSELIST SCHEDULE

1.   Line number

2.   Building number

3.   Census house number

Predominant material of the floor, wall and roof of the census house
(Give Code number from the respective list below)

4.   Floor

5.   Wall

6.   Roof

7.   Ascertain use of census house

(Write the actual purpose. Then choose the appropriate Code number for that purpose from among the different purposes listed below and enter that Code number in the box at the right hand side of this column)

Code No.

> *Residenc-1/Residence-cum-Other Use-2/Shop, Office-3/School, College etc.-4/Hotel, Lodge, Guest House etc.-5/Hospital, Dispensaries, etc.-6/ Factory, Workshop, Workshed, etc-7/Place of Worship-8/Other non-residential use-9/Vacant-0.*

8.   If code '1' or '2' in column 7, condition of this census house:

> *Good-1/Livable-2/Dilapidated-3*

These columns are to be filled if the census house is used wholly or partly as a residence. Do not fill columns 14 and 15 for institutional households.

9.   Household number*

Total number of persons normally residing in this household

10. Persons

11. Males

12. Females

Information relating to the head of the household

Name of the head of the household

13. Name of the head of the household

14. Male-1/Female-2

15. If SC⁺ or ST⁺ or Other? *SC-1/ST-2/Other-3*

Fill columns 16 to 34 for normal households. Put dash (-) in case of institutional households and non-residential census houses

16. Ownership status of this house? *Owned-1/Rented-2/Any other-3*

17. Number of dwelling rooms with this household# *(Record 0,1,2,3....)*

18. Number of married couple(s) living in this household *(Record 0,1,2,3....)*

19. Number of married couple(s) having independent room for sleeping *(Record 0,1,2,3....)*

20. Drinking water source : *(Give Code number from the list below)*

21. Drinking water source : *Within the premises-1/Near the premises-2/ Away-3*

22. Source of lighting : *(Give Code number from the list below)*

23. Latrine within the house : *No latrine-0/Service latrine-1/Pit latrine-2/ Water closet-3*

24. Waste water outlet connected to : *Closed drainage-1/Open drainage-2/ No drainage-3*

25. Bathroom within the house : *Yes-1/No-2*

26. Kitchen within the house : *Yes-1/No-2/Cooking in open-3/No cooking-4*

27. Fuel used for cooking : *(Give Code number from the list below)*

28. Radio/Transistor : *Yes-1/No-2*

29. Television : *Yes-1/No-2*

30. Telephone : *Yes-1/No-2*

31. Bicycle : *Yes-1/No-2*

32. Scooter/Motor Cycle/Moped : *Yes-1/No-2*

33. Car/Jeep/Van : *Yes-1/No-2*

34. Availing Banking Services : *Yes-1/No-2*

INDIA 2001 : HOUSEHOLD SCHEDULE

Confidential when filled A

Schedule number

**** Arabic Numerals as indicated below:

0 1 2 3 4 5 6 7 8 9

Part - I Location particulars

Name of State/UT....

Code No.

Name of Tahsil/Taluk/P.S./

Dev. Block/Circle/Mandal etc....

Code No.

Number and/or Name of Ward

Code No.

Name of District

Code No.

Name of Town/Village

Code No.

Enumeration Block Number

Serial number of household (*to be copied from column 7 of the Abridged Houselist*)

Type of household:

(*give appropriate Code number*)

Normal-1/Institutional-2/Houseless-3

Part II - Individual particulars

GENERAL AND SOCIO-CULTURAL CHARACTERISTICS

Serial Number

Q.1 Name of the person

Persons

ITEM-1

Q.2 Relationship to head (*record the relationship in full*)

Q.3. Sex : **Male**-1/**Female**-2

ITEM-2

Total No. of 1's

Total No. of 2's

Q.4. Age last birthday (*in completed years*)

ITEM-3

Males (0-6)

Females (0-6)

Q.5. Current marital status

(*give Code number from the list below*)

Code numbers for Q. 5

(*Marital status*)

Never Married   1

Currently married   2

Widowed   3

Divorced or Separated   4

Q. 6. Age at marriage (*in completed years*), if Code '2' or '3' or '4' in column 6

Q. 7. Religion (*write name of the religion in full*)

For following religions, also give Code number in box

Hindu   **1**

Muslim   **2**

Christian   **3**

Sikh   **4**

Buddhist   **5**

Jain   **6**

For other religions, write name of the religion in full but do not give any Code number

Q. 8. If Scheduled Caste, write name of the Scheduled Caste from the list supplied

(*Scheduled Castes can be only among Hindus, Sikhs and Buddhists*)

Q. 9. If Scheduled Tribe, write name of the Scheduled Tribe from the list supplied

(*Scheduled Tribes can be from any religion*)

Q. 10. Mother tongue

Q. 11. Other languages known (*enter upto two languages in order of proficiency*)

Q.12. Literacy status **Literate-1/Illiterate-2**

M/F

Literates (Total of 1's)

ITEM-4

Illiterates (Total of 2's)

ITEM-5

Q.13. Highest educational level attained (*for diploma or degree holder, also write the subject of specialisation*)

Q.14. If attending educational institution : **School-1/College-2/Vocational Institute-3/Other Institute-4/Literacy Centre-5 or if not attending -0**

Q.15. If the person is physically, mentally disabled, give appropriate Code number from the list below

Code Numbers for Q. 15

(*Type of disability*)

In Seeing   1

In Speech   2

In Hearing   3

In Movement 4

Mental   5

Name of the Respondent...................................

Relationship to head ....

Dated signature or thumb impression of the Respondent.....................................

Dated signature of the Enumerator.....................................

Dated signature of the Supervisor.......................................

Notes for striking Page Totals:

1. Count the number of persons from column 2 and give total in the box provided for item-1.

2. Strike 'Page Totals' for Items - 2 for items - 2 to 12 in respect of males and females separately below Questions 3,4,12,16 and 17 (I).

CHARACTERISTICS OF WORKERS AND NON-WORKERS

Q.16. Did the person work any time last year? (*includes even part time help or unpaid work on farm, family enterprise or in any other economic activity*)

Yes : If worked for 6 months or

more (**Main Worker**).

write "I" and proceed to

Q. 17. or If worked for less than 6 months

(**Marginal Worker**).

write "2" and proceed to Q. 17 or

No. If not worked at all (**Non-Worker**). write "3" and proceed to Qs. 18 & 19.

M/F

Main Workers (Total of 1's)

ITEM-6

Marginal Workers (Total of 2's)

ITEM-7

Non-Workers (Total of 3's)

ITEM-8

Q. 17.

Economic activity of the Main or Marginal Worker

Q.17. (i) Category of the economic activity of the Main or Marginal Worker

C-1/AL-2/HHI-3/OW-4

M/F

C (Total of 1's)

    ITEM-9

AL (Total of 2's)

    ITEM-10

HHI (Total of 3's)

    ITEM-11

OW (Total of 4's)

ITEM-12

Abbreviations used in Q. 17 (I)

C   Cultivator

AL   Agricultural Labourer

HHI   Worker in Household Industry

OW   Other Worker

If Code '3' (HHI) or Code '4' (OW) in column 20 or 21

Q.17. (ii) Occupation of the person

(*describe the actual work of the person*)

Q.17. (iii) Describe in detail the **nature of industry, trade or service** where the person works/worked or of self employment

Q.17. (iv) Class of Worker : - **Employer-1/Employee-2/Single Worker-3/Family Worker-4**

Q.18. If Code '2' (Marginal Worker) or Code '3' (Non-Worker) in Column 18 or 19, record Code of non-economic activity from : **Student -1/Household duties-2/Dependent-3/Pensioner-4/Beggar-5/Other-6**

Q.19. If Marginal Worker or Non-Worker, is the person seeking/available for work? **Yes-1/No-2**

Q.20. Travel to place of work

If Code '4' (OW) in column 20 or 21

Q.20 (i) Distance from residence to place of work in kilometres

Q.20 (ii) Mode of travel of place of work (*give Code number from the list below*)

Code numbers for Q. 20 (ii)

(*Mode of travel*)

On foot	1
Bicycle	2
Moped/Scooter/Motor cycle	3
Car/Jeep/Van	4
Tempo/Autorickshaw/Taxi	5
Bus	6
Train	7
Water transport	8
Any other	9
No Travel	0

MIGRATION CHARACTERISTICS

Q.21. Birth Place Is the person born in this village/town? If '**Yes**' put dash (-) against Qs. 21(I) and Q.21(ii) or If '**No**', enter particulars:

Birth place

Q.21. (i) State Country

(*if birth place within India, write the present name of the state or at birth place outside India write the present name of the country*)

Q.21. (ii) District

(*if birth place within India, write the present name of the district or if birth place outside India, put dash (-)*)

Q.22. Place of Last Residence

Has the person come to this village/town from elsewhere?

If '**No**', put dash (-) against Qs. 22(i) to 22 (v) or

If '**Yes**', give following particulars:

Place of last residence:

Q.22 (i) State/Country

(*if place of last residence **within India**, write the present name of the state or if place of last residence **outside India**. write the present name of the country*)

Q.22 (ii) District

(*if place of last residence **within India**, write the present name of the district or if place of last residence **outside India**, put dash (-))*

Q.22 (iii) At the time of migration, was the place of last residence **Rural**-1/ **Urban**-2

Q.22 (iv) Reason for migration of the person (give Code number from the list below)

Code numbers for Q. 22 (iv)

(*Reason for migration from place of last residence*)

Work/Employment	1
Business	2
Education	3
Marriage	4
Moved after birth	5
Moved with household	6
Any other reason	7

Q.22 (v) Duration of stay in this village or town since migration

(in completed years)

FERTILITY PARTICULARS

Q. 23 Fertility

For ever married women only (*currently Married, Widowed, Divorced or Separated*)

Q.23 (i) Number of children surviving at present (also include daughters and sons presently not staying in his household)

Daughter(s)

Son(s)

Q.23 (ii) Total number of children ever born alive (include both living and dead daughters and sons)

Daughter(s)

Son(s)

For currently married women only

Q.23 (iii) Number of children born alive during last one year (after 9th Feb., 2000)

Daughter(s)

Son(s)

Part III- For Household engaged in cultivation/plantation:

(i) Total net area of land under cultivation/plantation

                                                          Hectare   Ares

(ii) Net area of irrigated land

                                                          Hectare   Ares

(iii) Tenure status of land under cultivation/plantation.................

Owned-1/Rented-2/Owned and Rented-3

PART TWO

DEMOGRAPHIC PROFILE OF INDIA/STATES/UTs, 2001

Sections :

1. Demographic Profile of India
2. BIMARU States (Bihar, Madhya Pradesh, Rajasthan & Uttar Pradesh)
3. Offshoots of BIMARU States : Three New States (Chhatisgarh, Jharkhand & Uttaranchal)
4. Southern States (Andhra Pradesh, Karnataka, Kerala, Tamil Nadu, Goa & Pondicherry)
5. Jammu & Kashmir (where there was no Census in 1991)
6. North-Western States/UTs (Haryana, Himachal Pradesh, Punjab, Chandigarh and Delhi)
7. Western States (Gujarat, Maharashtra, Dadra & Nagar Haveli and Daman & Diu)
8. North-Eastern States (Arunachal Pradesh, Assam, Manipur, Meghalaya, Mizoram, Nagaland, Sikkim and Tripura)
9. West Bengal (where the urban birth rate is lowest)
10. Orissa (where the infant mortality rate is highest)
11. Islands (Andaman & Nicobar Islands, Lakshadweep)

1. DEMOGRAPHIC PROFILE OF INDIA

Census Paper 1 of 2001 presents the following 11 tables

Table 1 : Distribution of population, sex ratio, density and growth rate of population, India/State/UT

Table 2 : Total Population, child population in the age group 0-6, population 7 years and above, literates and literacy rates by sex : 2001, India/State/UT

Table 3 : Percentage decadal growth in population 1901-11 to 1991-2001, India/State/UT

Table 4 : States and Union territories arranged in descending order of percentage decadal growth of population : 1961-71 to 1991-2001

Table 5 : Projected, provisional and actual population of India, States and Union territories : 1971

Table 6 : Projected, provisional and actual population of India, States and Union territories : 1981

Table 7 : Projected, provisional and actual population of India, States and Union territories : 1991

Table 8 : Projected, provisional and actual population of India, States and Union territories : 1991

Table 9 : Projected population of India in 2000/2001 by different individuals and organizations in the last fifty years

Table 10 : Sex Ratio (females per 1,000 males) : 1901-2001, India/State/UT

Table 11 : States and Union territories arranged in descending order of Sex Ratio : 1961-2001, India/State/UT

The 28 States and 7 Union Territories are *not* arranged in alphabetical order as per the census practice. Instead, the states are arranged in some sort of geographical order as follows.

1.Jammu & Kashmir, 2. Himachal Pradesh, 3. Punjab, 4. Chandigarh, 5. Uttaranchal, 6. Haryana, 7. Delhi, 8. Rajasthan, 9. Uttar Pradesh, 10. Bihar, 11. Sikkim, 12. Arunachal Pradesh, 13. Nagaland, 14. Manipur, 15. Mizoram, 16. Tripura, 17. Meghalaya, 18. Assam, 19. West Bengal, 20. Jharkhand, 21. Orissa, 22. Chhatisgarh, 23. Madhya Pradesh, 24. Gujarat, 25. Daman & Diu, 26. Dadra & Nagar Haveli, 27. Maharashtra, 28. Andhra Pradesh, 29. Karnataka, 30. Goa, 31. Lakshadweep, 32. Kerala, 33. Tamil Nadu, 34. Pondicherry, 35. Andaman & Nicobar Islands.

The Census Commissioner deserves full credit for producing an impressive volume of 183 pages with maps, charts, graphs, and all the provisional tables in a record time. He also deserves credit for making it a priced publication so that even the provisional results are available to the wider public. However, we do not find the presentation of tables reader-friendly Jammu & Kashmir to Andaman Nicobar Islands listed haphazardly may promote national integration but is of little help to the reader who wants to locate quickly the data for the state in which he is interested. We, have therefore, taken the liberty of reorganising the data.

Since we consider size to be the most important factor in the context of population stabilization, we have classifed the 28 States and 7 UTs as follows:

A. Mega States (9)

(population : Over 50 million and more than 5 per cent of India's total population)
Uttar Pradesh, Maharashtra, Bihar, West Bengal, Andhra Pradesh, Tamil Nadu, Madhya Pradesh, Rajasthan, Karnataka

B. Bigger States/UTs (10)

(population : Over 10 million and more than 1 per cent of India's total population)
Gujarat, Orissa, Kerala, Jharkhand, Assam, Punjab, Haryana, Chhatisgarh, Delhi NCT, Jammu & Kashmir

C. Smaller States/UTs (16)

(population : Less than 10 million and less than 1 per cent of India's total population)

Uttaranchal , Himachal Pradesh, Tripura, Manipur, Meghalaya, Nagaland, Goa, Pondicherry UT, Chandigarh UT, Mizoram, Arunachal Pradesh, Sikkim, Andaman & Nicobar Islands UT, Dadra & Nagar Haveli UT, Daman & Diu UT, Lakshadweep UT

Before presenting statewise data (in 10 categories) we shall present the demographic profile of India as it emerges from the data in provisional tables. We have also included the vital statistics for India and the states as given in the latest issue of *Sample Registration Systems (SRS) Bulletin* issued by the Registrar General in October 2000.

It may be noted that the census decadal growth rates for states/UTs are a combination of natural growth rates and migration. The SRS data give the natural growth rates (births minus deaths) and this enables one to have an estimate of migration. The 2001 census did collect detailed data on migration but the tabulation and publication of such data will take considerable time. We have, therefore, included the latest SRS data on birth and death rates along with the census data. The SRS data are not given for the decade but only for the latest year (1999) for which such data are available.

Table 2.1 : Demographic Profile of India, 2001

Geographical Coverage

Number of States	28
Number of UTs	7
Number of Districts	593
Number of Tahsils/Talukas	5,564
Number of Towns	5,161
Number of Villages	640,000

Population Growth

Year	Population	Decadal Growth	
		Absolute	Per cent
1951[1]	361,088,090	42,427,510	13.31
1961[1]	439,234,771	78,146,681	21.64
1971	548,159,652	108,924,881	24.8
1981[2]	683,329,097	135,169,445	24.66
1991[3]	843,387,888	163,058,791	23.86
2001[4]	1,027,015,247	180,627,359	21.34

Note:

1. In working out 'Decadal Growth' and 'Percentage Decadal Growth' for India 1941-51 and 1951-61 the population of Tuensang district for 1951 (7,025) and the population of Tuensang (83,501) and Mon (5,774) districts for 1961 Census of Nagaland state have not been taken into account as the areas were censused for the first time in 1951 and the same are not comparable

2. The 1981 census could not be held owing to disturbed conditions prevailing in Assam. Hence the population figures for 1981 of Assam have been worked out by 'interpolation'.

3. The 1991 census could not be held owing to disturbed conditions prevailing in Jammu & Kashmir. Hence the population figures for 1991 of Jammu & Kashmir have been worked out by 'interpolation'

4. The population of India includes the estimated population of entire Kachchh district, Morvi, Maliya-Miyana and Wankaner talukas of Rajkot district, Jodiya taluka of Jamnagar district of Gujarat State and entire Kinnaur district of Himachal Pradesh where population enumeration of Census of India, 2001, could not be conducted due to natural calamities.

Fig. 2.1. Population of India, 2001 (in million)

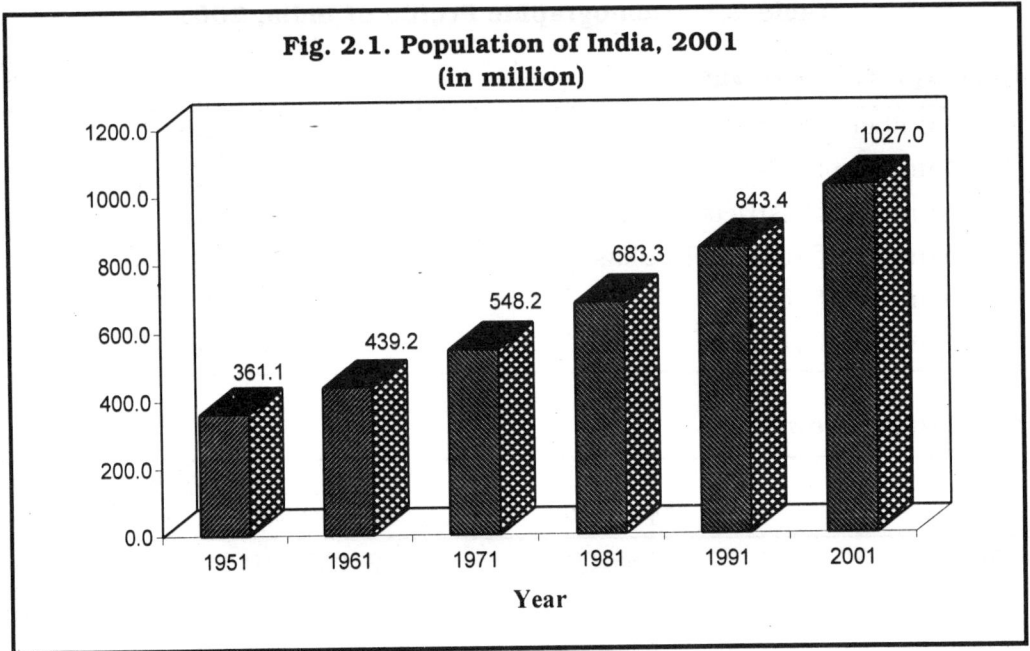

Fig. 2.2. Decadal Growth, Absolute Increase, 1951 to 2001 (in million)

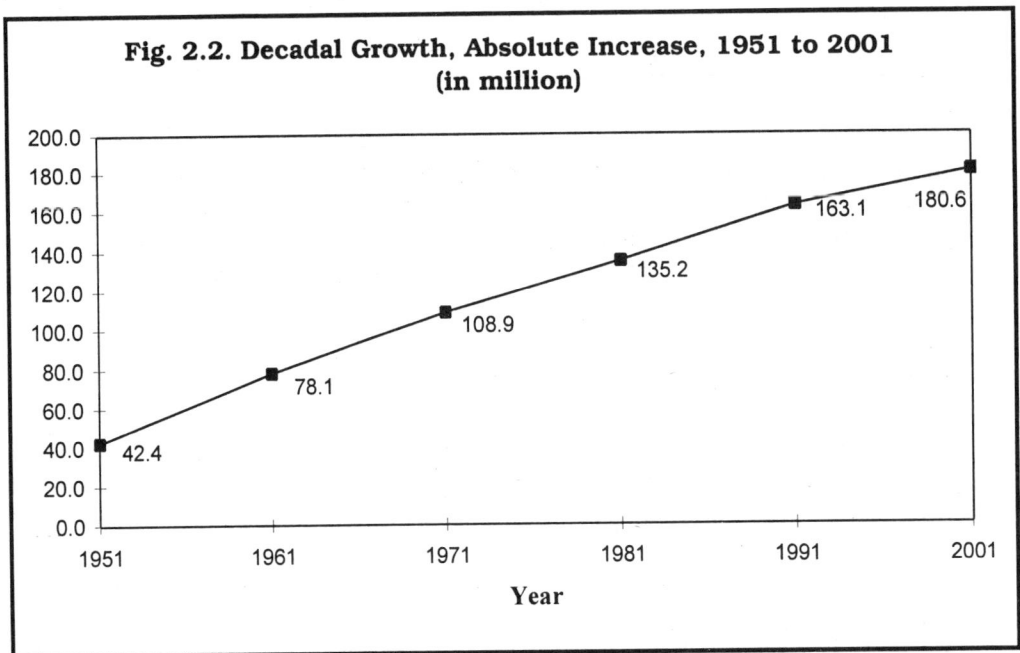

Fig. 2.3. Decadal Population Growth, 1951 to 2001 (per cent)

Year	Growth (%)
1951	13.3
1961	21.6
1971	24.8
1981	24.7
1991	23.9
2001	21.3

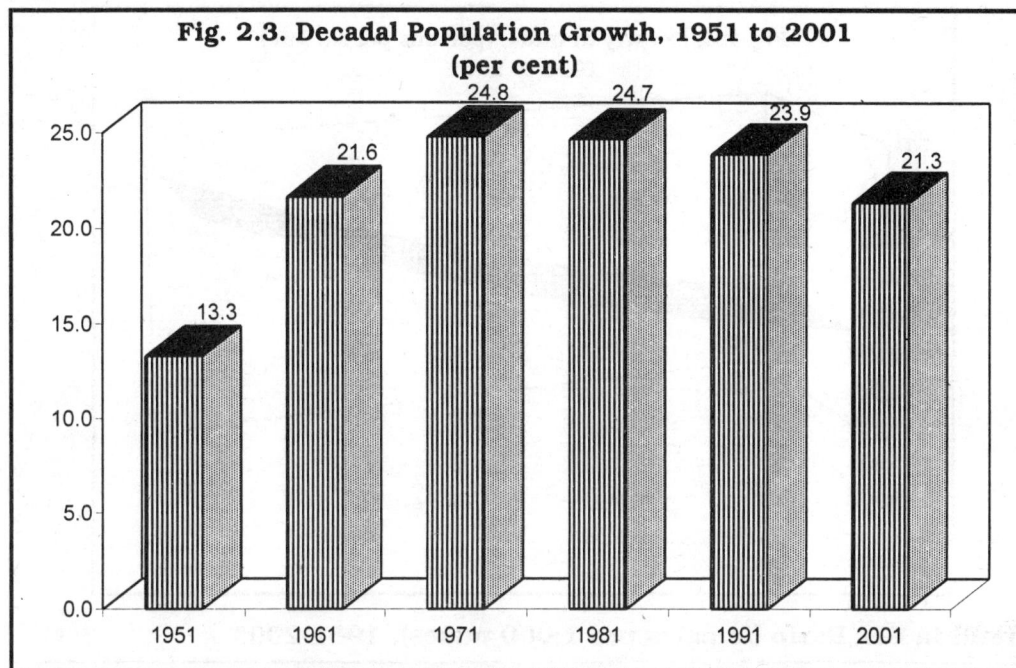

Difference in the Actual and Projected Population (in '000), 2001

Actual	Projected	Difference	Percent Difference
1,027,015	1,012,386	14,629	1.45

Child Population (age group 0-6), 2001

Persons	157,863,145
Male	81,911,041
Female	75,952,104

Percent of Child Population (age group 0-6) to Total Population

	1991	2001	Variation
Persons	17.94	15.42	-2.52
Male	17.77	15.47	-2.30
Female	18.12	15.36	-2.76

Density of Population

Year	Density (per sq.km)	Variation
1951	117	—
1961	142	25
1971	177	35
1981	216	39
1991	267	51
2001	324	57

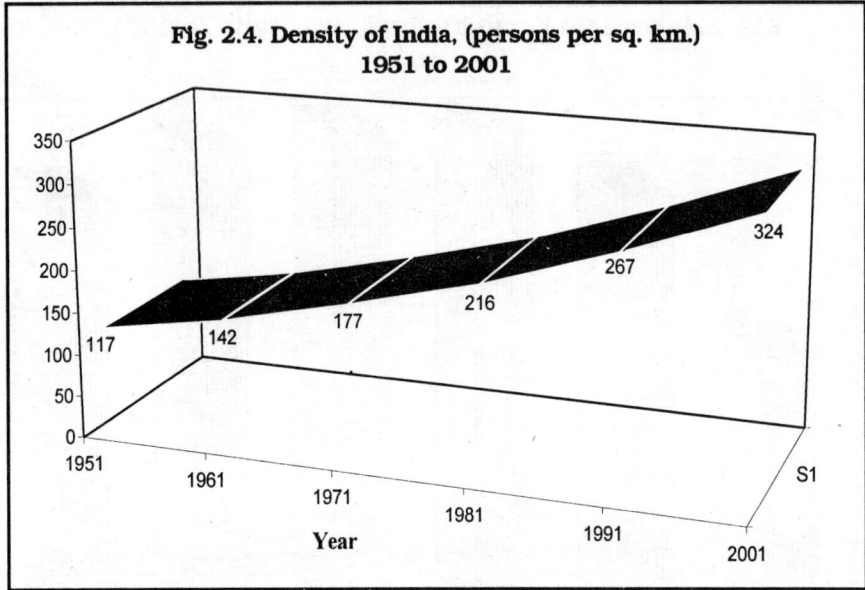

Fig. 2.4. Density of India, (persons per sq. km.) 1951 to 2001

Trend in Sex Ratio (females per 1,000 males), 1961-2001

Year	Sex ratio (females per 1,000 males)	Variation	0-6 population	Variation
1961	941	—	976	—
1971	930	-11	964	-12
1981	934	+4	962	-2
1991	927	-7	945	-17
2001	933	+6	927	-18

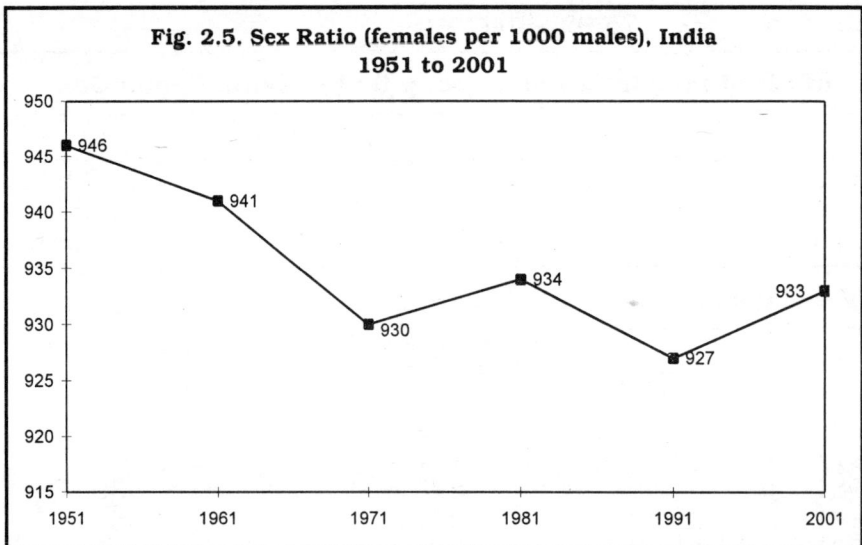

Fig. 2.5. Sex Ratio (females per 1000 males), India 1951 to 2001

Sex Ratio (females per 1,000 males)

	1991	*2001*	*Variation*
Total Population	927	933	+6
0-6	945	927	-18
7+	923	935	+12

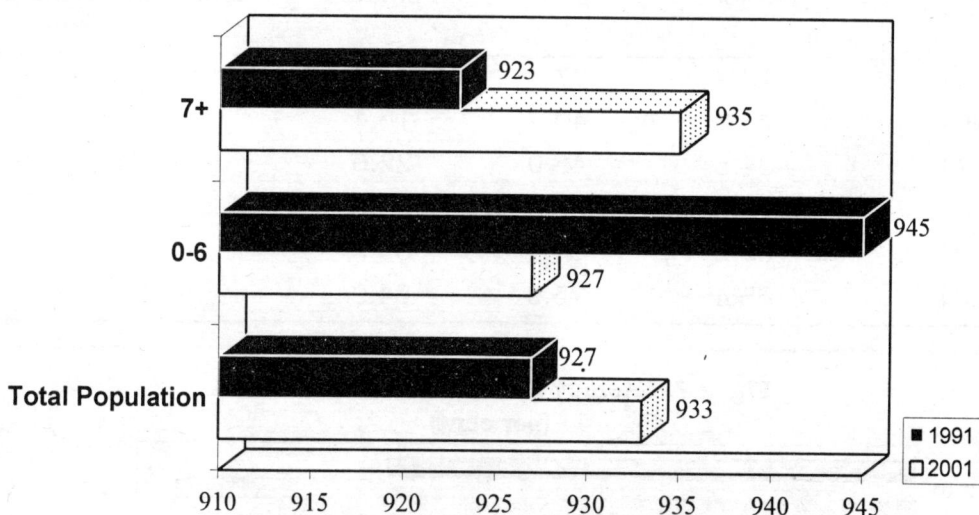

Fig. 2.6. Sex Ratio of 0-6 and 7+ age groups, India 1991 and 2001

Literate Population 7+

Year	*Persons*	*Male*	*Female*
1991	358,402,626	228,983,134	129,419,492
2001	562,010,743	336,969,695	225,041,048
Absolute increase in 2001 over 1991	203,608,117	107,986,561	95,621,556
Percentage decadal increase during 1991-2001	56.8	47.1	73.9

Illiterate Population 7+

Year	Persons	Male	Female
1991	328,167,288	128,099,211	200,068,077
2001	296,208,952	106,654,066	189,554,886
Absolute decline	-31,958,336	-21,445,145	-10,513,191
Percentage decadal decline during 1991-2001	-9.7	-16.7	-5.3

Literacy Rate in India (7+) Percent

Year	Persons	Males	Females	Male-female gap in literacy rate
1951	18.3	27.2	8.9	18.3
1961	28.3	40.4	15.4	25.1
1971	34.5	46.0	22.0	24.0
1981	43.6	56.4	29.8	26.6
1991	52.2	64.1	39.3	24.8
2001	65.4	75.9	54.2	21.7

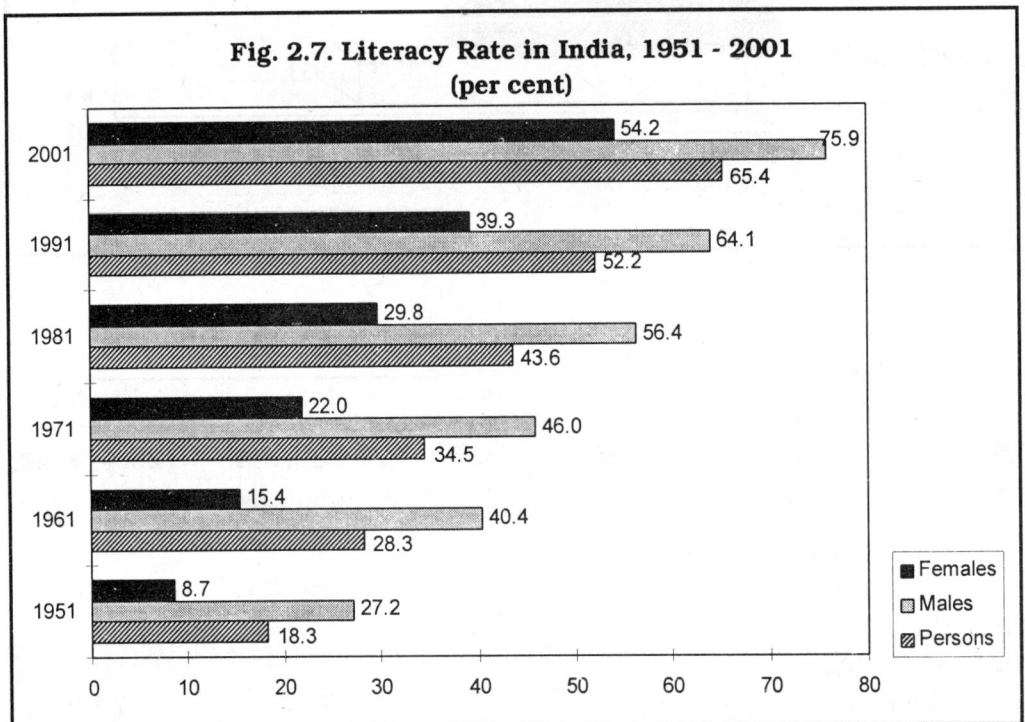

Fig. 2.7. Literacy Rate in India, 1951 - 2001 (per cent)

Vital Statistics (SRS Data, 1999)

	Birth Rate per 1000	Death Rate per 1000	Natural Growth Rate per 1000	Infant Mortality Rate per 1000
Total	26.1	8.7	17.4	70
Rural	27.6	9.4	18.2	75
Urban	20.8	6.3	14.5	44

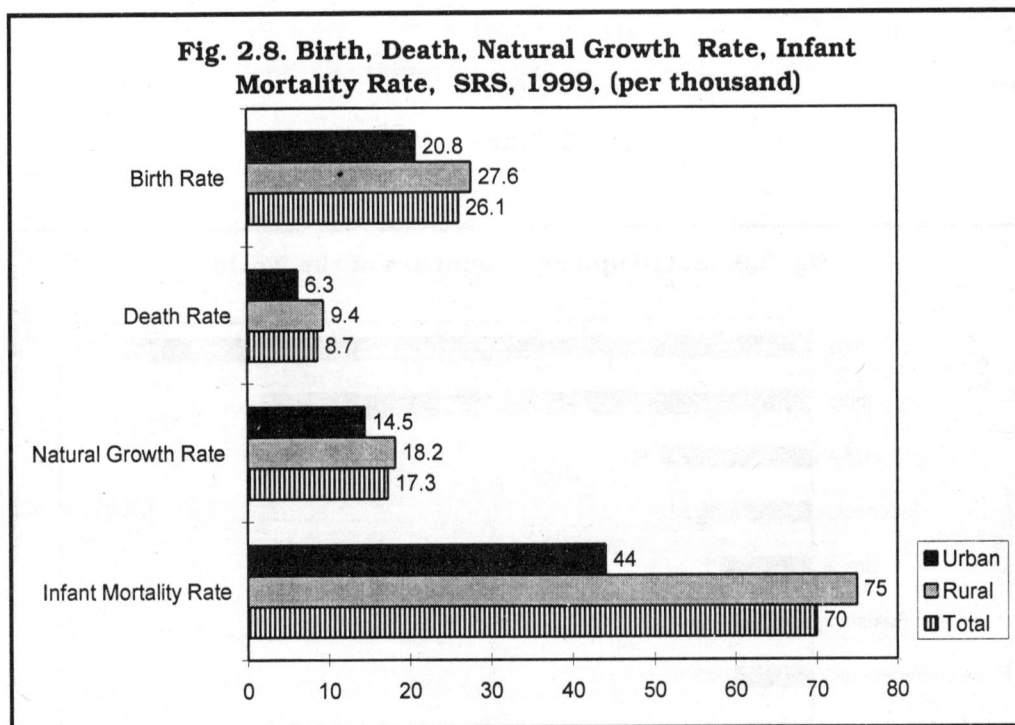

Fig. 2.8. Birth, Death, Natural Growth Rate, Infant Mortality Rate, SRS, 1999, (per thousand)

International Comparisions

Most Populous Countries of the World

Country	Reference date	Population (in million)
China	01.02.2000	1,278
India	01.03.2001	1,027
U.S.A.	April, 2000	281
Indonesia	01.07.2000	212
Brazil	01.07.2000	170
Pakistan	01.07.2000	157
Russian Federation	01.07.2000	147
Bangladesh	01.07.2000	129
Japan	01.10.2000	127
Nigeria	01.02.2000	112

Fig. 2.9. Most Populous Countries of the World

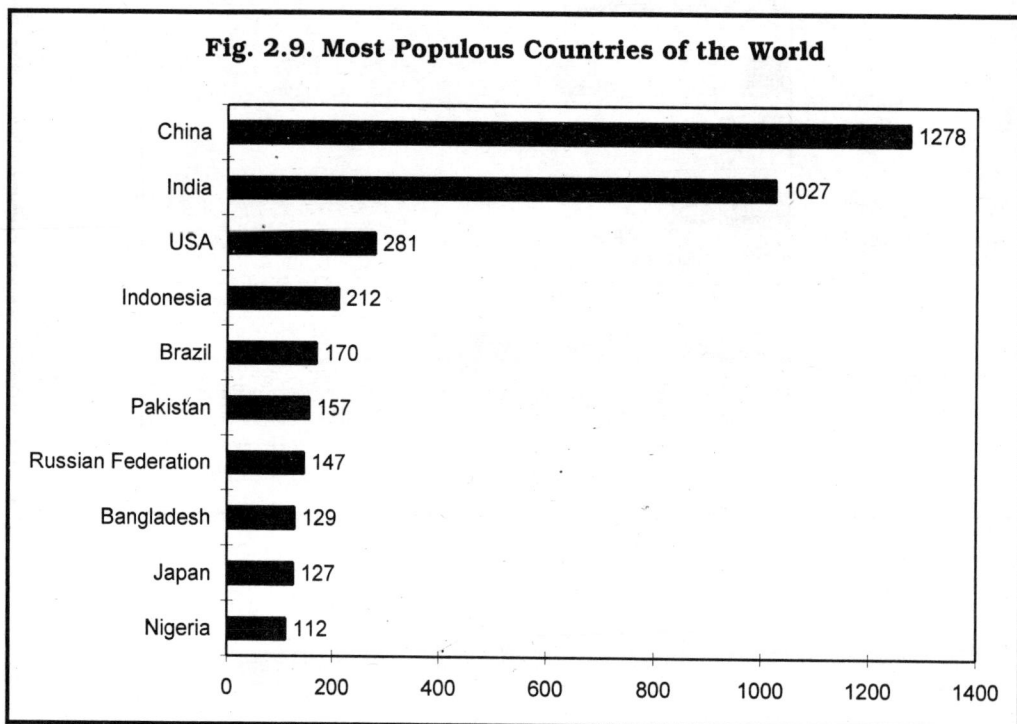

Country	Population
China	1278
India	1027
USA	281
Indonesia	212
Brazil	170
Pakistan	157
Russian Federation	147
Bangladesh	129
Japan	127
Nigeria	112

Table 2.2 : Demographic Diversity of India, 2001

	Maximum value	State/UT	Minimum value	State/UT
Area		Rajasthan		Lakshadweep
Population	166,052,859	Uttar Pradesh	60,595	Lakshadweep
Density (per sq. km)	9,294	Delhi	13	Arunachal Pradesh
Sex ratio (females per 1000 males)	1,058	Kerala	709	Daman & Diu
Growth rate (1991-2001), Percent	64.4	Nagaland	9.4	Kerala
Literacy Rate (percent)				
Persons	90.9	Kerala	47.5	Bihar
Males	94.2	Kerala	60.3	Bihar
Females	87.9	Kerala	33.6	Bihar
No. of Literates				
Persons	77,770,275	Uttar Pradesh	45,281	Lakshadweep
Males	50,256,119	Utlar Pradesh	24,806	Lakshadweep
Females	27,514,156	Utt r Pradesh	20,475	Lakshadweep
No. of Illiterates				
Persons	57,810,542	Utta. Pradesh	6,454	Lakshadweep
Males	21,306,282	Uttar Pradesh	1,824	Lakshadweep
Females	36,504,260	Uttar Pradesh	4,630	Lakshadweep
Vital Statistics, SRS (1999) Bigger States				
Birth Rate (per 1,000)				
Total	32.1	Uttar Pradesh	18.0	Kerala
Rural	33.1	Uttar Pradesh	18.1	Kerala
Urban	26.7	Uttar Pradesh	14.3	West Bengal
Death Rate (per 1,000)				
Total	10.6	Orissa	6.4	Kerala
Rural	11.2	Madhya Pradesh	6.5	Kerala
Urban	7.7	Uttar Pradesh	5.5	Karnataka
Natural Growth Rate (per 1,000)				
Total	22.7	Rajasthan	11.3	Tamil Nadu
Rural	23.6	Rajasthan	11.1	Tamil Nadu
Urban	19.0	Uttar Pradesh	7.5	West Bengal
Infant Mortality Rate (per 1,000)				
Total	97	Orissa	14	Kerala
Rural	100	Orissa	14	Kerala
Urban	65	Orissa	16	Kerala

Table 2.3 : Size, Distribution and Density of States and UTs, 2001

A. Mega States (9)
(population : Over 50 million and more than 5 per cent of India's total population)

Rank	State	Population (in million)	Per cent of India's Population	Density (per sq. km)
1	Uttar Pradesh	166.1	16.2	689
2	Maharashtra	96.8	9.4	314
3	Bihar	82.9	8.1	880
4	West Bengal	80.2	7.8	904
5	Andhra Pradesh	75.7	7.4	275
6	Tamil Nadu	62.1	6.1	478
7	Madhya Pradesh	60.4	5.9	196
8	Rajasthan	56.5	5.5	165
9	Karnataka	52.7	5.1	275

B. Bigger States/UTs (10)
(population : Over 10 million and more than 1 per cent of India's total population)

1	Gujarat	50.6	4.9	258
2	Orissa	36.7	3.6	236
3	Kerala	31.8	3.1	819
4	Jharkhand	26.9	2.6	338
5	Assam	26.6	2.6	340
6	Punjab	24.3	2.4	482
7	Haryana	21.1	2.1	477
8	Chhatisgarh	20.8	2.0	154
9	Delhi NCT	13.8	1.3	9,294
10	Jammu & Kashmir	10.1	1.0	99

C. Smaller States/UTs (16)
(population : Less than 10 million and less than 1 per cent of India's total population)

1	Uttaranchal	8.48	0.83	159
2	Himachal Pradesh	6.08	0.59	109
3	Tripura	3.19	0.31	304
4	Manipur	2.39	0.23	107
5	Meghalaya	2.31	0.22	103
6	Nagaland	1.99	0.19	120
7	Goa	1.34	0.13	363
8	Arunachal Pradesh	1.09	0.11	13
9	Pondicherry UT	0.97	0.09	2,029
10	Chandigarh UT	0.90	0.09	7,903
11	Mizoram	0.89	0.09	42
12	Sikkim	0.54	0.05	76
13	Andaman & Nicobar Islands UT	0.36	0.03	43
14	Dadra & Nagar Haveli UT	0.22	0.02	449
15	Daman & Diu UT	0.16	0.02	1,411
16	Lakshadweep UT	0.06	0.01	1,894
	INDIA	**1,027**	**100.00**	**324**

Table 2.4 : Increase in Density of States/UTs, 1991-2001
(States/UTs ranked according to increase in density between 1991-2001)

Rank	States/UTs	2001	1991	Increase in Denisty in 2001
	India	**324**	**267**	**57**
1	Delhi NCT	9,294	6,352	2,942
2	Chandigarh UT	7,903	5,632	2,271
3	Daman & Diu UT	1,411	907	504
4	Pondicherry UT	2,029	1,683	346
5	Lakshadweep UT	1,894	1,616	278
6	Bihar	880	685	195
7	Dadra & Nagar Haveli UT	449	282	167
8	Uttar Pradesh	689	548	141
9	West Bengal	904	767	137
10	Haryana	477	372	105
11	Punjab	482	403	79
12	Kerala	819	749	70
13	Jharkhand	338	274	64
14	Maharashtra	314	257	57
15	Assam	340	286	54
16	Tamil Nadu	478	429	49
17	Nagaland	120	73	47
18	Gujarat	258	211	47
19	Goa	363	316	47
20	Tripura	304	263	41
21	Karnataka	275	235	40
22	Madhya Pradesh	196	158	38
23	Rajasthan	165	129	36
24	Orissa	236	203	33
25	Andhra Pradesh	275	242	33
26	Uttaranchal	159	133	26
27	Manipur	107	82	25
28	Meghalaya	103	79	24
29	Chhatisgarh	154	130	24
30	Jammu & Kashmir	99	77	22
31	Sikkim	76	57	19
32	Himachal Pradesh	109	93	16
33	Mizoram	42	33	9
34	Andaman & Nicobar Islands UT	43	34	9
35	Arunachal Pradesh	13	10	3

Table 2.5 : Percentage Decadal Growth Rate of Population 1951-2001

A. Mega States (9) (population : Over 50 million and more than 5 per cent of India's total population)

Rank	State	1951-1961	1961-1971	1971-1981	1981-1991	1991-2001
1	Uttar Pradesh	16.4	19.5	25.4	25.6	25.8
2	Maharashtra	23.6	27.5	24.5	25.7	22.6
3	Bihar	19.8	20.9	24.2	23.4	28.4
4	West Bengal	32.8	26.9	23.2	24.7	17.8
5	Andhra Pradesh	15.7	20.9	23.1	24.2	13.9
6	Tamil Nadu	11.9	22.3	17.5	15.4	11.2
7	Madhya Pradesh	24.7	29.3	27.2	27.2	24.3
8	Rajasthan	26.2	27.8	33.0	28.4	28.3
9	Karnataka	21.6	24.2	26.8	21.1	17.3

B. Bigger States/UTs (10) (population : Over 10 million and more than 1 per cent of India's total population)

Rank	State	1951-1961	1961-1971	1971-1981	1981-1991	1991-2001
1	Gujarat	26.9	29.4	27.7	21.2	22.5
2	Orissa	19.8	25.1	20.2	20.1	15.9
3	Kerala	24.8	26.3	19.2	14.3	9.4
4	Jharkhand	19.7	22.6	23.8	24.0	23.2
5	Assam	35.0	35.0	23.4	24.2	18.9
6	Punjab	21.6	21.7	23.9	20.8	19.8
7	Haryana	33.8	32.2	28.8	27.4	28.1
8	Chhatisgarh	22.8	27.1	20.4	25.7	18.1
9	Delhi NCT	52.4	52.9	53.0	51.5	46.3
10	Jammu & Kashmir	9.4	29.7	29.7	30.3	29.0

C. Smaller States/UTs (16) (population : Less than 10 million and less than 1 per cent of India's total population)

Rank	State	1951-1961	1961-1971	1971-1981	1981-1991	1991-2001
1	Uttaranchal	22.6	24.4	27.5	24.2	19.2
2	Himachal Pradesh	17.9	23.0	23.7	20.8	17.5
3	Tripura	78.7	36.3	31.9	34.3	15.7
4	Manipur	35.0	37.5	32.5	29.3	30.0
5	Meghalaya	27.0	31.5	32.0	32.9	29.9
6	Nagaland	73.4	39.9	50.1	56.1	64.4
7	Goa	7.8	34.8	26.7	16.1	14.9
8	Pondicherry UT	16.3	27.8	28.2	33.6	20.6
9	Chandigarh UT	394.1	114.6	75.6	42.2	40.3
10	Mizoram	35.6	24.9	48.6	39.7	29.2
11	Arunachal Pradesh	NA	38.9	35.2	36.8	26.2
12	Sikkim	17.8	29.4	50.8	28.5	33.0
13	Andaman & Nicobar Islands UT	105.2	81.2	63.9	48.7	26.9
14	Dadra & Nagar Haveli UT	39.6	28.0	39.8	33.6	59.2
15	Daman & Diu UT	-24.6	70.9	26.1	28.6	55.6
16	Lakshadweep UT	14.6	32.0	26.5	28.5	17.2
	INDIA	**21.6**	**24.8**	**24.7**	**23.9**	**21.3**

Table 2.6 : Percentage Decadal Growth Rate of States and UTs Ranked According to Growth Rate during 1991-2001

Rank	State	1991-2001	Variation in decadal growth rate (per cent points), 1999-2001 compared to 1981-91
	INDIA	**21.3**	**-2.5**
1	Nagaland	64.4	8.3
2	Dadra & Nagar Haveli UT	59.2	25.6
3	Daman & Diu UT	55.6	27.0
4	Delhi NCT	46.3	-5.1
5	Chandigarh UT	40.3	-1.8
6	Sikkim	33.0	4.5
7	Manipur	30.0	0.7
8	Meghalaya	29.9	-2.9
9	Mizoram	29.2	-10.5
10	Jammu & Kashmir	29.0	-1.3
11	Bihar	28.4	5.1
12	Rajasthan	28.3	-0.1
13	Haryana	28.1	0.7
14	Andaman & Nicobar Islands UT	26.9	-21.8
15	Arunachal Pradesh	26.2	-10.6
16	Uttar Pradesh	25.8	0.3
17	Madhya Pradesh	24.3	-2.9
18	Jharkhand	23.2	-0.8
19	Maharashtra	22.6	-3.2
20	Gujarat	22.5	1.3
21	Pondicherry UT	20.6	-13.1
22	Punjab	19.8	-1.1
23	Uttaranchal	19.2	-5.0
24	Assam	18.9	-5.4
25	Chhatisgarh	18.1	-7.7
26	West Bengal	17.8	-6.9
27	Himachal Pradesh	17.5	-3.3
28	Karnataka	17.3	-3.9
29	Lakshadweep UT	17.2	-11.3
30	Orissa	15.9	-4.1
31	Tripura	15.7	-18.6
32	Goa	14.9	-1.2
33	Andhra Pradesh	13.9	-10.3
34	Tamil Nadu	11.2	-4.2
35	Kerala	9.4	-4.9

Table 2.7 : State/UTs Ranked According to Decline in Annual Growth Rate, 1981-2001 and SRS Data 2001

Rank	India/States/UT	1981-91	1991-2001	Difference points	CBR (per 1000)	CDR (per 1000)	Natural Growth Rate
	INDIA	**2.14**	**1.93**	**-0.21**	**26.1**	**8.7**	**1.73**
1	Daman & Diu UT	2.52	4.42	1.90	26.9	7.1	1.99
2	Dadra & Nagar Haveli UT	2.89	4.65	1.76	32.4	5.9	2.65
3	Nagaland	4.45	4.97	0.52	NA	NA	NA
4	Bihar	2.10	2.50	0.40	30.4	9.1	2.14
5	Sikkim	2.51	2.85	0.34	21.6	5.8	1.58
6	Gujarat	1.92	2.03	0.11	25.4	7.9	1.76
7	Manipur	2.57	2.63	0.06	18.6	5.4	1.31
8	Haryana	2.42	2.47	0.05	26.8	7.7	1.91
9	Uttar Pradesh	2.28	2.30	0.02	32.1	10.5	2.16
10	Rajasthan	2.50	2.49	-0.01	31.1	8.4	2.27
11	Jharkhand	2.15	2.09	-0.06	—	—	—
12	Punjab	1.89	1.80	-0.09	21.5	7.4	1.41
13	Jammu & Kashmir	2.65	2.55	-0.10	NA	NA	NA
14	Goa	1.49	1.39	-0.10	14.3	7.2	0.71
15	Chandigarh	3.52	3.39	-0.13	17.9	3.9	1.40
16	Meghalaya	2.84	2.62	-0.22	28.7	9.1	1.95
17	Madhya Pradesh	2.41	2.18	-0.23	30.7	10.6	2.01
18	Maharashtra	2.29	2.04	-0.25	21.1	7.5	1.36
19	Himachal Pradesh	1.89	1.62	-0.27	23.8	7.3	1.64
20	Karnataka	1.92	1.59	-0.33	22.3	7.7	1.46
21	Delhi NCT	4.15	3.81	-0.34	19.4	4.8	1.46
22	Orissa	1.83	1.48	-0.35	24.1	10.6	1.34
23	Tamil Nadu	1.43	1.06	-0.37	19.3	8.0	1.13
24	Uttaranchal	2.17	1.76	-0.41	—	—	—
25	Assam	2.17	1.73	-0.44	27.0	9.7	1.73
26	Kerala	1.34	0.90	-0.44	18.0	6.4	1.15
27	West Bengal	2.21	1.64	-0.57	20.7	7.1	1.36
28	Chhatisgarh	2.29	1.66	-0.63	—	—	—
29	Mizoram	3.34	2.56	-0.78	17.0	5.5	1.15
30	Arunachal Pradesh	3.14	2.33	-0.81	22.3	6.0	1.63
31	Andhra Pradesh	2.17	1.30	-0.87	21.7	8.2	1.35
32	Lakshadweep UT	2.51	1.59	-0.92	25.1	4.7	2.04
33	Pondicherry UT	2.90	1.87	-1.03	17.7	6.9	1.08
34	Tripura	2.95	1.46	-1.49	17.0	5.7	1.13
35	Andaman & Nicobar Islands UT	3.97	2.39	-1.58	18.1	5.5	1.26

Table 2.8 : Sex Ratio (females per 1,000 males), 1951-2001

A. **Mega States (9) (population : Over 50 million and more than 5 per cent of India's total population)**

Rank	State	1951	1961	1971	1981	1991	2001
1	Uttar Pradesh	908	907	876	882	876	898
2	Maharashtra	941	936	930	937	934	922
3	Bihar	1000	1005	957	948	907	921
4	West Bengal	865	878	891	911	917	934
5	Andhra Pradesh	986	981	977	975	972	978
6	Tamil Nadu	1007	992	978	977	974	986
7	Madhya Pradesh	945	932	920	921	912	920
8	Rajasthan	921	908	911	919	910	922
9	Karnataka	966	959	957	963	960	964

B. **Bigger States/UTs (10) (population : Over 10 million and more than 1 per cent of India's total population)**

Rank	State	1951	1961	1971	1981	1991	2001
1	Gujarat	952	940	934	942	934	921
2	Orissa	1022	1001	988	981	971	972
3	Kerala	1028	1022	1016	1032	1036	1,058
4	Jharkhand	961	960	945	940	922	941
5	Assam	868	869	896	910	923	932
6	Punjab	844	854	865	879	882	874
7	Haryana	871	868	867	870	865	861
8	Chhatisgarh	1024	1008	998	996	985	990
9	Delhi NCT	768	785	801	808	827	821
10	Jammu & Kashmir	873	878	878	892	896	900

C. **Smaller States/UTs (16) (population : Less than 10 million and less than 1 per cent of India's total population)**

Rank	State	1951	1961	1971	1981	1991	2001
1	Uttaranchal	940	947	940	936	936	964
2	Himachal Pradesh	912	938	958	973	976	970
3	Tripura	904	932	943	946	945	950
4	Manipur	1,036	1,015	980	971	958	978
5	Meghalaya	949	937	942	954	955	975
6	Nagaland	999	933	871	863	886	909
7	Goa	1,128	1,066	981	975	967	960
8	Pondicherry UT	1,030	1,013	989	985	979	1,001
9	Chandigarh UT	781	652	749	769	790	773
10	Mizoram	1,041	1,009	946	919	921	938
11	Arunachal Pradesh	NA	894	861	862	859	901
12	Sikkim	907	904	863	835	878	875
13	Andaman & Nicobar Islands UT	625	617	644	760	818	846
14	Dadra & Nagar Haveli UT	946	963	1,007	974	952	811
15	Daman & Diu UT	1,125	1,169	1,099	1,062	969	709
16	Lakshadweep UT	1,043	1,020	978	975	943	947
	INDIA	**946**	**941**	**930**	**934**	**927**	**933**

Table 2.9 : Child Population (0-6 years), 2001

A. Mega States (9) (population : Over 50 million and more than 5 per cent of India's total population)

Rank	State	Persons	Males	Females
1	Uttar Pradesh	30,472,042	15,903,900	14,568,142
2	Maharashtra	13,187,087	6,878,579	6,308,508
3	Bihar	16,234,539	8,375,532	7,859,007
4	West Bengal	11,132,824	5,671,152	5,461,672
5	Andhra Pradesh	9,673,274	4,926,200	4,747,074
6	Tamil Nadu	6,817,669	3,515,562	3,302,107
7	Madhya Pradesh	10,618,323	5,504,422	5,113,901
8	Rajasthan	10,451,103	5,474,965	4,976,138
9	Karnataka	6,826,168	3,501,499	3,324,669

B. Bigger States/UTs (10) (population : Over 10 million and more than 1 per cent of India's total population)

1	Gujarat	6,867,958	3,656,956	3,211,002
2	Orissa	5,180,551	2,656,046	2,524,505
3	Kerala	3,653,578	1,861,669	1,791,909
4	Jharkhand	4,796,188	2,440,025	2,356,163
5	Assam	4,350,248	2,215,104	2,135,144
6	Punjab	3,055,492	1,704,142	1,351,350
7	Haryana	3,259,080	1,790,758	1,468,322
8	Chhatisgarh	3,469,774	1,756,441	1,713,333
9	Delhi NCT	1,923,995	1,031,584	892,411
10	Jammu & Kashmir	1,431,182	738,839	692,343

C. Smaller States/UTs (16) (population : Less than 10 million and less than 1 per cent of India's total population)

1	Uttaranchal	1,319,393	692,272	627,121
2	Himachal Pradesh	769,424	405,618	363,806
3	Tripura	427,012	216,244	210,768
4	Manipur	312,691	159,448	153,243
5	Meghalaya	457,442	231,571	225,871
6	Nagaland	280,172	141,852	138,320
7	Goa	142,152	73,547	68,605
8	Pondicherry UT	113,010	57,722	55,288
9	Chandigarh UT	109,293	59,238	50,055
10	Mizoram	141,537	71,817	69,720
11	Arunachal Pradesh	200,055	102,010	98,045
12	Sikkim	77,170	38,856	38,314
13	Andaman & Nicobar Islands UT	44,674	22,733	21,941
14	Dadra & Nagar Haveli UT	39,173	19,856	19,317
15	Daman & Diu UT	20,012	10,394	9,618
16	Lakshadweep UT	8,860	4,488	4,372
	INDIA	**157,863,145**	**81,911,041**	**75,952,104**

Table 2.10 : Proportion of Child Population in the Age Group 0-6 to Total Population, 2001

A. Mega States (9) (population : Over 50 million and more than 5 per cent of India's total population)

Rank	State	Total	Male	Female
1	Uttar Pradesh	18.35	18.18	18.54
2	Maharashtra	13.63	13.67	13.59
3	Bihar	19.59	19.41	19.78
4	West Bengal	13.88	13.67	14.10
5	Andhra Pradesh	12.77	12.87	12.68
6	Tamil Nadu	10.98	11.24	10.71
7	Madhya Pradesh	17.58	17.50	17.68
8	Rajasthan	18.51	18.63	18.37
9	Karnataka	12.94	13.04	12.85

B. Bigger States/UTs (10) (population : Over 10 million and more than 1 per cent of India's total population)

1	Gujarat	14.2	14.5	13.9
2	Orissa	14.1	14.3	14.0
3	Kerala	11.5	12.0	11.0
4	Jharkhand	17.8	17.6	18.1
5	Assam	16.3	16.1	16.6
6	Punjab	12.6	13.2	11.9
7	Haryana	15.5	15.8	15.1
8	Chhatisgarh	16.7	16.8	16.6
9	Delhi NCT	14.0	13.6	14.4
10	Jammu & Kashmir	14.2	13.9	14.5

C. Smaller States/UTs (16) (population : Less than 10 million and less than 1 per cent of India's total population)

1	Uttaranchal	15.6	16.0	15.1
2	Himachal Pradesh	12.8	13.3	12.3
3	Tripura	13.4	13.2	13.6
4	Manipur	13.1	13.2	13.0
5	Meghalaya	19.8	19.8	19.8
6	Nagaland	14.1	13.6	14.6
7	Goa	10.6	10.7	10.4
8	Pondicherry UT	11.6	11.9	11.4
9	Chandigarh UT	12.1	11.7	12.8
10	Mizoram	15.9	15.6	16.2
11	Arunachal Pradesh	18.3	17.8	19.0
12	Sikkim	14.3	13.5	15.2
13	Andaman & Nicobar Islands UT	12.5	11.8	13.4
14	Dadra & Nagar Haveli UT	17.8	16.3	19.6
15	Daman & Diu UT	12.7	11.2	14.7
16	Lakshadweep UT	14.6	14.4	14.8
	INDIA	**15.4**	15.5	15.4

Table 2.11 : Sex Ratio (females per 1,000 males), of
Child Population, (0-6 and 7+ age group), 2001

A. Mega States (9) (population : Over 50 million and more than 5 per cent of India's total population)

Rank	State	0-6, age group	7+ age group
1	Uttar Pradesh	916	895
2	Maharashtra	917	923
3	Bihar	938	916
4	West Bengal	963	929
5	Andhra Pradesh	964	980
6	Tamil Nadu	939	992
7	Madhya Pradesh	929	918
8	Rajasthan	909	925
9	Karnataka	949	966

B. Bigger States/UTs (10) (population : Over 10 million and more than 1 per cent of India's total population)

Rank	State	0-6, age group	7+ age group
1	Gujarat	878	927
2	Orissa	950	976
3	Kerala	963	1071
4	Jharkhand	966	936
5	Assam	964	926
6	Punjab	793	886
7	Haryana	820	869
8	Chhatisgarh	975	992
9	Delhi NCT	865	813
10	Jammu & Kashmir	937	894

C. Smaller States/UTs (16) (population : Less than 10 million and less than 1 per cent of India's total population)

Rank	State	0-6, age group	7+ age group
1	Uttaranchal	906	976
2	Himachal Pradesh	897	981
3	Tripura	975	947
4	Manipur	961	981
5	Meghalaya	975	974
6	Nagaland	975	899
7	Goa	933	964
8	Pondicherry UT	958	1007
9	Chandigarh UT	845	763
10	Mizoram	971	932
11	Arunachal Pradesh	961	888
12	Sikkim	986	858
13	Andaman & Nicobar Islands UT	965	830
14	Dadra & Nagar Haveli UT	973	779
15	Daman & Diu UT	925	682
16	Lakshadweep UT	974	943
	INDIA	**927**	**935**

Table 2.12 : Literacy Rate by Sex, 2001

A. Mega States (9) (population : Over 50 million and more than 5 per cent of India's total population)

Rank	State	Persons	Males	Females
1	Uttar Pradesh	57.4	70.2	43.0
2	Maharashtra	77.3	86.3	67.5
3	Bihar	47.5	60.3	33.6
4	West Bengal	69.2	77.6	60.2
5	Andhra Pradesh	61.1	70.9	51.2
6	Tamil Nadu	73.5	82.3	64.6
7	Madhya Pradesh	64.1	76.8	50.3
8	Rajasthan	61.0	76.5	44.3
9	Karnataka	67.0	76.3	57.5

B. Bigger States/UTs (10) (population : Over 10 million and more than 1 per cent of India's total population)

Rank	State	Persons	Males	Females
1	Gujarat	70.0	80.5	58.6
2	Orissa	63.6	76.0	51.0
3	Kerala	90.9	94.2	87.9
4	Jharkhand	54.1	67.9	39.4
5	Assam	64.3	71.9	56.0
6	Punjab	70.0	75.6	63.6
7	Haryana	68.6	79.3	56.3
8	Chhatisgarh	65.2	77.9	52.4
9	Delhi NCT	81.8	87.4	75.0
10	Jammu & Kashmir	54.5	65.8	41.8

C. Smaller States/UTs (16) (population : Less than 10 million and less than 1 per cent of India's total population)

Rank	State	Persons	Males	Females
1	Uttaranchal	72.3	84.0	60.3
2	Himachal Pradesh	77.1	86.0	68.1
3	Tripura	73.7	81.5	65.4
4	Manipur	68.9	77.9	59.7
5	Meghalaya	63.3	66.1	60.4
6	Nagaland	67.1	71.8	61.9
7	Goa	82.3	88.9	75.5
8	Pondicherry UT	81.5	88.9	74.1
9	Chandigarh UT	81.8	85.7	76.7
10	Mizoram	88.5	90.7	86.1
11	Arunachal Pradesh	54.7	64.1	44.2
12	Sikkim	69.7	76.7	61.5
13	Andaman & Nicobar Islands UT	81.2	86.1	75.3
14	Dadra & Nagar Haveli UT	60.0	73.3	43.0
15	Daman & Diu UT	81.1	88.4	70.4
16	Lakshadweep UT	87.5	93.2	81.6
	INDIA	**65.4**	**75.9**	**54.2**

Table 2.13 : Distribution of Illiterate Population, 2001

India/State/UTs	Absolute		
	Persons	*Male*	*Female*
India	**296,208,952**	**106,654,066**	**189,554,886**
Uttar Pradesh	57,810,542	21,306,282	36,504,260
Bihar	34,968,650	13,799,477	21,169,173
Andhra Pradesh	25,689,502	9,724,534	15,964,968
West Bengal	21,266,590	8,031,792	13,234,798
Maharashtra	18,998,379	5,968,562	13,029,817
Rajasthan	17,935,918	5,627,181	12,308,737
Madhya Pradesh	17,860,686	6,020,438	11,840,248
Karnataka	15,132,802	5,537,162	9,595,640
Tamil Nadu	14,668,772	4,905,357	9,763,415
Gujarat	12,469,293	4,202,730	8,266,563
Orissa	11,472,584	3,838,038	7,634,546
Jharkhand	10,143,063	3,661,286	6,481,777
Assam	7,960,619	3,248,618	4,712,001
Punjab	6,379,994	2,743,910	3,636,084
Chhatisgarh	6,033,286	1,925,087	4,108,199
Haryana	5,598,873	1,978,457	3,620,416
Kerala	2,559,343	789,032	1,770,311
Delhi NCT	2,155,932	826,149	1,329,783
Uttaranchal	1,984,993	579,642	1,405,351
Himachal Pradesh	1,194,777	368,182	826,595
Tripura	727,997	263,070	464,927
Meghalaya	678,184	316,995	361,189
Manipur	646,287	231,946	414,341
Nagaland	561,941	254,027	307,914
Arunachal Pradesh	403,266	169,570	233,696
Goa	212,484	68,064	144,420
Pondicherry UT	159,372	47,656	111,716
Chandigarh UT	144,413	64,423	79,990
Sikkim	140,495	58,035	82,460
Mizoram	86,259	36,115	50,144
Dadra & Nagar Haveli UT	72,448	27,184	45,264
Andaman & Nicobar Islands UT	58,646	23,716	34,930
Daman & Diu UT	26,108	9,525	16,583
Lakshadweep UT	6,454	1,824	4,630

Table 2.14 : Per cent Distribution of Illiterate Population, 2001

States/UTs	Persons	Male	Female
Uttar Pradesh	19.52	19.98	19.26
Bihar	11.81	12.94	11.17
Andhra Pradesh	8.67	9.12	8.42
West Bengal	7.18	7.53	6.98
Maharashtra	6.41	5.60	6.87
Rajasthan	6.06	5.28	6.49
Madhya Pradesh	6.03	5.64	6.25
Karnataka	5.11	5.19	5.06
Tamil Nadu	4.95	4.60	5.15
Gujarat	4.21	3.94	4.36
Orissa	3.87	3.60	4.03
Jharkhand	3.42	3.43	3.42
Assam	2.69	3.05	2.49
Punjab	2.15	2.57	1.92
Chhatisgarh	2.04	1.80	2.17
Haryana	1.89	1.86	1.91
Kerala	0.86	0.74	0.93
Delhi NCT	0.73	0.77	0.70
Uttaranchal	0.67	0.54	0.74
Himachal Pradesh	0.40	0.35	0.44
Tripura	0.25	0.25	0.25
Meghalaya	0.23	0.30	0.19
Manipur	0.22	0.22	0.22
Nagaland	0.19	0.24	0.16
Arunachal Pradesh	0.14	0.16	0.12
Goa	0.07	0.06	0.08
Pondicherry UT	0.05	0.04	0.06
Chandigarh UT	0.05	0.06	0.04
Sikkim	0.05	0.05	0.04
Mizoram	0.03	0.03	0.03
Dadar & Nagar Haveli UT	0.02	0.03	0.02
Andaman & Nicobar Islands UT	0.02	0.02	0.02
Daman & Diu UT	0.01	0.01	0.01
Lakshadweep UT	0.00	0.00	0.00
India	**100.00**	**100.00**	**100.00**

2. BIMARU STATES

BIHAR, 2001

Population

Total Population	Male	Female	Per cent of Total Population of India	Density (per sq km)
82,878,796	43,153,964	39,724,832	8.07	880

Projected Population (Bihar + Jharkhand)

Total Pop ('000)	Projected Pop ('000)	Difference ('000) (T-P)
109,788	101,819	7,969

Percentage Decadal Growth Rates 1951-2001

1951-61	1961-71	1971-81	1981-91	1991-2001
19.8	20.9	24.2	23.4	28.4

Annual Exponential Growth Rate (percent)

1981-91	1991-2001
2.1	2.5

Sex Ratio 1951-2001(females per 1000 males)

1951	1961	1971	1981	1991	2001
1,000	1,005	957	948	907	921

Child Population (0-6 years) and Sex Ratio (0-6 years, 7+)

Child Population (0-6 years)			Sex Ratio (0-6)		Sex Ratio (7+)	
Total	Male	Female	1991	2001	1991	2001
16,234,539	8,375,532	7,859,007	953	938	895	916

Literate Population and Literacy Rate (Per cent)

Literates 7+			Literacy rate (%)		
Total	Male	Female	Total	Male	Female
31,675,607	20,978,955	10,696,652	47.5	60.3	33.6

Illiterate Population

Persons		Male		Female	
1991	2001	1991	2001	1991	2001
31,986,516	34,968,650	13,128,759	13,799,477	18,857,757	21,169,173

Vital Statistics, SRS (1999)

	Total	Rural	Urban
Birth Rate (per 1,000)	30.4	31.3	22.6
Death Rate (per 1,000)	9.1	9.3	6.6
Natural Growth Rate (per 1,000)	21.4	22.0	16.0
Infant Mortality Rate (per 1,000)	66	67	51

MADHYA PRADESH, 2001

Population

Total Population	Male	Female	Per cent of Total Population of India	Density (per sq km)
60,385,118	31,456,873	28,928,245	5.88	196

Projected Population (Madhya Pradesh + Chhatisgarh)

Total Pop ('000)	Projected Pop ('000)	Difference ('000) (T-P)
81,181	81,189	-8

Percentage Decadal Growth Rates 1951-2001

1951-61	1961-71	1971-81	1981-91	1991-2001
24.7	29.3	27.2	27.2	24.3

Annual Exponential Growth Rate (percent)

1981-91	1991-2001
2.4	2.2

Sex Ratio 1951-2001 (females per 1000 males)

1951	1961	1971	1981	1991	2001
945	932	920	921	912	920

Child Population (0-6 years) and Sex Ratio (0-6 years, 7+)

Child Population (0-6 years)			Sex Ratio (0-6)		Sex Ratio (7+)	
Total	Male	Female	1991	2001	1991	2001
10,618,323	5,504,422	5,113,901	941	929	905	918

Literate Population and Literacy Rate (Per cent)

Literates 7+			Literacy rate (%)		
Total	Male	Female	Total	Male	Female
31,906,109	19,932,013	11,974,096	64.1	76.8	50.3

Illiterate Population

Persons		Male		Female	
1991	2001	1991	2001	1991	2001
21,512,377	17,860,686	8,459,594	6,020,438	13,052,783	11,840,248

Vital Statistics, SRS (1999)

	Total	Rural	Urban
Birth Rate (per 1,000)	30.7	32.1	23.4
Death Rate (per 1,000)	10.6	11.2	7.4
Natural Growth Rate (per 1,000)	20.1	20.9	15.9
Infant Mortality Rate (per 1,000)	91	96	55

RAJASTHAN, 2001

Population

Total Population	Male	Female	Per cent of Total Population of India	Density (per sq km)
56,473,122	29,381,657	27,091,465	5.50	165

Projected Population

Total Pop ('000)	Projected Pop ('000)	Difference ('000) (T-P)
56,473	54,509	1,964

Percentage Decadal Growth Rates 1951-2001

1951-61	1961-71	1971-81	1981-91	1991-2001
26.2	27.8	33.0	28.4	28.3

Annual Exponential Growth Rate (percent)

1981-91	1991-2001
2.5	2.5

Sex Ratio 1951-2001(females per 1000 males)

1951	1961	1971	1981	1991	2001
921	908	911	919	910	922

Child Population (0-6 years) and Sex Ratio (0-6 years, 7+)

Child Population (0-6 years)			Sex Ratio (0-6)		Sex Ratio (7+)	
Total	Male	Female	1991	2001	1991	2001
10,451,103	5,474,965	4,976,138	916	909	908	925

Literate Population and Literacy Rate (Per cent)

Literates 7+			Literacy rate (%)		
Total	Male	Female	Total	Male	Female
28,086,101	18,279,511	9,806,590	61.0	76.5	44.3

Illiterate Population

Persons		Male		Female	
1991	2001	1991	2001	1991	2001
21,597,410	17,935,918	8,290,337	5,627,181	13,307,073	12,308,737

Vital Statistics, SRS (1999)

	Total	Rural	Urban
Birth Rate (per 1,000)	31.1	32.5	24.9
Death Rate (per 1,000)	8.4	8.9	6.4
Natural Growth Rate (per 1,000)	22.7	23.6	18.5
Infant Mortality Rate (per 1,000)	81	85	59

UTTAR PRADESH, 2001

Population

Total Population	Male	Female	Per cent of Total Population of India	Density (per sq km)
166,052,859	87,466,301	78,586,558	16.17	689

Projected Population (Uttar Pradesh + Uttaranchal)

Total Pop ('000)	Projected Pop ('000)	Difference ('000) (T-P)
174,532	174,290	242

Percentage Decadal Growth Rates 1951-2001

1951-61	1961-71	1971-81	1981-91	1991-2001
16.4	19.5	25.4	25.6	25.8

Annual Exponential Growth Rate (percent)

1981-91	1991-2001
2.3	2.3

Sex Ratio 1951-2001(females per 1000 males)

1951	1961	1971	1981	1991	2001
908	907	876	882	876	898

Child Population (0-6 years) and Sex Ratio (0-6 years, 7+)

Child Population (0-6 years)			Sex Ratio (0-6)		Sex Ratio (7+)	
Total	Male	Female	1991	2001	1991	2001
30,472,042	15,903,900	14,568,142	927	916	863	895

Literate Population and Literacy Rate (Per cent)

Literates 7+			Literacy rate (%)		
Total	Male	Female	Total	Male	Female
77,770,275	50,256,119	27,514,156	57.4	70.2	43.0

Illiterate Population

Persons		Male		Female	
1991	2001	1991	2001	1991	2001
62,313,875	57,810,542	25,480,524	21,306,282	36,833,351	36,504,260

Vital Statistics, SRS (1999)

	Total	Rural	Urban
Birth Rate (per 1,000)	32.1	33.1	26.7
Death Rate (per 1,000)	10.5	11.0	7.7
Natural Growth Rate (per 1,000)	21.6	22.1	19.0
Infant Mortality Rate (per 1,000)	84	87	64

2. HIGHLIGHTS OF BIMARU STATES
(Bihar, Madhya Pradesh, Rajasthan and Uttar Pradesh)

➢ It must be noted that the 2001 Census figures relate to the truncated states of Bihar, Madhya Pradesh and Uttar Pradesh, and separate figures are available for the three newly formed states of Jharkhand, Chhatisgarh and Uttaranchal.

➢ Uttar Pradesh has a population of 166 million, followed by Bihar (82.9 million), Madhya Pradesh (60.3 million) and Rajasthan (56.5 million).

➢ The density of population ranges from 880 in Bihar, to 689 in Uttar Pradesh, 196 in Madhya Pradesh and 165 in Rajasthan.

➢ The decadal growth rate in Bihar increased from 23.4 per cent during 1981-91 to 28.4 per cent during 1991-2001. In Rajasthan the growth rate was stagnant (28.4 per cent and 28.3 per cent respectively), in Uttar Pradesh it increased marginally from 25.6 per cent to 25.8 per cent, and in Madhya Pradesh, the decadal growth rate declined from 27.2 per cent to 24.3 per cent.

➢ The drop in the growth rate in Madhya Pradesh by itself is not enough to exclude it from BIMARU states. According to the latest SRS data, the birth rate in Madhya Pradesh is as high as 30.7 and infant mortality rate is highest in India (91 per thousand), with the exception of Orissa where it is 97.

➢ While the overall sex ratio has increased from 912 to 920, the sex ratio of the child population in Madhya Pradesh has declined sharply from 941 to 929 (i.e., by 12 points).

➢ In Bihar the overall sex ratio increased from 907 to 921 but the sex ratio of the child population decreased from 953 to 938 (i.e., by 17 points). In Rajasthan, the overall sex ratio increased from 910 to 922 but the sex ratio of the child population decreased from 916 to 909 points (i.e., by 7 points). In Uttar Pradesh, the overall sex ratio increased from 876 to 898 but the sex ratio of the child population decreased from 927 to 916 (i.e., by 11 points).

➢ The literacy rate in the BIMARU states ranged from 64.1 per cent in Madhya Pradesh to 61 per cent in Rajasthan, 57.4 per cent in Uttar Pradesh and 47.5 per cent in Bihar.

➤ In Bihar only 33.6 per cent of the females (7+) are literate and the number of both male and female illiterate increased during the last decade.

➤ In Uttar Pradesh, the female literacy rate was 43 per cent, in Rajastahn 44.3 per cent and in Madhya Pradesh 50.3 per cent.

➤ There was a decrease of both male and female illiterates in Madhya Pradesh and Rajasthan, while in Uttar Pradesh, there was a marginal decrease in the number of female illiterates.

➤ The natural growth rate of population (births minus deaths) was the highest in Rajasthan (22.7 per thousand), followed by Uttar Pradesh (21.6), Bihar (21.4) and Madhya Pradesh (20.1)

➤ In short, the 2001 Census data and the SRS data confirm our classification of these four states as BIMARU (sick) states. Considering the birth rate, death rate, infant mortality rate, female literacy rate and the gap between male and female literacy rate, one cannot but classify Madhya Pradesh as a BIMARU state, though it is true that among the four BIMARU states, Madhya Pradesh gets the best rating followed by Rajasthan while Bihar and Uttar Pradesh have the worst rating.

➤ In fact, there is a good case for classifying Bihar as an *ati-BIMARU* (intensely BIMARU or sick) state.

3. OFFSHOOTS OF BIMARU STATES (THREE NEW STATES)

CHHATISGARH, 2001

Population

Total Population	Male	Female	Per cent of Total Population of India	Density (per sq km)
20,795,956	10,452,426	10,343,530	2.03	154

Percentage Decadal Growth Rates 1951-2001

1951-61	1961-71	1971-81	1981-91	1991-2001
22.8	27.1	20.4	25.7	18.1

Annual Exponential Growth Rate (percent)

1981-91	1991-2001
2.3	1.7

Sex Ratio 1951-2001(females per 1000 males)

1951	1961	1971	1981	1991	2001
1,024	1,008	998	996	985	990

Child Population (0-6 years) and Sex Ratio (0-6 years, 7+)

Child Population (0-6 years)			Sex Ratio (0-6)		Sex Ratio (7+)	
Total	Male	Female	1991	2001	1991	2001
3,469,774	1,756,441	1,713,333	984	975	986	992

Literate Population and Literacy Rate (Per cent)

Literates 7+			Literacy rate (%)		
Total	Male	Female	Total	Male	Female
11,292,896	6,770,898	4,521,998	65.2	77.9	52.4

Illiterate Population

Persons		Male		Female	
1991	2001	1991	2001	1991	2001
8,111,922	6,033,286	3,000,310	1,925,087	5,111,612	4,108,199

JHARKHAND, 2001

Population

Total Population	Male	Female	Per cent of Total Population of India	Density (per sq km)
26,909,428	13,861,277	13,048,151	2.6	338

Percentage Decadal Growth Rates 1951-2001

1951-61	1961-71	1971-81	1981-91	1991-2001
19.7	22.6	23.8	24.0	23.2

Annual Exponential Growth Rate (percent)

1981-91	1991-2001
2.2	2.1

Sex Ratio 1951-2001(females per 1000 males)

1951	1961	1971	1981	1991	2001
961	960	945	940	922	941

Child Population (0-6 years) and Sex Ratio (0-6 years, 7+)

Child Population (0-6 years)			Sex Ratio (0-6)		Sex Ratio (7+)	
Total	Male	Female	1991	2001	1991	2001
4,796,188	2,440,025	2,356,163	979	966	908	936

Literate Population and Literacy Rate (Per cent)

Literates 7+			Literacy rate (%)		
Total	Male	Female	Total	Male	Female
11,970,177	7,759,966	4,210,211	54.1	67.9	39.4

Illiterate Population

Persons		Male		Female	
1991	2001	1991	2001	1991	2001
10,220,865	10,143,063	4,038,827	3,661,286	6,182,038	6,481,777

UTTARANCHAL, 2001

Population

Total Population	Male	Female	Per cent of Total Population of India	Density (per sq km)
8,479,562	4,316,401	4,163,161	0.83	159

Percentage Decadal Growth Rates 1951-2001

1951-61	1961-71	1971-81	1981-91	1991-2001
22.6	24.4	27.5	24.2	19.2

Annual Exponential Growth Rate (percent)

1981-91	1991-2001
2.2	1.8

Sex Ratio 1951-2001(females per 1000 males)

1951	1961	1971	1981	1991	2001
940	947	940	936	936	964

Child Population (0-6 years) and Sex Ratio (0-6 years, 7+)

Child Population (0-6 years)			Sex Ratio (0-6)		Sex Ratio (7+)	
Total	Male	Female	1991	2001	1991	2001
1,319,393	692,272	627.121	948	906	933	976

Literate Population and Literacy Rate (Per cent)

Literates 7+			Literacy rate (%)		
Total	Male	Female	Total	Male	Female
5,175,176	3,044,487	2,130,689	72.3	84.0	60.3

Illiterate Population

Persons		Male		Female	
1991	2001	1991	2001	1991	2001
2,454,593	1,984,993	817,685	579,642	1,636,908	1,405,351

3. HIGHLIGHTS OF THE THREE NEW STATES
(Chhatisgarh, Jharkhand and Uttaranchal)

➢ Among the three new states, the state of Jharkhand had the highest population of 26.9 million followed by Chhatisgarh 20.8 million and Uttaranchal 8.5 million.

➢ Chhatisgarh recorded the highest decline in the decadal growth rate, a decline of 7.6 per cent point followed by Uttaranchal, a decline of 5.0 per cent points and Jharkhand, a decline of 0.8 per cent point during the decade 1991-2001.

➢ Among the three new states, Jharkhand is the most densly populated state, followed by Chhatisgarh and Uttaranchal, in 2001.

➢ There was an increase in the overall sex ratio (females per 1,000 males) in all the three states during the decade 1991-2001. Sex ratio was highest in Chhatisgarh, 990, followed by Uttaranchal, 964 and Jharkhand, 941 during the year 2001. Highest increase of 28 points was recorded in the state of Uttaranchal, followed by Jharkhand (19 points) and Chhatisgarh (5 points).

➢ In contrast there was decline in the child sex ratio (0-6 age group) in all the three states in 2001. The decline was more pronounced in Uttaranchal, a decline of 42 points during the last 10 years, followed by Jharkhand (13 points) and Chhatisgarh (9 points).

➢ Uttaranchal has the highest literacy rate of , 72.3 per cent followed by Chhatisgarh (65.2 per cent) and Jharkhand (54.1 per cent) in the year 2001.

➢ Male literacy rate (for population 7 years and above) was highest in Uttaranchal (84.0 per cent) followed by Chhatisgarh (77.9 per cent) and Jharkhand (67.9 per cent).

➢ Female literacy rate (for population 7 years and above) was highest in Uttaranchal (60.3 per cent) followed by Chhatisgarh (52.4 per cent) and Jharkhand (39.4 per cent).

➢ In all three states the absolute number of illiterate population has declined during the last decade, except for the females in Jharkhand, where female illiterates have increased from 1991 to 2001.

4. SOUTHERN STATES/UTs

ANDHRA PRADESH, 2001

Population

Total Population	Male	Female	Per cent of Total Population of India	Density (per sq km)
75,727,541	38,286,811	37,440,730	7.37	275

Projected Population

Total Pop ('000)	Projected Pop ('000)	Difference ('000) (T-P)
75,728	76,392	-664

Percentage Decadal Growth Rates 1951-2001

1951-61	1961-71	1971-81	1981-91	1991-2001
15.7	20.9	23.1	24.2	13.9

Annual Exponential Growth Rate (percent)

1981-91	1991-2001
2.2	1.3

Sex Ratio 1951-2001(females per 1000 males)

1951	1961	1971	1981	1991	2001
986	981	977	975	972	978

Child Population (0-6 years) and Sex Ratio (0-6 years, 7+)

Child Population (0-6 years)			Sex Ratio (0-6)		Sex Ratio (7+)	
Total	Male	Female	1991	2001	1991	2001
9,673,274	4,926,200	4,747,074	975	964	972	980

Literate Population and Literacy Rate (Per cent)

Literates 7+			Literacy rate (%)		
Total	Male	Female	Total	Male	Female
40,364,765	23,636,077	16,728,688	61.1	70.9	51.2

Illiterate Population

Persons		Male		Female	
1991	2001	1991	2001	1991	2001
31,056,061	25,689,502	12,639,933	9,724,534	18,416,128	15,964,968

Vital Statistics, SRS (1999)

	Total	Rural	Urban
Birth Rate (per 1,000)	21.7	22.0	20.6
Death Rate (per 1,000)	8.2	9.0	5.7
Natural Growth Rate (per 1,000)	13.5	13.1	15.0
Infant Mortality Rate (per 1,000)	66	75	37

KARNATAKA, 2001

Population				
Total Population	Male	Female	Per cent of Total Population of India	Density (per sq km)
52,733,958	26,856,343	25,877,615	5.14	275

Projected Population

Total Pop ('000)	Projected Pop ('000)	Difference ('000) (T-P)
52,734	52,719	15

Percentage Decadal Growth Rates 1951-2001

1951-61	1961-71	1971-81	1981-91	1991-2001
21.6	24.2	26.8	21.1	17.3

Annual Exponential Growth Rate (percent)

1981-91	1991-2001
1.9	1.6

Sex Ratio 1951-2001(females per 1000 males)

1951	1961	1971	1981	1991	2001
966	959	957	963	960	964

Child Population (0-6 years) and Sex Ratio (0-6 years, 7+)

Child Population (0-6 years)			Sex Ratio (0-6)		Sex Ratio (7+)	
Total	Male	Female	1991	2001	1991	2001
6,826,168	3,501,499	3,324,669	960	949	960	966

Literate Population and Literacy Rate (Per cent)

Literates 7+			Literacy rate (%)		
Total	Male	Female	Total	Male	Female
30,774,988	17,817,682	12,957,306	67.0	76.3	57.5

Illiterate Population

Persons		Male		Female	
1991	2001	1991	2001	1991	2001
16,486,397	15,132,802	6,264,457	5,537,162	10,221,940	9,595,640

Vital Statistics, SRS (1999)

	Total	Rural	Urban
Birth Rate (per 1,000)	22.3	23.7	19.2
Death Rate (per 1,000)	7.7	8.7	5.5
Natural Growth Rate (per 1,000)	14.6	15.0	13.6
Infant Mortality Rate (per 1,000)	58	69	24

KERALA, 2001

Population

Total Population	Male	Female	Per cent of Total Population of India	Density (per sq km)
31,838,619	15,468,664	16,369,955	3.10	819

Projected Population

Total Pop ('000)	Projected Pop ('000)	Difference ('000) (T-P)
31,839	32,530	-691

Percentage Decadal Growth Rates 1951-2001

1951-61	1961-71	1971-81	1981-91	1991-2001
24.8	26.3	19.2	14.3	9.4

Annual Exponential Growth Rate (percent)

1981-91	1991-2001
1.3	0.9

Sex Ratio 1951-2001(females per 1000 males)

1951	1961	1971	1981	1991	2001
1,028	1,022	1,016	1,032	1,036	1,058

Child Population (0-6 years) and Sex Ratio (0-6 years, 7+)

Child Population (0-6 years)			Sex Ratio (0-6)		Sex Ratio (7+)	
Total	Male	Female	1991	2001	1991	2001
3,653,578	1,861,669	1,791,909	958	963	1049	1071

Literate Population and Literacy Rate (Per cent)

Literates 7+			Literacy rate (%)		
Total	Male	Female	Total	Male	Female
25,625,698	12,817,963	12,807,735	90.9	94.2	87.9

Illiterate Population

Persons		Male		Female	
1991	2001	1991	2001	1991	2001
2,575,157	2,559,343	786,620	789,032	1,788,537	1,770,311

Vital Statistics, SRS (1999)

	Total	Rural	Urban
Birth Rate (per 1,000)	18.0	18.1	17.7
Death Rate (per 1,000)	6.4	6.5	6.3
Natural Growth Rate (per 1,000)	11.5	11.6	11.4
Infant Mortality Rate (per 1,000)	14	14	16

TAMIL NADU, 2001

Population

Total Population	Male	Female	Per cent of Total Population of India	Density (per sq km)
62,110,839	31,268,654	30,842,185	6.05	478

Projected Population

Total Pop ('000)	Projected Pop ('000)	Difference ('000) (T-P)
62,111	62,252	-141

Percentage Decadal Growth Rates 1951-2001

1951-61	1961-71	1971-81	1981-91	1991-2001
11.9	22.3	17.5	15.4	11.2

Annual Exponential Growth Rate (percent)

1981-91	1991-2001
1.4	1.1

Sex Ratio 1951-2001(females per 1000 males)

1951	1961	1971	1981	1991	2001
1,007	992	978	977	974	986

Child Population (0-6 years) and Sex Ratio (0-6 years, 7+)

Child Population (0-6 years)			Sex Ratio (0-6)		Sex Ratio (7+)	
Total	Male	Female	1991	2001	1991	2001
6,817,669	3,515,562	3,302,107	948	939	978	992

Literate Population and Literacy Rate (Per cent)

Literates 7+			Literacy rate (%)		
Total	Male	Female	Total	Male	Female
40,624,398	22,847,735	17,776,663	73.5	82.3	64.6

Illiterate Population

Persons		Male		Female	
1991	2001	1991	2001	1991	2001
18,074,652	14,668,772	6,425,791	4,905,357	11,648,861	9,763,415

Vital Statistics, SRS (1999)

	Total	Rural	Urban
Birth Rate (per 1,000)	19.3	19.8	18.2
Death Rate (per 1,000)	8.0	8.7	6.6
Natural Growth Rate (per 1,000)	11.3	11.1	11.6
Infant Mortality Rate (per 1,000)	52	58	39

GOA, 2001

Population				
Total Population	Male	Female	Per cent of Total Population of India	Density (per sq km)
1,343,998	685,617	658,381	0.13	363

Projected Population		
Total Pop ('000)	Projected Pop ('000)	Difference ('000) (T-P)
1,344	1,627	-283

Percentage Decadal Growth Rates 1951-2001				
1951-61	1961-71	1971-81	1981-91	1991-2001
7.8	34.8	26.7	16.1	14.9

Annual Exponential Growth Rate (percent)	
1981-91	1991-2001
1.5	1.4

Sex Ratio 1951-2001(females per 1000 males)					
1951	1961	1971	1981	1991	2001
1,128	1,066	981	975	967	960

Child Population (0-6 years) and Sex Ratio (0-6 years, 7+)						
Child Population (0-6 years)			Sex Ratio (0-6)		Sex Ratio (7+)	
Total	Male	Female	1991	2001	1991	2001
142,152	73,547	68,605	964	933	967	964

Literate Population and Literacy Rate (Per cent)					
Literates 7+			Literacy rate (%)		
Total	Male	Female	Total	Male	Female
989,362	544,006	445,356	82.3	88.9	75.5

Illiterate Population					
Persons		Male		Female	
1991	2001	1991	2001	1991	2001
252,881	212,484	85,846	68,064	167,035	144,420

Vital Statistics, SRS (1999)	Total	Rural	Urban
Birth Rate (per 1,000)	14.3	14.4	14.1
Death Rate (per 1,000)	7.2	7.6	6.6
Natural Growth Rate (per 1,000)	7.1	6.8	7.5
Infant Mortality Rate (per 1,000)	21	23	17

PONDICHERRY, 2001

Population

Total Population	Male	Female	Per cent of Total Population of India	Density (per sq km)
973,829	486,705	487,124	0.09	2,029

Projected Population

Total Pop ('000)	Projected Pop ('000)	Difference ('000) (T-P)
974	1,134	-160

Percentage Decadal Growth Rates 1951-2001

1951-61	1961-71	1971-81	1981-91	1991-2001
16.3	27.8	28.2	33.6	20.6

Annual Exponential Growth Rate (percent)

1981-91	1991-2001
2.9	1.9

Sex Ratio 1951-2001(females per 1000 males)

1951	1961	1971	1981	1991	2001
1,030	1,013	989	985	979	1,001

Child Population (0-6 years) and Sex Ratio (0-6 years, 7+)

Child Population (0-6 years)			Sex Ratio (0-6)		Sex Ratio (7+)	
Total	Male	Female	1991	2001	1991	2001
113,010	57,722	55,288	963	958	982	1,007

Literate Population and Literacy Rate (Per cent)

Literates 7+			Literacy rate (%)		
Total	Male	Female	Total	Male	Female
701,447	381,327	320,120	81.5	88.9	74.1

Illiterate Population

Persons		Male		Female	
1991	2001	1991	2001	1991	2001
176,177	159,372	57,403	47,656	118,774	111,716

Vital Statistics, SRS (1999)

	Total	Rural	Urban
Birth Rate (per 1,000)	17.7	18.0	17.5
Death Rate (per 1,000)	6.9	7.9	6.1
Natural Growth Rate (per 1,000)	10.8	10.1	11.4
Infant Mortality Rate (per 1,000)	22	32	15

4. HIGHLIGHTS OF SOUTHERN STATES
(Andhra Pradesh, Karnataka, Kerala, Tamil Nadu, Goa and Pondicherry)

➤ In 2001, the population of Andhra Pradesh was 75.7 million, folllowed by Tamil Nadu (62.1 million), Karnataka (52.7 million), Kerala (31.8 million), Goa (1.3 million) and Pondicherry (974 thousand)

➤ The density ranged from 819 in Kerala to 478 in Tamil Nadu, 275 in Karnataka and Andhra Pradesh and 363 in Goa. In the Union Territory of Pondicherry it was 2029 persons per sq km.

➤ The decadal growth rate was lowest in Kerala (9.4 per cent), followed by 11.2 per cent in Tamil Nadu, 13.9 per cent in Andhra Pradesh, 14.9 per cent in Goa, 17.3 per cent in Karnataka and 20.6 per cent in Pondicherry

➤ The fall in the growth rate was highest in Andhra Pradesh, from 2.2 per cent per year to 1.3 per cent per year during 1991-2001. In decadal percentage terms, the fall was of the order of 10.3 per cent points during the last decade.

➤ The overall sex ratio increased from 1036 to 1058 in Kerala, from 974 to 986 in Tamil Nadu, from 972 to 978 in Andhra Pradesh, from 960 to 964 in Karnataka and from 979 to 1001 in Pondicherry. In Goa it *decreased* from 967 to 960 during the last decade.

➤ Sex ratio of the child population increased from 958 to 963 (i.e., by 5 points) in Kerala, but in the other states it decreased. In Andhra Pradesh, the juvenile sex ratio decreased from 975 to 964 (11 points), in Karnataka from 960 to 949 (21 points) in Tamil Nadu from 948 to 939 (9 points) in Goa from 964 to 933 (31 points) and in Pondicherry from 963 to 958 (5 points). The fall in the sex ratio of the child population in the demographically progressive states calls for an explanation. Is the practice of female foeticide widespread in South India also? Is the son complex as high as in the northern states, with the exception of Kerala? We must await the publication of detailed data from the Census before we can explain this perverse phenomenon.

➤ Kerala has the highest literacy rate (90.9 per cent), followed by Tamil Nadu (73.5 per cent), Karnataka (67.0 per cent), and Andhra Pradesh (61.1 per cent). In Goa, the literacy rate was 82.3 per cent and in Pondicherry 81.5 per cent.

> ➢ Surprisingly, during 1991-2001, the number of illiterate males *increased* in Kerala while the number of illiterate females decreased. In all other states, the number of illiterate male as well as females decreased during the last decade.

> ➢ The lowest birth rate according to the SRS data was in Goa (14.3 per thousand), followed by Pondicherry (17.7), Kerala (18), Tamil Nadu (19.3), Andhra Pradesh (21.7) and Karnataka (22.3)

> ➢ The death rate was lowest in Kerala (6.4), followed by 6.9 in Pondicherry, Karnataka (7.7), Goa (7.2), Tamil Nadu (8) and Andhra Pradesh (8.2)

> ➢ The infant mortality rate was very low in Kerala (14 per thousand) followed by Goa (21), Pondicherry (22), Tamil Nadu (52), Karnataka (58), and Andhra Pradesh (66)

> ➢ The natural growth rate was lowest in Goa (7.1 per thousand) followed by Pondicherry (10.8), Tamil Nadu (11.3), Kerala (11.5), Andhra Pradesh (13.5) and Karnataka (14.6)

> ➢ To sum up, all the southern states are demographically progressive and the 2001 census data and SRS data confirm our analysis in terms of North-South Demographic divide.

5. JAMMU & KASHMIR (WHERE THERE WAS NO CENSUS ENUMERATION IN 1991)

JAMMU & KASHMIR, 2001

Population				
Total Population	Male	Female	Per cent of Total Population of India	Density (per sq km)
10,069,917	5,300,574	4,769,343	0.98	99

Projected Population		
Total Pop ('000)	Projected Pop ('000)	Difference ('000) (T-P)
10,070	10,071	-1

Percentage Decadal Growth Rates 1951-2001				
1951-61	1961-71	1971-81	1981-91	1991-2001
9.4	29.7	29.7	30.3	29.0

Annual Exponential Growth Rate (percent)	
1981-91	1991-2001
2.7	72.6

Sex Ratio 1951-2001(females per 1000 males)					
1951	1961	1971	1981	1991	2001
873	878	878	892	896	900

Child Population (0-6 years) and Sex Ratio (0-6 years, 7+)						
Child Population (0-6 years)			Sex Ratio (0-6)		Sex Ratio (7+)	
Total	Male	Female	1991	2001	1991	2001
1,431,182	738,839	692,343	NA	937	NA	894

Literate Population and Literacy Rate (Per cent)					
Literates 7+			Literacy rate (%)		
Total	Male	Female	Total	Male	Female
4,704,252	2,999,353	1,704,899	54.5	65.8	41.8

5. HIGHLIGHTS OF JAMMU & KASHMIR STATE

➤ The population of Jammu & Kashmir as on 1st March 2001 was 10.1 million

➤ Jammu & Kashmir has 0.98 per cent of India's population.

➤ Density of Jammu & Kashmir is 99 per sq. km.

➤ Decadal growth rate in Jammu & Kashmir has declined from 30.3 (1981-91) per cent to 29.0 per cent (1991-2001). A decline of 1.3 per cent point during 1991-2001 decade.

➤ Annual exponential growth rate declined by 0.1 per cent point during 1991-2001 decade.

➤ The sex ratio (females per 1000 males) is 900 in 2001 compared to 896 in 1991, an increase of 4 points during the last decade

➤ Child population in the state of Jammu & Kashmir was 1.4 million.

➤ The Child sex ratio (0-6 age group) was 937 to 2001.

➤ Literate population (for population 7 years and above) in the state was 4.7 million of which 3 million were male literates and 1.7 million female literates.

➤ The literacy rate (for population 7 years and above) was 54. 5 per cent in 2001. The male literacy rate was 65.8 and the female literacy rate was 41.8 per cent.

6. NORTH-WESTERN STATES/UTs

HARYANA, 2001

Population

Total Population	Male	Female	Per cent of Total Population of India	Density (per sq km)
21,082,989	11,327,658	9,755,331	2.05	477

Projected Population

Total Pop ('000)	Projected Pop ('000)	Difference ('000) (T-P)
21,083	20,120	963

Percentage Decadal Growth Rates 1951-2001

1951-61	1961-71	1971-81	1981-91	1991-2001
33.8	32.2	28.8	27.4	28.1

Annual Exponential Growth Rate (percent)

1981-91	1991-2001
2.4	2.5

Sex Ratio 1951-2001 (females per 1000 males)

1951	1961	1971	1981	1991	2001
871	868	867	870	865	861

Child Population (0-6 years) and Sex Ratio (0-6 years, 7+)

Child Population (0-6 years)			Sex Ratio (0-6)		Sex Ratio (7+)	
Total	Male	Female	1991	2001	1991	2001
3,259,080	1,790,758	1,468,322	879	820	862	869

Literate Population and Literacy Rate (Per cent)

Literates 7+			Literacy rate (%)		
Total	Male	Female	Total	Male	Female
12,225,036	7,558,443	4,666,593	68.6	79.3	56.3

Illiterate Population

Persons		Male		Female	
1991	2001	1991	2001	1991	2001
5,889,463	5,598,873	2,214,011	1,978,457	3,675,452	3,620,416

Vital Statistics, SRS (1999)

	Total	Rural	Urban
Birth Rate (per 1,000)	26.8	27.7	23.3
Death Rate (per 1,000)	7.7	8.0	6.4
Natural Growth Rate (per 1,000)	19.1	19.7	16.9
Infant Mortality Rate (per 1,000)	68	70	58

HIMACHAL PRADESH, 2001

Population

Total Population	Male	Female	Per cent of Total Population of India	Density (per sq km)
6,077,248	3,085,256	2,991,992	0.59	109

Projected Population

Total Pop ('000)	Projected Pop ('000)	Difference ('000) (T-P)
6,077	6,805	-728

Percentage Decadal Growth Rates 1951-2001

1951-61	1961-71	1971-81	1981-91	1991-2001
17.9	23.0	23.7	20.8	17.5

Annual Exponential Growth Rate (percent)

1981-91	1991-2001
1.9	1.6

Sex Ratio 1951-2001(females per 1000 males)

1951	1961	1971	1981	1991	2001
912	938	958	973	976	970

Child Population (0-6 years) and Sex Ratio (0-6 years, 7+)

Child Population (0-6 years)			Sex Ratio (0-6)		Sex Ratio (7+)	
Total	Male	Female	1991	2001	1991	2001
769,424	405,618	363,806	951	897	980	981

Literate Population and Literacy Rate (Per cent)

Literates 7+			Literacy rate (%)		
Total	Male	Female	Total	Male	Female
4,029,097	2,266,103	1,762,994	77.1	86.0	68.1

Illiterate Population

Persons		Male		Female	
1991	2001	1991	2001	1991	2001
1,540,150	1,194,777	529,694	3,68,182	1,010,456	826,595

Vital Statistics, SRS (1999)

	Total	Rural	Urban
Birth Rate (per 1,000)	23.8	24.3	16.8
Death Rate (per 1,000)	7.3	7.5	5.2
Natural Growth Rate (per 1,000)	16.4	16.8	11.6
Infant Mortality Rate (per 1,000)	62	63	38

PUNJAB, 2001

Population				
Total Population	*Male*	*Female*	*Per cent of Total Population of India*	*Density (per sq km)*
24,289,296	12,963,362	11,325,934	2.37	482

Projected Population		
Total Pop ('000)	*Projected Pop ('000)*	*Difference ('000) (T-P)*
24,289	23,794	495

Percentage Decadal Growth Rates 1951-2001				
1951-61	*1961-71*	*1971-81*	*1981-91*	*1991-2001*
21.6	21.7	23.9	20.8	19.8

Annual Exponential Growth Rate (percent)	
1981-91	*1991-2001*
1.9	1.8

Sex Ratio 1951-2001(females per 1000 males)					
1951	*1961*	*1971*	*1981*	*1991*	*2001*
844	854	865	879	882	874

Child Population (0-6 years) and Sex Ratio (0-6 years, 7+)

Child Population (0-6 years)			*Sex Ratio (0-6)*		*Sex Ratio (7+)*	
Total	*Male*	*Female*	*1991*	*2001*	*1991*	*2001*
3,055,492	1,704,142	1,351,350	875	793	883	886

Literate Population and Literacy Rate (Per cent)

Literates 7+			*Literacy rate (%)*		
Total	*Male*	*Female*	*Total*	*Male*	*Female*
14,853,810	8,515,310	6,338,500	70.0	75.6	63.6

Illiterate Population

Persons		*Male*		*Female*	
1991	*2001*	*1991*	*2001*	*1991*	*2001*
7,043,608	6,379,994	3,095,357	2,743,910	3,948,251	3,636,084

Vital Statistics, SRS (1999)

	Total	*Rural*	*Urban*
Birth Rate (per 1,000)	21.5	22.5	18.6
Death Rate (per 1,000)	7.4	7.9	6.1
Natural Growth Rate (per 1,000)	14.1	14.6	12.5
Infant Mortality Rate (per 1,000)	53	57	39

CHANDIGARH, 2001

Population

Total Population	Male	Female	Per cent of Total Population of India	Density (per sq km)
900,914	508,224	392,690	0.09	7,903

Projected Population

Total Pop ('000)	Projected Pop ('000)	Difference ('000) (T-P)
901	907	-6

Percentage Decadal Growth Rates 1951-2001

1951-61	1961-71	1971-81	1981-91	1991-2001
394.1	114.6	75.6	42.2	40.3

Annual Exponential Growth Rate (percent)

1981-91	1991-2001
3.5	3.4

Sex Ratio 1951-2001 (females per 1000 males)

1951	1961	1971	1981	1991	2001
781	652	749	769	790	773

Child Population (0-6 years) and Sex Ratio (0-6 years, 7+)

Child Population (0-6 years)			Sex Ratio (0-6)		Sex Ratio (7+)	
Total	Male	Female	1991	2001	1991	2001
109,293	59.238	50,055	899	845	772	763

Literate Population and Literacy Rate (Per cent)

Literates 7+			Literacy rate (%)		
Total	Male	Female	Total	Male	Female
647,208	384,563	262,645	81.8	85.7	76.7

Illiterate Population

Persons		Male		Female	
1991	2001	1991	2001	1991	2001
121,185	144,413	55,336	64,423	65,849	79,990

Vital Statistics, SRS (1999)

	Total	Rural	Urban
Birth Rate (per 1,000)	17.9	24.5	17.1
Death Rate (per 1,000)	3.9	2.6	4.1
Natural Growth Rate (per 1,000)	14.0	21.9	13.0
Infant Mortality Rate (per 1,000)	28	36	27

DELHI, 2001

Population

Total Population	Male	Female	Per cent of Total Population of India	Density (per sq km)
13,782,976	7,570,890	6,212,086	1.34	9,294

Projected Population

Total Pop ('000)	Projected Pop ('000)	Difference ('000) (T-P)
13,783	14,366	-583

Percentage Decadal Growth Rates 1951-2001

1951-61	1961-71	1971-81	1981-91	1991-2001
52.4	52.9	53.0	51.5	46.3

Annual Exponential Growth Rate (percent)

1981-91	1991-2001
4.2	3.8

Sex Ratio 1951-2001(females per 1000 males)

1951	1961	1971	1981	1991	2001
768	785	801	808	827	821

Child Population (0-6 years) and Sex Ratio (0-6 years, 7+)

Child Population (0-6 years)			Sex Ratio (0-6)		Sex Ratio (7+)	
Total	Male	Female	1991	2001	1991	2001
1,923,995	1,031,584	892,411	915	865	810	813

Literate Population and Literacy Rate (Per cent)

Literates 7+			Literacy rate (%)		
Total	Male	Female	Total	Male	Female
9,703,049	5,713,157	3,989,892	81.8	87.4	75.0

Illiterate Population

Persons		Male		Female	
1991	2001	1991	2001	1991	2001
1,930,951	2,155,932	776,591	826,149	1,154,360	1,329,783

Vital Statistics, SRS (1999)

	Total	Rural	Urban
Birth Rate (per 1,000)	19.4	20.7	19.3
Death Rate (per 1,000)	4.8	4.5	4.9
Natural Growth Rate (per 1,000)	14.6	16.2	14.4
Infant Mortality Rate (per 1,000)	31	33	31

6. HIGHLIGHTS OF NORTH-WESTERN STATES/UTs
(Haryana, Himachal Pradesh, Punjab, Chandigarh & Delhi)

➤ The population of Punjab as of March 1st, 2001 was 24.3 million followed by Haryana (21.1 million), Delhi (13.8 million), Himachal Pradesh (6.1 million), and Chandigarh (0.9 million) respectively.

➤ The highest decline in the decadal growth rate was in Delhi (5.2 per cent points) followed by Himachal Pradesh (3.3 per cent points), Chandigarh (1.9 per cent points)and Punjab (1.0 per cent points). In contrast, Haryana registered an increase of 0.7 per cent points in the decadal growth rate during the last decade.

➤ Density of Delhi was recorded highest at 9294 persons per sq km., followed by Chandigarh (7903 per sq. km), Punjab (482 per sq km), Haryana (477 per sq km), and Himachal Pradesh (109 per sq km).

➤ Sex Ratio (females per 1,000 males) was highest in Himachal Pradesh (970), followed by Punjab (874), Haryana (861), Delhi (821) and Chandigarh (773). In all the north-western states and UTs the sex ratio declined over the decade. The highest decline was registered in Chandigarh (17 points) followed by Punjab (8 points), Delhi (6 points), Himachal Pradesh (6 points) and Haryana (4 points).

➤ Sex ratio (females per 1,000 males) in 0-6 age group declined sharply in Punjab (82 points), Himachal Pradesh (72 points), Haryana (59 points), Chandigarh (54 points) and Delhi (50 points) during the last decade.

➤ Sex ratio in 7+ age group increased in all the five north-western states and UTs during the last decade.

➤ Literacy rate (for population 7 years and above) was highest in Chandigarh and Delhi (81.8 per cent) followed by Himachal Pradesh (77.1 per cent), Punjab (70.o per cent), and Haryana (68.6 per cent).

➤ Gap between male female literacy rate in 2001 was highest in Haryana (23.0 per cent points) followed by Himachal Pradesh (18.2 per cent points), Delhi (12.4 per cent points), Punjab (12.0 per cent points), and Chandigarh (9.0 per cent points).

➤   There was an increase in the absolute number of illiterates in Chandigarh and Delhi while it has gone down in Haryana, Himachal Pradesh and Punjab.

➤   The highest birth rate (per 1,000 population), was recorded in Haryana (26.8) followed by Himachal Pradesh (23.8), Punjab (21.5), Delhi (19.4), and Chandigarh (17.9).

➤   Death rate (per 1,000 population) was highest in Haryana (7.7) followed by Punjab (7.4), Himachal Pradesh (7.3), Delhi (4.8) and Chandigarh (3.9) respectively

➤   Infant mortality rate (per 1,000 live births) was highest in Haryana (68) followed by Himachal Pradesh (62), Punjab (53), Delhi (31) and Chandigarh (28).

7. WESTERN STATES/UTs

GUJARAT, 2001

Population

Total Population	Male	Female	Per cent of Total Population of India	Density (per sq km)
50,596,992	26,344,053	24,252,939	4.93	258

Projected Population

Total Pop ('000)	Projected Pop ('000)	Difference ('000) (T-P)
50,597	48,971	1,626

Percentage Decadal Growth Rates 1951-2001

1951-61	1961-71	1971-81	1981-91	1991-2001
26.9	29.4	27.7	21.2	22.5

Annual Exponential Growth Rate (percent)

1981-91	1991-2001
1.9	2.0

Sex Ratio 1951-2001(females per 1000 males)

1951	1961	1971	1981	1991	2001
952	940	934	942	934	921

Child Population (0-6 years) and Sex Ratio (0-6 years, 7+)

Child Population (0-6 years)			Sex Ratio (0-6)		Sex Ratio (7+)	
Total	Male	Female	1991	2001	1991	2001
6,867,958	3,656,956	3,211,002	928	878	936	927

Literate Population and Literacy Rate (Per cent)

Literates 7+			Literacy rate (%)		
Total	Male	Female	Total	Male	Female
29,050,019	17,349,179	11,700,840	70.0	80.5	58.6

Illiterate Population

Persons		Male		Female	
1991	2001	1991	2001	1991	2001
12,661,634	12,469,293	4,532,658	4,202,730	8,128,976	8,266,563

Vital Statistics, SRS (1999)

	Total	Rural	Urban
Birth Rate (per 1,000)	25.4	27.0	22.0
Death Rate (per 1,000)	7.9	8.8	5.9
Natural Growth Rate (per 1,000)	17.6	18.2	16.1
Infant Mortality Rate (per 1,000)	63	70	45

MAHARASHTRA, 2001

Population

Total Population	Male	Female	Per cent of Total Population of India	Density (per sq km)
96,752,247	50,334,270	46,417,977	9.42	314

Projected Population

Total Pop ('000)	Projected Pop ('000)	Difference ('000) (T-P)
96,752	92,057	4,695

Percentage Decadal Growth Rates 1951-2001

1951-61	1961-71	1971-81	1981-91	1991-2001
23.6	27.5	24.5	25.7	22.6

Annual Exponential Growth Rate (percent)

1981-91	1991-2001
2.3	2.0

Sex Ratio 1951-2001(females per 1000 males)

1951	1961	1971	1981	1991	2001
941	936	930	937	934	922

Child Population (0-6 years) and Sex Ratio (0-6 years, 7+)

Child Population (0-6 years)			Sex Ratio (0-6)		Sex Ratio (7+)	
Total	Male	Female	1991	2001	1991	2001
13,187,087	6,878,579	6,308,508	946	917	931	923

Literate Population and Literacy Rate (Per cent)

Literates 7+			Literacy rate (%)		
Total	Male	Female	Total	Male	Female
64,566,781	37,487,129	27,079,652	77.3	86.3	67.5

Illiterate Population

Persons		Male		Female	
1991	2001	1991	2001	1991	2001
22,985,512	18,998,379	7,943,119	5,968,562	15,042,393	13,029,817

Vital Statistics, SRS (1999)

	Total	Rural	Urban
Birth Rate (per 1,000)	21.1	21.6	20.3
Death Rate (per 1,000)	7.5	8.7	5.6
Natural Growth Rate (per 1,000)	13.6	12.9	14.7
Infant Mortality Rate (per 1,000)	48	58	31

DADRA & NAGAR HAVELI, 2001

Population

Total Population	Male	Female	Per cent of Total Population of India	Density (per sq km)
220,451	121,731	98,720	0.02	449

Projected Population

Total Pop ('000)	Projected Pop ('000)	Difference ('000) (T-P)
220	194	26

Percentage Decadal Growth Rates 1951-2001

1951-61	1961-71	1971-81	1981-91	1991-2001
39.6	28.0	39.8	33.6	59.2

Annual Exponential Growth Rate (percent)

1981-91	1991-2001
2.9	4.7

Sex Ratio 1951-2001(females per 1000 males)

1951	1961	1971	1981	1991	2001
946	963	1,007	974	952	811

Child Population (0-6 years) and Sex Ratio (0-6 years, 7+)

Child Population (0-6 years)			Sex Ratio (0-6)		Sex Ratio (7+)	
Total	Male	Female	1991	2001	1991	2001
39,173	19,856	19,317	1,013	973	937	779

Literate Population and Literacy Rate (Per cent)

Literates 7+			Literacy rate (%)		
Total	Male	Female	Total	Male	Female
108,830	74,691	34,139	60.0	73.3	43.0

Illiterate Population

Persons		Male		Female	
1991	2001	1991	2001	1991	2001
65,306	72,448	26,412	27,184	38,894	45,264

Vital Statistics, SRS (1999)

	Total	Rural	Urban
Birth Rate (per 1,000)	32.4	35.2	23.5
Death Rate (per 1,000)	5.9	7.0	2.3
Natural Growth Rate (per 1,000)	26.5	28.1	21.2
Infant Mortality Rate (per 1,000)	56	61	7

DAMAN & DIU, 2001

Population				
Total Population	Male	Female	Per cent of Total Population of India	Density (per sq km)
158,059	92,478	65,581	0.02	1,411

Projected Population		
Total Pop ('000)	Projected Pop ('000)	Difference ('000) (T-P)
158	142	16

Percentage Decadal Growth Rates 1951-2001

1951-61	1961-71	1971-81	1981-91	1991-2001
-24.6	70.9	26.1	28.6	55.6

Annual Exponential Growth Rate (percent)

1981-91	1991-2001
2.5	4.4

Sex Ratio 1951-2001(females per 1000 males)

1951	1961	1971	1981	1991	2001
1,125	1,169	1,099	1,062	969	709

Child Population (0-6 years) and Sex Ratio (0-6 years, 7+)

Child Population (0-6 years)			Sex Ratio (0-6)		Sex Ratio (7+)	
Total	Male	Female	1991	2001	1991	2001
20,012	10,394	9,618	958	925	971	682

Literate Population and Literacy Rate (Per cent)

Literates 7+			Literacy rate (%)		
Total	Male	Female	Total	Male	Female
111,939	72,559	39,380	81.1	88.4	70.4

Illiterate Population

Persons		Male		Female	
1991	2001	1991	2001	1991	2001
24,712	26,108	7,548	9,525	17,164	16,583

Vital Statistics, SRS (1999)

	Total	Rural	Urban
Birth Rate (per 1,000)	26.9	24.9	28.8
Death Rate (per 1,000)	7.1	8.9	5.4
Natural Growth Rate (per 1,000)	19.9	16.1	23.3
Infant Mortality Rate (per 1,000)	35	34	36

7. HIGHLIGHTS OF WESTERN STATES/UTs
(Gujarat, Maharashtra, Dadra & Nagar Haveli, Daman & Diu)

➤ Among the four Western states (Maharashtra, Gujarat, Dadra & Nagar Haveli and Daman & Diu), the state of Maharashtra had the highest population of 96.7 million followed by Gujarat 50.6 million, Dadra & Nagar Haveli 2.2 lakhs and Daman & Diu 1.5 lakh.

➤ Maharashtra contributed 9.42 per cent to the total population of India followed by Gujarat 4.93 per cent, Dadra & Nagar Haveli and Daman & Diu, both 0.02 per cent respectively.

➤ Population density was highest in Daman & Diu, 1,411 persons per sq km. followed by Dadra & Nagar Haveli 449 persons per sq km., Maharashtra 314 persons per sq. km. and Gujarat, 258 persons per sq. km.

➤ Maharashtra recorded a decline in the decadal growth rate, a decline of 3.7 per cent points during the last decade. The decadal growth rate increased sharply in Daman & Diu, an increase of 27 per cent points, followed by Dadra & Nagar Haveli (25.6 per cent) and Gujarat (1.3 per cent), during the last decade.

➤ There was a decline in the overall sex ratio (females per 1,000 males) in all the four states and UTs during the decade 1991-2001. The highest decline in the sex ratio was in Daman & Diu, a decline of 260 points followed by Dadra & Nagar Haveli (41 points), Gujarat (13 points) and Maharashtra, a decline of 12 points.

➤ Child sex ratio (age group 0-6 and 7+) has declined sharply in all the four states and UTs during the last decade.

➤ Daman & Diu has the highest literacy rate of 81.1 per cent followed by Maharashtra (77.3 per cent), Gujarat (70 per cent) and Dadra & Nagar Haveli (60.0 per cent) in the year 2001.

➤ Male literacy rate (for population 7 years and above) was highest in Daman & Diu (88.4 per cent) followed by Maharashtra (86.3 per cent), Gujarat (80.5) and Dadra & Nagar Haveli (73.3 per cent).

➤ Female literacy rate (for population 7 years and above) was highest in Daman & Diu (70.4 per cent) followed by Maharashtra (67.5 per cent), Gujarat (58.6) and Dadra & Nagar Haveli (43.0 per cent).

➤ In Maharashtra the absolute number of illiterate population has declined by 4 million while in Gujarat it has declined marginally during the last decade. In contrast it has increased in Dadra & Nagar Haveli and Daman & Diu during the last decade.

➤ Birth rate was highest in Dadra and Nagar Haveli followed by Daman & Diu, Gujarat and Maharashtra.

➤ Death rate was highest in Gujarat followed by Maharashtra, Daman & Diu and Dadra & Nagar Haveli.

➤ Infant Mortality Rate was highest in Gujarat, followed by Dadra & Nagar Haveli, Maharashtra and Daman & Diu.

8. NORTH-EASTERN STATES

ARUNACHAL PRADESH, 2001

Population

Total Population	Male	Female	Per cent of Total Population of India	Density (per sq km)
1,091,117	573,951	517,166	0.11	13

Projected Population

Total Pop ('000)	Projected Pop ('000)	Difference ('000) (T-P)
1,091	1,217	-126

Percentage Decadal Growth Rates 1951-2001

1951-61	1961-71	1971-81	1981-91	1991-2001
NA	38.9	35.2	36.8	26.2

Annual Exponential Growth Rate (percent)

1981-91	1991-2001
3.1	2.3

Sex Ratio 1951-2001(females per 1000 males)

1951	1961	1971	1981	1991	2001
NA	894	861	862	859	901

Child Population (0-6 years) and Sex Ratio (0-6 years, 7+)

Child Population (0-6 years)			Sex Ratio (0-6)		Sex Ratio (7+)	
Total	Male	Female	1991	2001	1991	2001
200,055	102,010	98,045	982	961	829	888

Literate Population and Literacy Rate (Per cent)

Literates 7+			Literacy rate (%)		
Total	Male	Female	Total	Male	Female
487,796	302,371	185,425	54.7	64.1	44.2

Illiterate Population

Persons		Male		Female	
1991	2001	1991	2001	1991	2001
398,323	403,266	181,007	169,570	217,316	233,696

Vital Statistics, SRS (1999)

	Total	Rural	Urban
Birth Rate (per 1,000)	22.3	23.2	13.5
Death Rate (per 1,000)	6.0	6.4	1.9
Natural Growth Rate (per 1,000)	16.3	16.7	11.6
Infant Mortality Rate (per 1,000)	43	45	10

ASSAM, 2001

Population

Total Population	Male	Female	Per cent of Total Population of India	Density (per sq km)
26,638,407	13,787,799	12,850,608	2.59	340

Projected Population

Total Pop ('000)	Projected Pop ('000)	Difference ('000) (T-P)
26,638	26,492	146

Percentage Decadal Growth Rates 1951-2001

1951-61	1961-71	1971-81	1981-91	1991-2001
35.0	35.0	23.4	24.2	18.9

Annual Exponential Growth Rate (percent)

1981-91	1991-2001
2.2	1.7

Sex Ratio 1951-2001(females per 1000 males)

1951	1961	1971	1981	1991	2001
868	869	896	910	923	932

Child Population (0-6 years) and Sex Ratio (0-6 years, 7+)

Child Population (0-6 years)			Sex Ratio (0-6)		Sex Ratio (7+)	
Total	Male	Female	1991	2001	1991	2001
4,350,248	2,215,104	2,135,144	975	964	910	926

Literate Population and Literacy Rate (Per cent)

Literates 7+			Literacy rate (%)		
Total	Male	Female	Total	Male	Female
14,327,540	8,324,077	6,003,463	64.3	71.9	56.0

Illiterate Population

Persons		Male		Female	
1991	2001	1991	2001	1991	2001
8,476,418	7,960,619	3,591,741	3,248,618	4,884,677	4,712,001

Vital Statistics, SRS (1999)

	Total	Rural	Urban
Birth Rate (per 1,000)	27.0	28.0	18.9
Death Rate (per 1,000)	9.7	10.1	6.2
Natural Growth Rate (per 1,000)	17.3	17.9	12.7
Infant Mortality Rate (per 1,000)	76	79	36

MANIPUR, 2001

Population

Total Population	Male	Female	Per cent of Total Population of India	Density (per sq km)
2,388,634	1,207,338	1,181,296	0.23	107

Projected Population

Total Pop ('000)	Projected Pop ('000)	Difference ('000) (T-P)
2,389	2,569	-180

Percentage Decadal Growth Rates 1951-2001

1951-61	1961-71	1971-81	1981-91	1991-2001
35.0	37.5	32.5	29.3	30.0

Annual Exponential Growth Rate (percent)

1981-91	1991-2001
2.6	2.6

Sex Ratio 1951-2001(females per 1000 males)

1951	1961	1971	1981	1991	2001
1,036	1,015	980	971	958	978

Child Population (0-6 years) and Sex Ratio (0-6 years, 7+)

Child Population (0-6 years)			Sex Ratio (0-6)		Sex Ratio (7+)	
Total	Male	Female	1991	2001	1991	2001
312,691	159,448	153,243	974	961	955	981

Literate Population and Literacy Rate (Per cent)

Literates 7+			Literacy rate (%)		
Total	Male	Female	Total	Male	Female
1,429,656	815,944	613,712	68.9	77.9	59.7

Illiterate Population

Persons		Male		Female	
1991	2001	1991	2001	1991	2001
613,840	646,287	222,167	231,946	391,673	414,341

Vital Statistics, SRS (1999)

	Total	Rural	Urban
Birth Rate (per 1,000)	18.6	19.4	16.4
Death Rate (per 1,000)	5.4	5.0	6.6
Natural Growth Rate (per 1,000)	13.1	14.3	9.8
Infant Mortality Rate (per 1,000)	25	22	24

MEGHALAYA, 2001

Population

Total Population	Male	Female	Per cent of Total Population of India	Density (per sq km)
2,306,069	1,167,840	1,138,229	0.22	103

Projected Population

Total Pop ('000)	Projected Pop ('000)	Difference ('000) (T-P)
2,306	2,484	-178

Percentage Decadal Growth Rates 1951-2001

1951-61	1961-71	1971-81	1981-91	1991-2001
27.0	31.5	32.0	32.9	29.9

Annual Exponential Growth Rate (percent)

1981-91	1991-2001
2.8	2.6

Sex Ratio 1951-2001(females per 1000 males)

1951	1961	1971	1981	1991	2001
949	937	942	954	955	975

Child Population (0-6 years) and Sex Ratio (0-6 years, 7+)

Child Population (0-6 years)			Sex Ratio (0-6)		Sex Ratio (7+)	
Total	Male	Female	1991	2001	1991	2001
457,442	231,571	225,871	986	975	947	974

Literate Population and Literacy Rate (Per cent)

Literates 7+			Literacy rate (%)		
Total	Male	Female	Total	Male	Female
1,170,443	619,274	551,169	63.3	66.1	60.4

Illiterate Population

Persons		Male		Female	
1991	2001	1991	2001	1991	2001
702,944	678,184	332,556	316,995	370,388	361,189

Vital Statistics, SRS (1999)

	Total	Rural	Urban
Birth Rate (per 1,000)	28.7	31.1	15.7
Death Rate (per 1,000)	9.1	10.2	3.3
Natural Growth Rate (per 1,000)	19.5	20.9	12.4
Infant Mortality Rate (per 1,000)	56	59	33

MIZORAM, 2001

Population

Total Population	Male	Female	Per cent of Total Population of India	Density (per sq km)
891,058	459,783	431,275	0.09	42

Projected Population

Total Pop ('000)	Projected Pop ('000)	Difference ('000) (T-P)
891	972	-81

Percentage Decadal Growth Rates 1951-2001

1951-61	1961-71	1971-81	1981-91	1991-2001
35.6	24.9	48.6	39.7	29.2

Annual Exponential Growth Rate (percent)

1981-91	1991-2001
3.3	2.6

Sex Ratio 1951-2001(females per 1000 males)

1951	1961	1971	1981	1991	2001
1,041	1,009	946	919	921	938

Child Population (0-6 years) and Sex Ratio (0-6 years, 7+)

Child Population (0-6 years)			Sex Ratio (0-6)		Sex Ratio (7+)	
Total	Male	Female	1991	2001	1991	2001
141,537	71,817	69,720	969	971	911	932

Literate Population and Literacy Rate (Per cent)

Literates 7+			Literacy rate (%)		
Total	Male	Female	Total	Male	Female
663,262	351,851	311,411	88.5	90.7	86.1

Illiterate Population

Persons		Male		Female	
1991	2001	1991	2001	1991	2001
99,553	86,259	42,286	36,115	57,267	50,144

Vital Statistics, SRS (1999)

	Total	Rural	Urban
Birth Rate (per 1,000)	17.0	18.7	14.8
Death Rate (per 1,000)	5.5	6.9	3.7
Natural Growth Rate (per 1,000)	11.5	11.8	11.1
Infant Mortality Rate (per 1,000)	19	22	14

NAGALAND, 2001

Population

Total Population	Male	Female	Per cent of Total Population of India	Density (per sq km)
1,988,636	1,041,686	946,950	0.19	120

Projected Population

Total Pop ('000)	Projected Pop ('000)	Difference ('000) (T-P)
1,989	1,721	268

Percentage Decadal Growth Rates 1951-2001

1951-61	1961-71	1971-81	1981-91	1991-2001
73.4	39.9	50.1	56.1	64.4

Annual Exponential Growth Rate (percent)

1981-91	1991-2001
4.5	5.0

Sex Ratio 1951-2001(females per 1000 males)

1951	1961	1971	1981	1991	2001
999	933	871	863	886	909

Child Population (0-6 years) and Sex Ratio (0-6 years, 7+)

Child Population (0-6 years)			Sex Ratio (0-6)		Sex Ratio (7+)	
Total	Male	Female	1991	2001	1991	2001
280,172	141,852	138,320	993	975	865	899

Literate Population and Literacy Rate (Per cent)

Literates 7+			Literacy rate (%)		
Total	Male	Female	Total	Male	Female
1,146,523	645,807	500,716	67.1	71.8	61.9

Illiterate Population

Persons		Male		Female	
1991	2001	1991	2001	1991	2001
384,323	561,941	173,951	254,027	210,372	307,914

Vital Statistics, SRS (1999)

	Total	Rural	Urban
Birth Rate (per 1,000)	NA	NA	11.8
Death Rate (per 1,000)	NA	NA	2.3
Natural Growth Rate (per 1,000)	NA	NA	9.5
Infant Mortality Rate (per 1,000)	NA	NA	16

SIKKIM, 2001

Population

Total Population	Male	Female	Per cent of Total Population of India	Density (per sq km)
540,493	288,217	252,276	0.05	76

Projected Population

Total Pop ('000)	Projected Pop ('000)	Difference ('000) (T-P)
540	570	-30

Percentage Decadal Growth Rates 1951-2001

1951-61	1961-71	1971-81	1981-91	1991-2001
17.8	29.4	50.8	28.5	33.0

Annual Exponential Growth Rate (percent)

1981-91	1991-2001
2.5	2.9

Sex Ratio 1951-2001(females per 1000 males)

1951	1961	1971	1981	1991	2001
907	904	863	835	878	875

Child Population (0-6 years) and Sex Ratio (0-6 years, 7+)

Child Population (0-6 years)			Sex Ratio (0-6)		Sex Ratio (7+)	
Total	Male	Female	1991	2001	1991	2001
77,170	38,856	38,314	965	986	860	858

Literate Population and Literacy Rate (Per cent)

Literates 7+			Literacy rate (%)		
Total	Male	Female	Total	Male	Female
322,828	191,326	131,502	69.7	76.7	61.5

Illiterate Population

Persons		Male		Female	
1991	2001	1991	2001	1991	2001
142,870	140,495	61,207	58,035	81,663	82,460

Vital Statistics, SRS (1999)

	Total	Rural	Urban
Birth Rate (per 1,000)	21.6	21.9	14.7
Death Rate (per 1,000)	5.8	5.9	3.4
Natural Growth Rate (per 1,000)	15.8	16.0	11.3
Infant Mortality Rate (per 1,000)	49	50	33

TRIPURA, 2001

Population

Total Population	Male	Female	Per cent of Total Population of India	Density (per sq km)
3,191,168	1,636,138	1,555,030	0.31	304

Projected Population

Total Pop ('000)	Projected Pop ('000)	Difference ('000) (T-P)
3,191	3,859	-668

Percentage Decadal Growth Rates 1951-2001

1951-61	1961-71	1971-81	1981-91	1991-2001
78.7	36.3	31.9	34.3	15.7

Annual Exponential Growth Rate (percent)

1981-91	1991-2001
3.0	1.5

Sex Ratio 1951-2001(females per 1000 males)

1951	1961	1971	1981	1991	2001
904	932	943	946	945	950

Child Population (0-6 years) and Sex Ratio (0-6 years, 7+)

Child Population (0-6 years)			Sex Ratio (0-6)		Sex Ratio (7+)	
Total	Male	Female	1991	2001	1991	2001
427,012	216,244	210,768	967	975	940	947

Literate Population and Literacy Rate (Per cent)

Literates 7+			Literacy rate (%)		
Total	Male	Female	Total	Male	Female
2,036,159	1,156,824	879,335	73.7	81.5	65.4

Illiterate Population

Persons		Male		Female	
1991	2001	1991	2001	1991	2001
894,103	727,997	342,804	263,070	551,299	464,927

Vital Statistics, SRS (1999)

	Total	Rural	Urban
Birth Rate (per 1,000)	17.0	17.5	14.4
Death Rate (per 1,000)	5.7	5.7	5.7
Natural Growth Rate (per 1,000)	11.3	11.8	8.7
Infant Mortality Rate (per 1,000)	42	43	33

8. HIGHLIGHTS OF NORTH-EASTERN STATES
(Arunachal Pradesh, Assam, Manipur, Meghalaya, Mizoram, Nagaland, Sikkim and Tripura)

➢ The population of Assam as of March 1st, 2001 was 26.6 million followed by Tripura (3.19 million) Manipur (2.39 million), Meghalaya (2.31 million), Nagaland (1.99 million), Arunachal Pradesh (1.09 million), Mizoram (0.89 million) and Sikkim (0.54 million).

➢ There has been a sharp decline in the decadal growth rate in Tripura (18.6 per cent points) followed by Arunachal Pradesh (10.6 per cent points), Mizoram (10.5 per cent points), Assam (5.3 per cent points) and Meghalaya (3.0 per cent points) during the last decade. In contrast Nagaland, Sikkim and Manipur had an increase of 8.3, 4.5 & 0.7 per cent points in the decadal growth rate during the last decade.

➢ Density of Assam was highest at 340 persons per sq km., followed by Tripura (304 per sq. km), Nagaland (120 per sq km), Manipur (107 per sq km), Meghalaya (103 per sq km), Sikkim (76 per km), Mizoram (42 per sq km) and Arunachal Pradesh (13 per sq km).

➢ Sex Ratio (females per 1,000 males) was highest in Manipur (978), followed by Meghalaya (975), Tripura (950), Mizoram (938), Assam (932), Nagaland (909), Arunachal Pradesh (901) and Sikkim (875). In all the north-eastern states the sex ratio increased over the decade except in Sikkim where there was a decline of 3 points during the previous decade. The highest increase was registered in Arunachal Pradesh (42 points), followed by Nagaland (23 points), Manipur (20 points), Meghalaya (20 points), Mizoram (17 points), Assam (9 points) and Tripura (5 points).

➢ Sex ratio (females per 1,000 males) in 0-6 age group declined in Arunachal Pradesh (21 points), Nagaland (18 points), Manipur (13 points), Assam (11 points) and Meghalaya (11 points) during the last decade. In contrast there was an increase of 21 points in Sikkim, 8 points in Tripura and an increase of 2 points in Mizoram.

➢ Sex ratio in 7+ age group increased in all the states except in Sikkim where there was a decline of 2 points in the last decade.

➢ Literacy rate (for population 7 years and above) in 2001 was highest in Mizoram (88.5 per cent) followed by Tripura (73.7 per cent), Sikkim (69.7 per cent), Manipur (68.9 per cent), Nagaland (67.1 per cent), Assam (64.3 per cent), Meghalaya (63.3 per cent) and Arunachal Pradesh (54.7 per cent).

➢ Gap between male and female literacy rate was highest in Arunachal Pradesh (19.9 per cent points), followed by Manipur (18.2 per cent points), Tripura (16.1 per cent points), Assam (15.9 per cent points), Sikkim (15.2 per cent points), Nagaland (10.2 per cent points), Meghalaya (5.7 per cent points) and Mizoram (4.6 per cent points).

➢ There was an increase in the absolute number of illiterates in Nagaland Manipur and Arunachal Pradesh while it has gone down in Assam, Meghalaya, Mizoram, Sikkim and Tripura.

➢ The highest birth rate (per 1,000 population), was recorded in the state of Meghalaya (28.7), followed by Assam (27.0), Arunachal Pradesh (22.3), Sikkim (21.6), Manipur (18.6), Mizoram (17) and Tripura (17).

➢ Death rate (per 1,000 population) was highest in Assam (9.7) followed by Meghalaya (9.1), Arunachal Pradesh (6.0), Sikkim (5.8), Tripura (5.7), Mizoram (5.5) and Manipur 5.4).

➢ Infant mortality rate (per 1,000 live births) was highest in Assam (76) followed by Meghalaya (56), Sikkim (49), Arunachal Pradesh (43), Tripura (42), Manipur (25) and Mizoram (19).

9. WEST BENGAL (LOWEST URBAN BIRTH RATE)

WEST BENGAL, 2001

Population

Total Population	Male	Female	Per cent of Total Population of India	Density (per sq km)
80,221,171	41,487,694	38,733,477	7.81	904

Projected Population

Total Pop ('000)	Projected Pop ('000)	Difference ('000) (T-P)
80,221	79,992	229

Percentage Decadal Growth Rates 1951-2001

1951-61	1961-71	1971-81	1981-91	1991-2001
32.8	26.9	23.2	24.7	17.8

Annual Exponential Growth Rate (percent)

1981-91	1991-2001
2.2	1.6

Sex Ratio 1951-2001(females per 1000 males)

1951	1961	1971	1981	1991	2001
865	878	891	911	917	934

Child Population (0-6 years) and Sex Ratio (0-6 years, 7+)

Child Population (0-6 years)			Sex Ratio (0-6)		Sex Ratio (7+)	
Total	Male	Female	1991	2001	1991	2001
11,132,824	5,671,152	5,461,672	967	963	907	929

Literate Population and Literacy Rate (Per cent)

Literates 7+			Literacy rate (%)		
Total	Male	Female	Total	Male	Female
47,821,757	27,784,750	20,037,007	69.2	77.6	60.2

Illiterate Population

Persons		Male		Female	
1991	2001	1991	2001	1991	2001
23,906,271	21,266,590	9,539,513	8,031,792	14,366,758	13,234,798

Vital Statistics, SRS (1999)

	Total	Rural	Urban
Birth Rate (per 1,000)	20.7	22.9	14.3
Death Rate (per 1,000)	7.1	7.2	6.8
Natural Growth Rate (per 1,000)	13.6	15.7	7.5
Infant Mortality Rate (per 1,000)	52	55	40

9. HIGHLIGHTS OF WEST BENGAL STATE

➤ The population of West Bengal as on 1st March 2001 was 80.2 million

➤ West Bengal has 7.81 per cent of India's population.

➤ Density in West Bengal is very high at 904 persons per sq. km.

➤ Decadal growth rate in West Bengal has declined significantly from 24.7 (1981-91) per cent to 17.8 per cent (1991-2001). A decline of 6.9 per cent point during 1991-2001 decade.

➤ Annual exponential growth rate declined by 0.6 per cent point during 1991-2001 decade.

➤ The sex ratio (females per 1000 males) is 934 in 2001 compared to 917 in 1991, an increase of 17 points during the last decade

➤ Child population in the state of West Bengal was recorded as 11.1 million.

➤ The Child sex ratio (0-6 age group) registered a decline of 4 points during the last decade.

➤ Child sex ratio (7+ age groups) has increased by 22 points over the last decade.

➤ Literate population (for population 7 years and above) in the state was 47.8 million of which 27.7 million were male literates and 20.1 million female literates.

➤ The literacy rate (for population 7 years and above) was 69.2 per cent in 2001. The male literacy rate was 77.6 per cent and the female literacy rate was 60.2 per cent.

➤ The absolute number of illiterate population declined nearly by 2.7 million over last decade.

➤ Birth rate (per 1,000) in West Bengal was 20.7. 22.9 births per 1,000 population were recorded in rural West Bengal while in Urban areas birth rates were lowest in the country.

➤ Death rate in West Bengal was 7.1 deaths per 1,000 population.

➤ Infant Mortality Rate in West Bengal was 52 per 1,000 live births.

10. ORISSA (HIGHEST INFANT MORTALITY)

ORISSA, 2001

Population

Total Population	Male	Female	Per cent of Total Population of India	Density (per sq km)
36,706,920	18,612,340	18,094,580	3.57	236

Projected Population

Total Pop ('000)	Projected Pop ('000)	Difference ('000) (T-P)
36,707	36,156	551

Percentage Decadal Growth Rates 1951-2001

1951-61	1961-71	1971-81	1981-91	1991-2001
19.8	25.1	20.2	20.1	15.9

Annual Exponential Growth Rate (percent)

1981-91	1991-2001
1.8	1.5

Sex Ratio 1951-2001(females per 1000 males)

1951	1961	1971	1981	1991	2001
1,022	1,001	988	981	971	972

Child Population (0-6 years) and Sex Ratio (0-6 years, 7+)

Child Population (0-6 years)			Sex Ratio (0-6)		Sex Ratio (7+)	
Total	Male	Female	1991	2001	1991	2001
5,180,551	2,656,046	2,524,505	967	950	972	976

Literate Population and Literacy Rate (Per cent)

Literates 7+			Literacy rate (%)		
Total	Male	Female	Total	Male	Female
20,053,785	12,118,256	7,935,529	63.6	76.0	51.0

Illiterate Population

Persons		Male		Female	
1991	2001	1991	2001	1991	2001
13,396,318	11,472,584	4,925,536	3,838,038	8,470,782	7,634,546

Vital Statistics, SRS (1999)

	Total	Rural	Urban
Birth Rate (per 1,000)	24.1	24.6	20.3
Death Rate (per 1,000)	10.6	11.1	7.1
Natural Growth Rate (per 1,000)	13.4	13.5	13.3
Infant Mortality Rate (per 1,000)	97	100	65

10. HIGHLIGHTS OF ORISSA STATE

➢ The population of Orissa as on 1st March 2001 was 36.7 million

➢ Orissa has 3.57 per cent of India's population.

➢ Density of Orissa is 236 persons per sq. km.

➢ Decadal growth rate in Orissa has declined from 20.1 (1981-91) per cent to 15.9 per cent (1991-2001). A decline of 4.2 per cent points during the 1991-2001 decade.

➢ Annual exponential growth rate declined by 0.3 per cent point during the 1991-2001 decade.

➢ The sex ratio (females per 1000 males) was 972 in 2001 compared to 971 in 1991, an increase of 1 point during the last decade

➢ Child population (0-6) in the state of Orissa was 5.1 million.

➢ The Child sex ratio (0-6 age group) was 950 to 2001, a decline of 17 points over the last decade.

➢ Literate population (for population 7 years and above) in the state was 20 million of which 12 million were male literates and 8 million female literates.

➢ The literacy rate (for population 7 years and above) was 63.6 per cent. The male literacy rate was 76.0 per cent and the female literacy rate was 51.0 per cent.

➢ The absolute number of illiterate population declined nearly by 2 million over the last decade.

➢ Birth rate was 24.1 per 1,000 population (SRS data).

➢ Death rate was 10.6 per 1,000 population.

➢ Infant Mortality Rate in Orissa was the highest in India (97 deaths per 1,000 live births). In rural areas it was even higher (100).

11. ISLANDS

ANDAMAN & NICOBAR ISLANDS, 2001

Population

Total Population	Male	Female	Per cent of Total Population of India	Density (per sq. km)
356,265	192,985	163,280	0.03	43

Projected Population

Total Pop ('000)	Projected Pop ('000)	Difference ('000) (T-P)
356	394	-38

Percentage Decadal Growth Rates 1951-2001

1951-61	1961-71	1971-81	1981-91	1991-2001
105.2	81.2	63.9	48.7	26.9

Annual Exponential Growth Rate (percent)

1981-91	1991-2001
4.0	2.4

Sex Ratio 1951-2001 (females per 1000 males)

1951	1961	1971	1981	1991	2001
625	617	644	760	818	846

Child Population (0-6 years) and Sex Ratio (0-6 years, 7+)

Child Population (0-6 years)			Sex Ratio (0-6)		Sex Ratio (7+)	
Total	Male	Female	1991	2001	1991	2001
44,674	22,733	21,941	973	965	790	830

Literate Population and Literacy Rate (Per cent)

Literates 7+			Literacy rate (%)		
Total	Male	Female	Total	Male	Female
252,945	146,536	106,409	81.2	86.1	75.3

Illiterate Population

Persons		Male		Female	
1991	2001	1991	2001	1991	2001
63,226	58,646	27,495	23,716	35,731	34,930

Vital Statistics, SRS (1999)

	Total	Rural	Urban
Birth Rate (per 1,000)	18.1	17.8	19.2
Death Rate (per 1,000)	5.5	6.2	3.5
Natural Growth Rate (per 1,000)	12.6	11.5	15.7
Infant Mortality Rate (per 1,000)	25	30	9

LAKSHADWEEP, 2001

Population				
Total Population	*Male*	*Female*	*Per cent of Total Population of India*	*Density (per sq km)*
60,595	31,118	29,447	0.01	1,894

Projected Population		
Total Pop ('000)	*Projected Pop ('000)*	*Difference ('000) (T-P)*
61	72	-11

Percentage Decadal Growth Rates 1951-2001				
1951-61	*1961-71*	*1971-81*	*1981-91*	*1991-2001*
14.6	32.0	26.5	28.5	17.2

Annual Exponential Growth Rate (percent)	
1981-91	*1991-2001*
2.5	1.6

Sex Ratio 1951-2001(females per 1000 males)					
1951	*1961*	*1971*	*1981*	*1991*	*2001*
1,043	1,020	978	975	943	947

Child Population (0-6 years) and Sex Ratio (0-6 years, 7+)						
Child Population (0-6 years)			*Sex Ratio (0-6)*		*Sex Ratio (7+)*	
Total	*Male*	*Female*	*1991*	*2001*	*1991*	*2001*
8,860	4,488	4,372	941	974	943	943

Literate Population and Literacy Rate (Per cent)					
Literates 7+			*Literacy rate (%)*		
Total	*Male*	*Female*	*Total*	*Male*	*Female*
45,281	24,806	20,475	87.5	93.2	81.6

Illiterate Population					
Persons		*Male*		*Female*	
1991	*2001*	*1991*	*2001*	*1991*	*2001*
7,695	6,454	2,136	1,824	5,559	4,630

Vital Statistics, SRS (1999)	*Total*	*Rural*	*Urban*
Birth Rate (per 1,000)	25.1	25.1	25.0
Death Rate (per 1,000)	4.7	4.3	5.0
Natural Growth Rate (per 1,000)	20.4	20.8	20.0
Infant Mortality Rate (per 1,000)	32	26	37

11. HIGHLIGHTS OF ISLANDS
(Andaman & Nicobar Islands and Lakshadweep)

➤ Among the two groups of Islands, Andaman & Nicobar Islands had a population of 356 thousand followed by Lakshadweep 60 thousands.

➤ Andaman & Nicobar Islands recorded the highest decline in the decadal growth rate, a decline of 21.8 per cent points followed by Lakshadweep, a decline of 11.3 per cent points.

➤ The density of Lakshadweep was 1,894 persons per sq km. followed by Andaman & Nicobar Islands (43 persons per sq km).

➤ The annual exponential growth rate declined by 0.9 per cent points.

➤ There was an increase in the overall sex ratio (females per 1,000 males) in both Islands during the decade 1991-2001. Sex ratio was highest in Lakshadweep (947) followed by Andaman & Nicobar Islands (846). In Andaman & Nicobar Islands it increased by 28 points followed by Lakhsadweep (5 points).

➤ The child sex ratio declined in Andaman & Nicobar Islands from 973 to 965 while it has increased in Lakshadweep (by 33 points), during the last decade.

➤ The Child sex ratio (age group 7+) in Lakshadweep remained unchanged at 943 during the last decade, while in Andaman and Nicobar Islands it incresed from 790 in 1991 to 830 in 2001 an increase of 40 points.

➤ Lakshadweep has the highest literacy rate of 87.5 per cent followed by Andaman & Nicobar Islands (81.2 per cent).

➤ Male literacy rate (for population 7 years and above) in Lakshadweep was 93.2 per cent followed by Andaman & Nicobar Islands (86.1 per cent).

➤ Female literacy rate (for population 7 years and above) in Lakshadweep was 81.6 per cent, followed by Andaman & Nicobar Islands (75.3 per cent).

➤ In both the groups of Islands the absolute number of illiterate population has declined during the last decade.

➤ Birth rate in Andaman & Nicobar Islands (18.1 births per 1,000 population) is much less than Lakshadweep (25.1 per 1,000 population).

➤ Death rate in both the Islands was low, in Andaman & Nicobar Islands it was 5.5 deaths per 1,000 population followed by 4.7 deaths in Lakshadweep.

➤ Infant Mortality Rate is higher in Lakshadweep (32 deaths per 1,000 live births) compared to Andaman & Nicobar Islands (25 deaths per 1,000 live births)

PART THREE

IMPLICATIONS

FIRST THOUGHTS ON THE PROVISIONAL RESULTS OF CENSUS OF INDIA 2001

IMPLICATIONS

1. Demographic astrology: How good were the population projections?

There is considerable literature in Demography about the pitfalls of population projections. Demographers always maintain that they do not make predictions but projections based an certain assumptions. These assumptions are in respect of expected declines in fertility and mortality and increase in the expectaction of life. Unlike in astrology, the rules of the game in Demography permit three projections – high, medium and low. Generally, the medium projection is accepted. Migration is assumed to be zero while making these projections.

The Census Commissioner for 2001 Census has devoted considerable space to population projections in Census Paper No. 1 of 2001. A whole section is devoted to Population Projections (pp. 63-70), and 5 detailed tables are presented (Tables 5 to 9). We reproduce below Table 9 of the Census paper, without the technical notes on the assumptions:

Table 3.1 : Projected Population of India in 2000/2001 by Different Individuals and Organisations in the Last Fifty Years

S. No.	Year of Projection/ Publication	Name of the individual /organisation	Population Projection for the year 2000/2001 (million)
1	1950	Kingsley Davis	790
2	1958	Coale-Hoover	1146
3	1984	Office of the Registrar General, India	992
4	1985	Planning Commission/O/o The Registrar General, India	986
5	1986	US Bureau of Census	1024
6	1987	Department of International Economic & Social Affairs, UN	1006
7	1989	Planning Commission	1003
8	1996	Planning Commission/O/o The Registrar General, India	1012
9	1996	USAID	1013
10	1998	Population Division, UN	1007
11	1999	Institute of Economic Growth, New Delhi	1043
12	1999	Population Division, UN	1014
13	2000	Population Foundation of India, New Delhi	1012
14	2000	Tim Dyson	1011

It is worth noting that fifty years back, Kingsley Davis, an outstanding demographer, thought that India's population will be 790 million in 2000, while Tim Dyson, another outstanding demographer, who made the projection in 2000 put the figure at 1011 million. According to the table presented by the Census Commissioner, the projection made by the US Bureau of Census in 1986 was the closest to the actual population of India in 2001.

It may be recalled that in 1996, an Expert Committee headed by the Registrar General was appointed at the instance of the Planning Commission. The committee made projections of population of India and states till the year 2016. In Table 3.2 we give the projected figures and the actual provisional population as of 2001.

Table 3.2 : Projected and Provisional Population of India, States and UTs as on March 1, 2001

A. **Mega States (9) (population : Over 50 million and more than 5 per cent of India's Total population)**

Rank	India/States/UTs	Projected population ('000)	Provisional Population ('000)	Difference ('000)	Percent difference*
1	2	3	4	5	6
1	Uttar Pradesh & Uttaranchal	174,290	174,532	242	0.14
2	Maharashtra	92,057	96,752	4,6955	5.10
3	Bihar & Jharkhand	101,819	109,788	7,969	7.83
4	West Bengal	79,992	80,221	229	0.29
5	Andhra Pradesh	76,392	75,728	-664	-0.87
6	Tamil Nadu	62,252	62,111	-141	-0.23
7	Madhya Pradesh & Chhatisgarh	81,189	81,181	-8	-0.01
8	Rajasthan	54,509	56,473	1,964	3.60
9	Karnataka	52,179	52,734	15	0.03

B. **Bigger States/UTs (8) (population : Over 10 million and more than 1 per cent of India's total population)**

Rank	India/States/UTs	Projected population ('000)	Provisional Population ('000)	Difference ('000)	Percent difference*
1	Gujarat	48,971	50,597	1,626	3.32
2	Orissa	36,156	36,707	551	1.52
3	Kerala	32,530	31,839	-691	-2.13
4	Assam	26,492	26,638	146	0.55
5	Punjab	23,794	24,289	495	2.08
6	Haryana	20,120	21,083	963	4.79
7	Delhi NCT	14,366	13,783	-583	-4.06
8	Jammu & Kashmir	10,071	10,070	-1	-0.01

(Contd...)

C. Smaller States/UTs (15) (population : Less than 10 million and less than 1 per cent of India's total population)

1	2	3	4	5	6
1	Himachal Pradesh	6,805	6,077	728	10.70
2	Tripura	3,859	3,191	-668	-17.31
3	Manipur	2,569	2,389	-180	-7.02
4	Meghalaya	2,484	2,306	-178	-7.16
5	Nagaland	1,721	1,989	268	15.55
6	Goa	1,627	1,344	-283	-17.39
7	Pondicherry UT	1,134	974	-160	-14.12
8	Chandigarh UT	907	901	-6	-0.67
9	Mizoram	972	891	-81	-8.33
10	Arunachal Pradesh	1,217	1,091	-126	-10.34
11	Sikkim	570	540	-30	-5.18
12	Andaman & Nicobar Islands UT	394	356	-38	-9.58
13	Dadra & Nagar Haveli UT	194	220	26	13.63
14	Daman & Diu UT	142	158	16	11.31
15	Lakshadweep UT	72	61	-11	-15.84
	INDIA	**1,021,386**	**1,027,015**	**14,629**	**1.45**

* (Provisional population minus projected population) x 100/projected population

It will be seen that the actual census count for India is higher than the projected figure by about 15 million. The final figure for the 2001 census count may be slightly higher than the provisional figure. In that case the difference will increase further.

If we ignore the small states and UTs, the picture which emerges is as follows:

Table 3.3 : Difference Between Projected and Provisional Population in Selected States, 2001 (in '000)

States	Projected Population ('000)	Provisional Population ('000)	Difference ('000)	Percent Difference
1	2	3	4	5
BIMARU States				
Bihar & Jharkhand	101,819	109,788	7,969	7.83
Madhya Pradesh & Chhatisgarh	81,189	81,181	-8	-0.01
Rajasthan	54,509	56,473	1,964	3.60
Uttar Pradesh & Uttaranchal	174,290	174,532	242	0.14
Southern States				
Andhra Pradesh	76,392	75,728	-664	-0.87
Karnataka	52,179	52,734	15	0.03
Tamil Nadu	62,252	62,111	-141	-0.23
Kerala	32,530	31,839	-691	-2.13

(Contd...)

1	2	3	4	5
Western States				
Gujarat	48,971	50,597	1,628	3.32
Maharashtra	92,057	96,752	4,695	5.10
Eastern States				
Assam	2,492	26,638	146	0.55
Orissa	36,156	36,707	551	1.52
West Bengal	79,992	80,221	229	0.29

It is not possible to make firm comments in the absence of detailed data but it appears to us that the failure of family planning is reflected in the fairly high degree of error in Bihar while the comparative success of family planning is reflected in the relative accuracy of the projections for the three Southern states. In Kerala the actual figure was less than the projected figure by 2.13 per cent, reflecting a faster decline in fertility than anticipated. In Rajasthan, the difference is fairly high (3.60 per cent), while in Madhya Pradesh the projection was almost correct. In Uttar Pradesh the difference is not much. It appears to us that among the BIMARU States, family planning performance has been best in Madhya Pradesh and worst in Bihar. The comparatively high degree of error in Maharashtra must be attributed to migration as the SRS data indicate a fairly low birth rate in that state. Gujarat is also in a similar situation.

The Census Commissioner has rightly observed that the data "clearly demonstrate some of the perils of long term projections and makes it mandatory for the country to go an revising its medium and long term projections on a continuous basis" (on p. 69)

Highlights

➤ The provisional population of India was 1027 million in 2001 compared to the projected figure of 1012 million.

➤ The enumerated figure was more than 15 million, compared to the projected population.

➤ The growth rate during the 1991-2001 decade was 1.93 per cent per year compared to 1.79 per cent implicit in the projected figure for 2001.

➤ In short, the rate of growth of population was higher during 1991-2001 than anticipated by the Technical Group on Population Projections.

➤ Where did the projections go wrong? In Bihar (including Jharkhand) the per cent difference in Projected and Actual Population was of the order of 7.8 per cent, followed by Maharashtra (5.1 per cent), and Rajasthan (3.6 per cent) where there was excess population.

➤ In contrast, in Kerala the actual population was less than the projected population (difference –2.13 per cent), followed by Andhra Pradesh (0.87 per cent), and Tamil Nadu (-0.23 per cent).

➤ These figures bring out the growing disparity between BIMARU states and Southern states in terms of decline in fertility and the adverse impact of BIMARU states on the demographic scene.

2. DEMARU States : Decline in the sex ratio of child population (0-6 years)

We shall discuss the implications of an increase in the overall sex ratio during the last decade, accompanied by a *decline* in the sex ratio of the child population. In Table 3.4 we give figures for the variation in the sex ratio of the total population of all the 35 states and UTs, arranged in descending order of magnitude of variation (in points). In Table 3.5 we give the sex ratio of two groups of population : (a) 0-6 age group and (b) 7+ age group. Table 3.6 gives the proportion of population in the 0-6 age group in 1991 and 2001 the states and UTs are ranked according to the variation (percentage points) in the *female* proportion during the last decade. We summarise the main findings below.

Highlights

➤ The overall sex ratio (females per 1,000 males) in India has improved during the last decade and there was an increase in 6 points: The sex ratio in 2001 was 933 compared to 927 in 1991.

➤ In sharp contrast, the sex ratio of the child population (0-6) declined sharply during this decade, from 945 in 1991 to 927 in 2001 – a decline of 18 points.

➤ What explanins this contradictory trend? The clue lies in the 7+ age group (the five-yearly age distribution is not yet available from the first results and hence we have to consider the 7+ age group, the data for which were tabulated in order to calculate the literacy rates). The sex ratio of the 7+ age group increased from 923 in 1991 to 935 in 2001 or an increase in 12 points. In short young girls on the age group 0-6 have fared badly while things have improved in the 7+ age group. This has happened because the mortality rates of females in the higher age groups are lower than of males and so also in the expectation of life. In the absence of data it is not possible to have a detailed analysis at this stage.

➤ A word of caution is called for while analysing the data on sex ratio. An increase in sex ratio does not necessarily indicate an improvement in the 'status of women' (to use an hackneyed phrase). For examples in Uttaranchal (the census paper gives adjusted figures for this newly formed state) the overall sex ratio increased from 936 in 1991 to 964 in 2001 – an increase of 28 points. This reflects increasing migration of males from Uttaranchal and the growing hardship of women who have to fend for themselves and take care of the children, the old people, their farming and animal husbandry. In Kerala also migration of males must have contributed to the improvement in the overall sex ratio, apart from the higher levels of expection of life of females compared to that of males.

➤ A dismal aspect of the 2001 Census first results is the *decline* in the overall sex ratio of several states during the last decade. Confining ourselves to the bigger states we find that in Gujarat the sex ratio *declined* by 17 points, in Maharashtra by 12, in Punjab by 8 points and in Himachal Pradesh by 6 points. Can selective migration alone explain this decline in sex ratio or is there a growing neglect of women and improvement of women in these economically advanced states? In Himachal Pradesh, there is outmigration of males, why should then the overall sex ratio decline? The clue is provided by the declining sex ratio in the 0-6 age group.

➢ Table 3.5 reveals a shocking state of affairs. In Punjab, the child sex ratio declined by 82 points duirng the last decade, followed by Haryana (59 points), Himachal Pradesh (54 points), Gujarat (50 points), Uttaranchal (42 points), and Maharashtra (29 points).

➢ The child sex ratio in 2001 was lowest in Punjab (793), followed by Haryana (820). It may be recalled that overall sex ratio was lowest in Haryana (861) followed by Punjab (874).

➢ The child sex ratio has declined in almost all the states. The states where it has *increased* during the decade are Sikkim (21 points), Tripura (8 points), Kerala (5 points) and Mizoram (2 points). In Lakshadweep Islands, the increase was of the order of 33 points. There may be statistical explanations of this phenomenon, apart from the socio-cultural aspects in states like Kerala and Mizoram, where the discrimination against the girl child is absent. In the absence of detailed districtwise data, no further comments can be made at this stage.

➢ With the spread of family planning and the decline in fertility, the proportion of population in the 0-6 age group is bound to decline as fewer children are born. But if comparatively fewer girls are born, the decline in the female child population will be more than that of the male child population. This is reflected by Table 3.6. In India as a whole, the proportion of male child (0-6) population declined from 17.8 per cent in 1991 to 15.5 per cent in 2001 or a decline of 2.3 per cent points. In the case of females, the decline was sharper – from 18.1 per cent to 15.4 per cent or a decline of 2.7 per cent points.

➢ The *decline* in the proportion of female child population was sharpest in Tripura (4.7 points) followed by Punjab (4.3 points), Sikkim (4.1 points) and Haryana (4.1 points).

➢ The proportion of both male and female child population declined in every state and UT during the last decade which confirms the decline in fertility.

Why is the sex ratio of the child population falling?

The Census Commissioner in his comments on the census results of 2001 (Census Paper No. 1 of 2001) sums up the causes of this decline commonly put forward as follows (P. 91):

> Neglect of the girl child resulting in their higher mortality at younger ages
> Higher maternal mortality
> Sex selective female abortion
> Female infanticide
> Change in sex ratio at birth

One could add to this list another factor – quality of census enumeration, the differential undercount of males and females, the quality of age data and methodological aspects of sucessive censuses. In the absence of the results of the post enumeration check for the 2001 census (which will be taken up shortly), it is not possible to make comparisions between the censuses of 1981, 1991 and 2001 in terms of enumeration and age data.

At this stage it is not possible to make firm comments on the declining child sex ratio and we must await the publication of detailed data by the Census Commissioner. It should be noted, however, that the decline in child sex ratio is not confined to this decade only as the following figures will indicate.

Table 3.4 : Sex Ratio in 0-6 Age Group, 1961-2001

Year	Sex ratio in 0-6 age group	Variation
1961	976	-
1971	964	-12
1981	962	-2
1991	945	-17
2001	927	-18

There is no doubt that increasing use of pre-natal sex determination tests and female foeticide must have contributed significantly to the significant decline in the sex ratio in the last two decades. The Census Commissioner asks cautiously in the Census Paper : "Are the sharp declines in the child sex ratios indicative of an underline trend of sex selective abortions in these areas ?" (p. 97).

In Part V, we have reproduced a recent article by Professor M.K. Premi who concludes :

"....in recent years the female death rates have become lower than the male death rates. This must have led to improvement in overall sex ratio in favour of females. SRB becoming more favourable to males would, however, influence the overall sex ratio in the opposite direction.

In contrast, the sex differential in infant mortality rate as also in child mortality rate has still not become favourable to female child. The two factors together, particularly in the latter part of the 1990s, should explain a part of decline in the child sex ratio during the 1990s.

Child sex ratio of 793 in Punjab and 820 in Haryana, especially with sex ratio at birth of 122.8 and 123.3 respectively point towards rampant practice of female foeticide along with a certain amount of infanticide in these two states. The districtwise data on child sex ratio as and when they become available will throw more light on this very important aspect".

Finally, we wish to refer to the most recent contribution on this subject – a thought provoking book on *Enduring Conundrum: India's Sex Ratio* edited by Vina Mazumdar and N. Krishnaji published for Centre for Women's Development Studies by Rainbow Publishers, New Delhi, released on 9 April 2001. Satish Agnihotri, known for his outstanding contribution on sex ratio (*Sex Ratio Patterns in the Indian Population*, Sage Publishers, New Delhi, 2000) writes a short piece on this new book titled "Rising sons and setting daughters". To quote him :

> *Interestingly, the increase in the overall sex ratio by 6 points in the face of an 18 point decline in the child sex ratio is rather counter intuitive. For a comparable decline of 17 points in the child sex ratio between 1981 and 1991, the overall sex ratio had declined by 7 points. This has happened through a rise in the sex ratio of the population above 6 years. This increase, according to the preliminary report, is as high as 12 points – from 923 to 935. Similar pattern is reflected in most of the states. While the increase in the sex ratio in the 6 years plus age group has been modest in the southern states, it is substantial in Uttar Pradesh, Bihar, Uttaranchal and Jharkhand. Have females suddenly surfaced everywhere? Have their life chances gone up so dramatically? One has to grapple with the answers after the final totals become available. Prima facie however, such increase in the background of drastic decline in the child ratio appears implausible.*

Pending the publication of detailed data from census and SRS and subsequent studies on the subject by demographers and other experts, all one can say at this stage is that even the provisional results clearly point out the growing malaise in Indian Society which has to be fought at all levels.

Table 3.5 : Sex Ratio in States/UTs Ranked According to Variation during 1991-2001

Rank	State	1991	2001	Variation
1	2	3	4	5
	INDIA	**927**	**933**	**6**
1	Arunachal Pradesh	859	901	42
2	Uttaranchal	936	964	28
3	Andaman & Nicobar Islands UT	818	846	28
4	Nagaland	886	909	23
5	Uttar Pradesh	876	898	22
6	Kerala	1036	1058	22
7	Pondicherry UT	979	1001	22
8	Manipur	958	978	20
9	Meghalaya	955	975	20
10	Jharkhand	922	941	19

(Contd...)

1	2	3	4	5
11	West Bengal	917	934	17
12	Mizoram	921	938	17
13	Bihar	907	921	14
14	Tamil Nadu	974	986	12
15	Rajasthan	910	922	12
16	Assam	923	932	9
17	Madhya Pradesh	912	920	8
18	Andhra Pradesh	972	978	6
19	Chhatisgarh	985	990	5
20	Tripura	945	950	5
21	Karnataka	960	964	4
22	Jammu & Kashmir	896	900	4
23	Lakshadweep UT	943	947	4
24	Orissa	971	972	1
25	Sikkim	878	875	-3
26	Haryana	865	861	-4
27	Delhi NCT	827	821	-6
28	Himachal Pradesh	976	970	-6
29	Goa	967	960	-7
30	Punjab	882	874	-8
31	Maharashtra	934	922	-12
32	Gujarat	934	921	-13
33	Chandigarh UT	790	773	-17
34	Dadra & Nagar Haveli UT	952	811	-141
35	Daman & Diu UT	969	709	-260

In Table 3.6 we present data for two groups: 0-6 age group and 7+ age group. It will be seen that in most of the states and UTs the child sex ratio has gone down in 2001 while in 7+ age group there has been an increase in the sex ratio in almost all the states.

Table 3.6 : Child Sex Ratio (0-6 age and 7+ age group) State/UTs Ranked According to Decline in Sex Ratio of 0-6 Population

Rank	India/States/UT	Sex ratio (0-6 age group)			Sex ratio (7+ age group)		
		1991	2001	Difference points	1991	2001	Difference points
1	2	3	4	5	6	7	8
	INDIA	**945**	**927**	**-18**	**923**	**935**	**12**
1	Punjab	875	793	-82	883	886	3
2	Haryana	879	820	-59	862	869	7
3	Himachal Pradesh	951	897	-54	980	981	1
4	Chandigarh UT	899	845	-54	772	763	-9

(Contd...)

1	2	3	4	5	6	7	8
5	Gujarat	928	878	-50	936	927	-9
6	Delhi	915	865	-50	810	813	3
7	Uttaranchal	948	906	-42	933	976	43
8	Dadra & Nagar Haveli UT	1,013	973	-40	936	779	-157
9	Daman & Diu UT	958	925	-33	971	682	-289
10	Goa	964	933	-31	967	964	-3
11	Maharashtra	946	917	-29	931	923	-8
12	Arunachal Pradesh	982	961	-21	829	888	59
13	Nagaland	993	975	-18	865	899	34
14	Orissa	967	950	-17	972	976	4
15	Bihar	953	938	-15	895	916	21
16	Manipur	974	961	-13	955	981	26
17	Jharkhand	979	966	-13	908	936	28
18	Madhya Pradesh	941	929	-12	905	918	13
19	Meghalaya	986	975	-11	947	974	27
20	Uttar Pradesh	927	916	-11	863	895	32
21	Assam	975	964	-11	910	926	16
22	Karnataka	960	949	-11	960	966	6
23	Andhra Pradesh	975	964	-11	972	980	8
24	Chhatisgarh	984	975	-9	986	992	6
25	Tamil Nadu	948	939	-9	978	992	14
26	Andaman & Nicobar Islands UT	973	965	-8	790	830	40
27	Rajasthan	916	909	-7	908	925	17
28	Pondicherry UT	963	958	-5	982	1007	25
29	West Bengal	967	963	-4	907	929	22
30	Mizoram	969	971	2	911	932	21
31	Kerala	958	963	5	1049	1071	22
32	Tripura	967	975	8	940	947	7
33	Sikkim	965	986	21	860	858	-2
34	Lakshadweep UT	941	974	33	943	943	0
35	Jammu & Kashmir	N.A	937	—	NA	894	—

In Table 3.7 we present the percentage of population in age group 0-6 years in 1991 and 2001. It will be seen that the proportion has declined in all the states and UTs in 2001.

**Table 3.7 : Percentage of Population in the Age Group 0-6 Ranked
According to the Decrease in the Female Percentage in 2001**

Rank	State	Male			Female		
		1991	*2001*	*Difference*	*1991*	*2001*	*Difference*
	INDIA	**17.77**	**15.47**	**-2.30**	**18.12**	**15.36**	**-2.76**
1	Tripura	17.82	13.22	-4.60	18.25	13.55	-4.70
2	Andaman & Nicobar Islands UT	15.22	11.78	-3.44	18.09	13.44	-4.65
3	Punjab	16.36	13.15	-3.21	16.23	11.93	-4.30
4	Sikkim	17.56	13.48	-4.08	19.29	15.19	-4.10
5	Haryana	18.84	15.81	-3.03	19.14	15.05	-4.09
6	Manipur	16.55	13.21	-3.34	16.83	12.97	-3.86
7	Andhra Pradesh	16.46	12.87	-3.59	16.51	12.68	-3.83
8	Karnataka	16.63	13.04	-3.59	16.63	12.85	-3.78
9	Himachal Pradesh	16.47	13.34	-3.13	16.03	12.32	-3.71
10	Arunachal Pradesh	19.82	17.77	-2.05	22.64	18.96	-3.68
11	Assam	19.2	16.07	-3.13	20.29	16.62	-3.67
12	Delhi NCT	16.28	13.63	-2.65	18.01	14.37	-3.64
13	Maharashtra	17.00	13.67	-3.33	17.23	13.59	-3.64
14	Nagaland	16.23	13.62	-2.61	18.19	14.61	-3.58
15	Lakshadweep UT	18.32	14.42	-3.90	18.28	14.83	-3.45
16	Uttaranchal	18.22	16.04	-2.18	18.46	15.06	-3.40
17	West Bengal	16.56	13.67	-2.89	17.45	14.10	-3.35
18	Chandigarh UT	14.06	11.66	-2.40	16.00	12.75	-3.25
19	Mizoram	18.15	15.62	-2.53	19.09	16.17	-2.92
20	Orissa	16.93	14.27	-2.66	16.85	13.95	-2.90
21	Chhatisgarh	19.36	16.80	-2.56	19.33	16.56	-2.77
22	Jharkhand	19.59	17.60	-1.99	20.80	18.06	-2.74
23	Meghalaya	21.84	19.83	-2.01	22.54	19.84	-2.70
24	Madhya Pradesh	19.64	17.50	-2.14	20.27	17.68	-2.59
25	Gujarat	16.53	14.51	-2.02	16.43	13.85	-2.58
26	Uttar Pradesh	19.84	18.18	-1.66	20.99	18.54	-2.45
27	Tamil Nadu	13.51	11.24	-2.27	13.15	10.71	-2.44
28	Pondicherry UT	13.78	11.86	-1.92	13.55	11.35	-2.20
29	Rajasthan	20.06	18.63	-1.43	20.21	18.37	-1.84
30	Kerala	13.71	12.04	-1.67	12.68	10.95	-1.73
31	Dadra & Nagar Haveli UT	19.84	16.31	-3.53	21.12	19.57	-1.55
32	Bihar	20.21	19.41	-0.8	21.24	19.78	-1.46
33	Goa	11.75	10.73	-1.02	11.72	10.42	-1.30
34	Daman & Diu UT	15.62	11.24	-4.38	15.44	14.67	-0.77
35	Jammu & Kashmir	NA	13.94	—	NA	14.52	—

The most dismal aspect of the 2001 census result is the sharp fall in the sex ratio (female per 1000 males) in the child population (0-6 age group). We have already given the relevant figures in the preceding pages. It will be seen that there has been an increase in the sex ratio of the overall population but a sharp *decrease* in the sex ratio of the child population in states like Punjab, Haryana, Himachal Pradesh and Gujarat, apart from Chandigarh and Delhi UTs. It has also decreased in Maharashtra, the most urbanised state in India. We present here the *districtwise* figures for these states which give an idea of the dramatic decline in the sex ratio. As discussed in the Overview, we call these states DEMARU – daughter killers (where D stands for daughters and E for elimination in English and MARU for killing in Hindi).

Table 3.8 : District Level Data on Sex Ratio, Selected States/UTs

PUNJAB

State/District	Sex Ratio 2001	Sex Ratio 1991	Variation 2001-1991
1	2	3	4
Punjab	**793**	**875**	**-82**
Gurdaspur	775	878	-103
Amritsar	783	861	-78
Kapurthala	775	879	-104
Jalandhar	797	886	-89
Hoshiarpur	810	884	-74
Nawanshahr	810	900	-90
Rupnagar	791	884	-93
Fatehgarh Sahib	754	874	-120
Ludhiana	814	877	-63
Moga	819	867	-48
Firozpur	819	887	-68
Muktsar	807	858	-51
Faridkot	805	865	-60
Bathinda	779	860	-81
Mansa	779	873	-94
Sangrur	784	873	-89
Patiala	770	871	-101

HARYANA

1	2	3	4
Haryana	**820**	**879**	**-59**
Panchkula	837	NA	NA
Ambala	784	888	-104
Yamunanagar	807	889	-82
Kurukshetra	770	867	-97
Kaithal	789	854	-65
Karnal	808	875	-67
Panipat	807	881	-74
Sonipat	783	879	-96
Jind	818	858	-40
Fatehabad	830	NA	NA
Sirsa	818	883	-65
Hisar	830	867	-37
Bhiwani	838	886	-48
Rohtak	.796	876	-80
Jhajjar	805	NA	NA
Mahendragarh	814	892	-78
Rewari	814	894	-80
Gurgaon	863	895	-32
Faridabad	856	884	-28

HIMACHAL PRADESH

1	2	3	4
Himachal Pradesh	**897**	**951**	**-54**
Chamba	962	965	-3
Kangra	836	939	-103
Lahul & Spiti	986	951	35
Kullu	960	966	-6
Mandi	916	968	-52
Hamirpur	864	938	-74
Una	839	923	-84
Bilaspur	884	923	-39
Solan	900	951	-51
Sirmaur	940	973	-33
Shimla	930	958	-28
Kinnaur	NA	958	—

CHANDIGARH

1	2	3	4
Chandigarh	845	899	-54

DELHI

Delhi	865	915	-50

GUJARAT

Gujarat	878	928	-50
Kachchh	NA	929	—
Banas Kantha	907	931	-24
Patan	862	NA	—
Mahesana	798	897	-99
Sabar Kantha	876	933	-57
Gandhinagar	816	879	-63
Ahmadabad	814	897	-83
Surendranagar	861	905	-44
Rajkot	844	916	-72
Jamnagar	894	916	-22
Porbandar	897	NA	—
Junagadh	898	926	-28
Amreli	894	932	-38
Bhavnagar	886	925	-39
Anand	873	NA	—
Kheda	880	898	-18
Panch Mahals	934	985	-51
Dohad	964	NA	—
Vadodara	873	934	-61
Narmada	952	NA	—
Bharuch	909	965	-56
Surat	873	944	-71
The Dangs	974	999	-25
Navsari	912	NA	—
Valsad	934	966	-32

MAHARASHTRA

1	2	3	4
Maharashtra	**917**	**946**	**-29**
Nandurbar	966	NA	—
Dhule	907	960	-53
Jalgaon	867	925	-58
Buldana	915	945	-30
Akola	936	934	2
Washim	921	NA	—
Amravati	947	950	-3
Wardha	934	952	-18
Nagpur	949	951	-2
Bhandara	958	971	-13
Gondiya	964	NA	—
Gadchiroli	974	980	-6
Chandrapur	944	965	-21
Yavatmal	942	961	-19
Nanded	944	960	-16
Hingoli	935	NA	—
Parbhani	926	955	-29
Jalna	914	951	-37
Aurangabad	884	933	-49
Nashik	936	954	-18
Thane	933	952	-19
Mumbai (Suburb)	919	NA	—
Mumbai	898	NA	—
Raigarh	943	961	-18
Pune	906	943	-37
Ahmadnagar	890	949	-59
Bid	898	939	-41
Latur	923	947	-24
Osmanabad	927	947	-20
Solapur	897	935	-38
Satara	884	941	-57
Ratnagiri	954	961	-7
Sindhudurg	946	963	-17
Kolhapur	859	931	-72
Sangli	850	924	-74

Source: Compiled from State reports on *Provisional Tables for 2001 Census* and
Ashish Bose, *Demographic Diversity of India, 1991 Census, Supplement 1998.*

3.   Role of BIMARU States

The 2001 Census results fully validate our diagnosis of India's population probelm in terms of the adverse role of four large states – Bihar, Madhya Pradesh, Rajasthan and Uttar Pradesh which are demographically, economically, socially and politically lagging behind most other states of India. Our acronym is BIMARU which means sick in Hindi dialect. On diplomatic grounds, we may designate this group of states as 'North' which may not be geographically correct. We present a set of tables which bring out the sharp contrast between North and South. The growing North-South disparity should be a cause for concern to all citizens of India.

In Table 3.8 we present the literacy rate of states and UTs by sex for the year 2001. The states are ranked according to the increase in the female literacy rate. The highest female literacy was recorded in the state of Kerala and the lowest in Bihar.

Table 3.9 : Population Growth Rates in BIMARU States, 1981-91 & 1991-2001

State	Population in million		Percent decadal growth rate		Average Annual exponential growth rate (per cent)	
	1991	2001	1981-91	1991-2001	1981-91	1991-2001
1	2	3	4	5	6	7
North						
Uttar Pradesh	132.0	166.1	25.6	25.8	2.28	2.30
Bihar	64.5	82.9	23.4	28.4	2.10	2.50
Madhya Pradesh	48.6	60.4	27.2	24.3	2.41	2.18
Rajasthan	44.0	56.5	28.4	28.3	2.50	2.49
Total	**289.1**	**365.9**	**NA**	**26.6**	**NA**	**2.36**
South						
Andhra Pradesh	53.55	66.5	75.7	24.2	13.9	2.17	1.30
Tamil Nadu	48.41	55.9	62.1	15.4	11.2	1.43	1.06
Karnataka	37.14	45.0	52.7	21.1	17.3	1.92	1.59
Kerala	25.45	29.1	31.8	14.3	9.4	1.34	0.90
Total	**164.55**	**196.5**	**222.3**	**19.42**	**13.13**	**1.77**	**1.23**

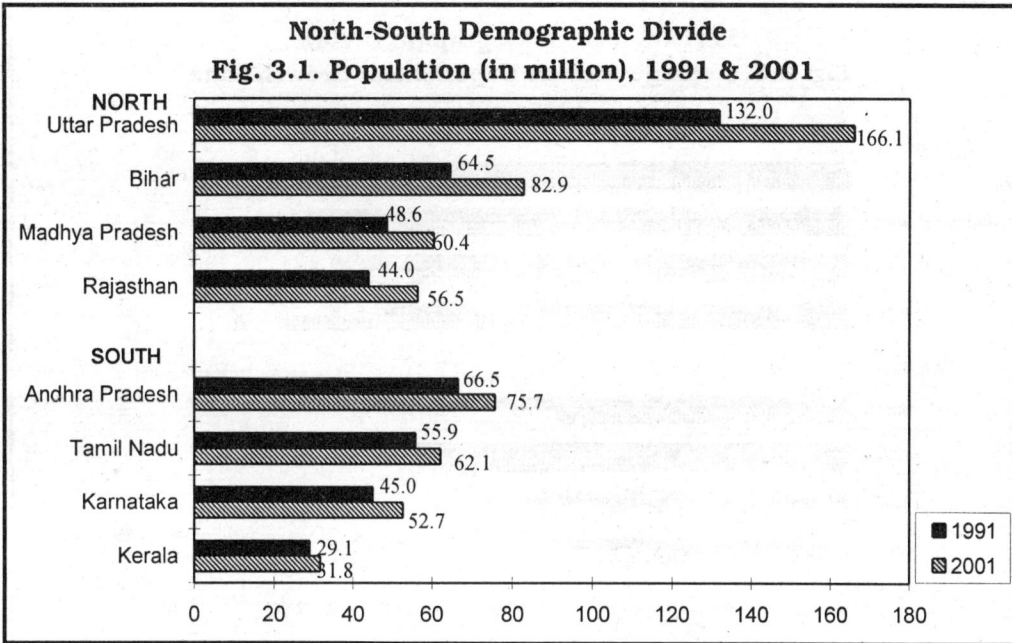

North-South Demographic Divide
Fig. 3.1. Population (in million), 1991 & 2001

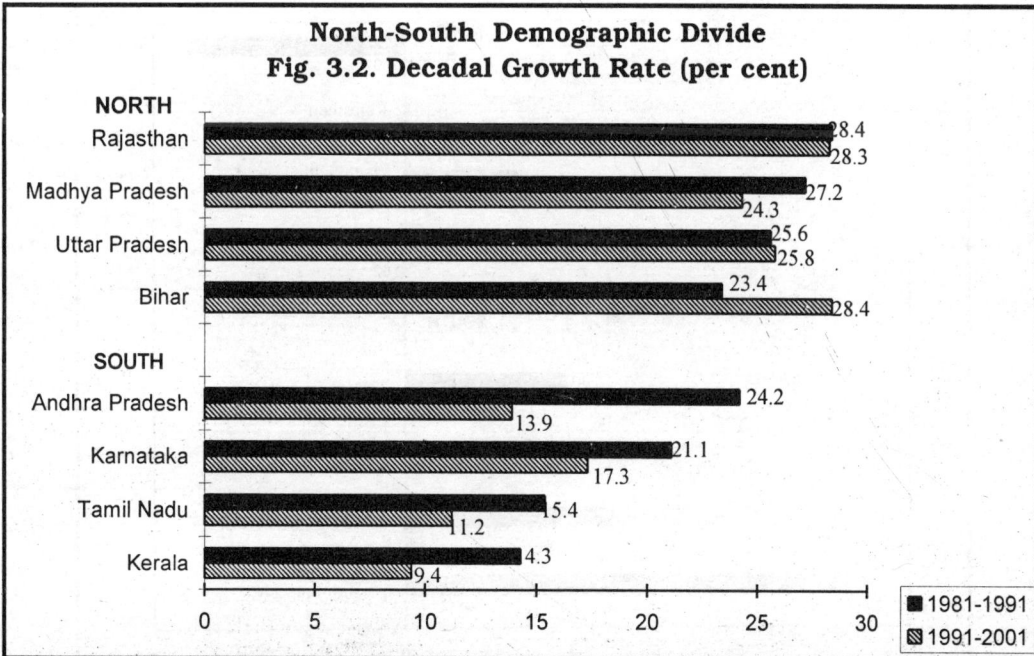

North-South Demographic Divide
Fig. 3.2. Decadal Growth Rate (per cent)

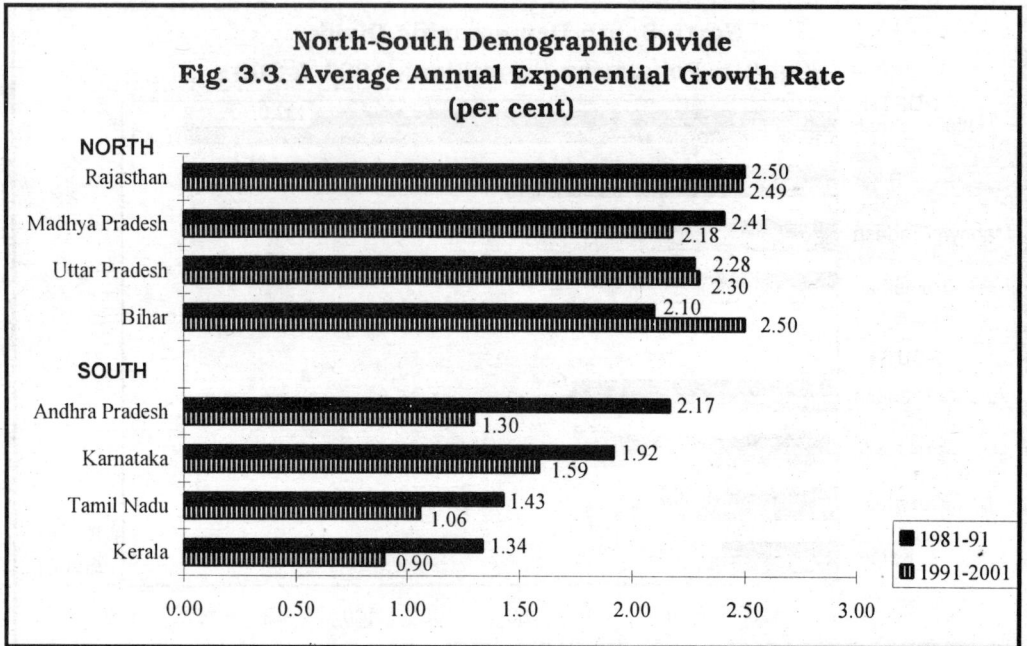

North-South Demographic Divide
Fig. 3.3. Average Annual Exponential Growth Rate
(per cent)

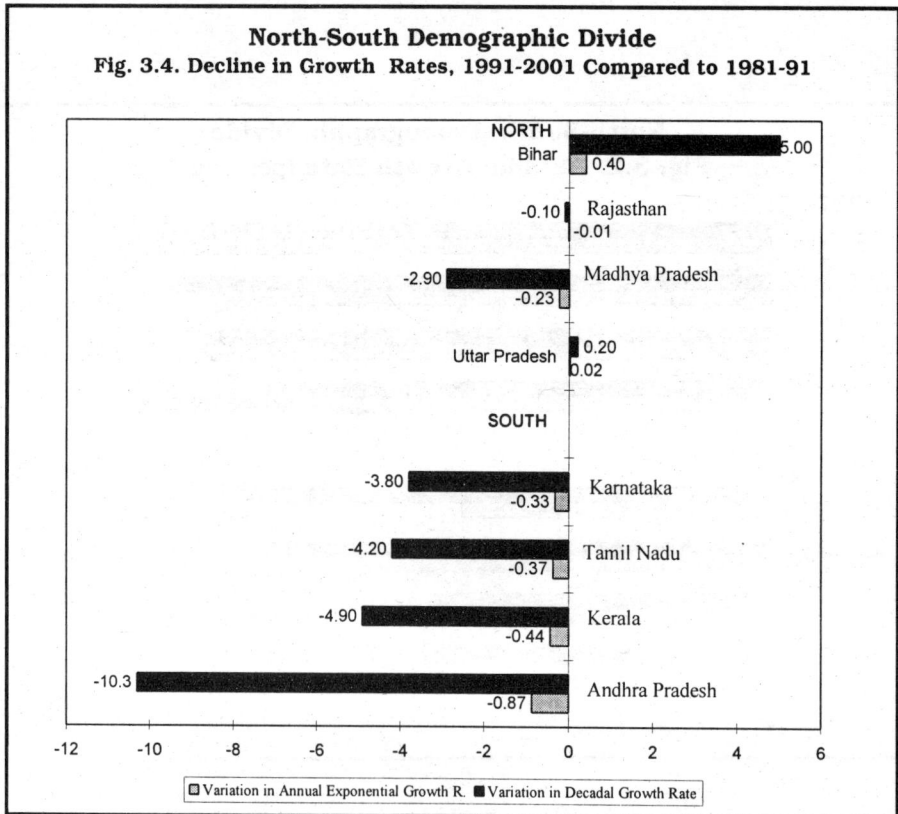

North-South Demographic Divide
Fig. 3.4. Decline in Growth Rates, 1991-2001 Compared to 1981-91

Table 3.10 : Population of Three New States Added to BIMARU States, 1981-91 & 1991-2001

State	Population in million			Percent decadal growth rate		Average Annual exponential growth rate (per cent)	
	1981	1991	2001	1981-91	1991-2001	1981-91	1991-2001
North							
Uttar Pradesh + Uttaranchal	110.9	139.1	174.6	25.43	25.5	2.27	2.27
Bihar + Jharkhand	69.9	86.4	109.5	23.61	26.7	2.12	2.34
Madhya Pradesh + Chhatisgarh	52.2	66.2	81.2	26.82	22.7	2.38	2.04
Rajasthan	34.3	44.0	56.5	28.28	28.4	2.49	2.50
Total	**267.3**	**335.7**	**421.8**	**25.59**	**25.7**	**2.27**	**2.28**

Table 3.11 : Share of Population and Increase in Population

State	Per cent of total population of India		Per cent contribution to total population growth of India	
	1991*	2001	1981-91	1991-2001
North				
Uttar Pradesh	15.60	16.17	16.5	18.8
Bihar	7.62	8.07	7.5	10.1
Madhya Pradesh	5.74	5.88	6.4	6.5
Rajasthan	5.20	5.50	6.0	6.9
Total	**34.16**	**35.62**	**36.4**	**42.3**
South				
Andhra Pradesh	7.86	7.37	8.0	5.1
Tamil Nadu	6.59	6.05	4.6	3.4
Karnataka	5.31	5.14	4.8	4.2
Kerala	3.44	3.10	2.2	1.5
Total	**23.20**	**21.66**	**19.6**	**14.2**

* The 1991 figures are adjusted to exclude the figures for Jharkhand, Chhatisgarh and Uttaranchal which were created in 2000. The figures given here, therefore, do not tally with the total population of these states given in 1991 census reports.

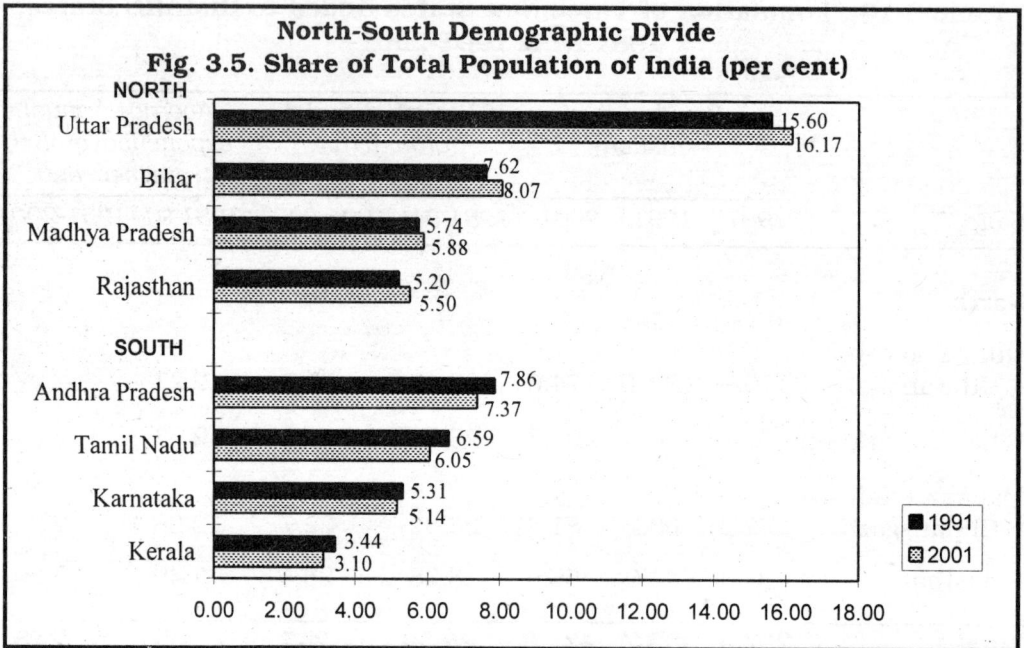

North-South Demographic Divide
Fig. 3.5. Share of Total Population of India (per cent)

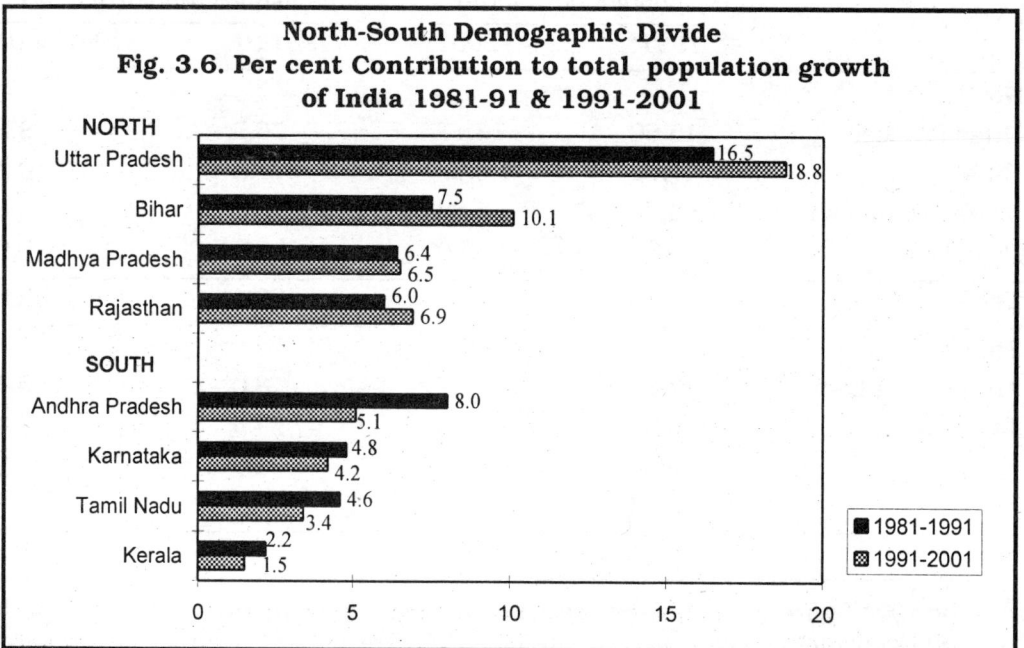

North-South Demographic Divide
Fig. 3.6. Per cent Contribution to total population growth of India 1981-91 & 1991-2001

**Table 3.12 : Share of Population of Three New States Added
to BIMARU States and Increase in Population**

State	Per cent of total population of India		Per cent contribution to total population growth of India	
	1991	2001	1981-91	1991-2001
North				
Uttar Pradesh + Uttaranchal	16.6	17.0	17.3	19.5
Bihar + Jharkhand	10.3	10.7	10.1	12.9
Madhya Pradesh + Chhatisgarh	7.9	7.9	8.6	8.2
Rajasthan	5.3	5.5	6.0	6.9
Total	**40.0**	**41.1**	**42.0**	**47.5**

Table 3.13 : Increase in Absolute Population (in million)

State	1981-91	1991-2001
North		
Uttar Pradesh	26.9	34.1
Bihar	12.2	18.4
Madhya Pradesh	10.4	11.8
Rajasthan	9.7	12.5
Total	**59.2**	**76.7**
South		
Andhra Pradesh	13.0	9.2
Tamil Nadu	7.5	6.3
Karnataka	7.8	7.8
Kerala	3.6	2.7
Total	**31.9**	**26.0**
INDIA	**63.1**	**180.6**

North-South Demographic Divide
Fig. 3.7. Increase in Absolute Population (in million)

	NORTH		
Uttar Pradesh	26.86	34.05	
Bihar	12.23	18.35	
Madhya Pradesh	10.40 / 11.82		
Rajasthan	9.74 / 12.47		
	SOUTH		
Andhra Pradesh	12.96 / 9.22		
Karnataka	7.84 / 7.76		
Tamil Nadu	7.45 / 6.25		
Kerala	3.64 / 2.74		

■ 1981-1991
▨ 1991-2001

Scale: 0 5 10 15 20 25 30 35 40

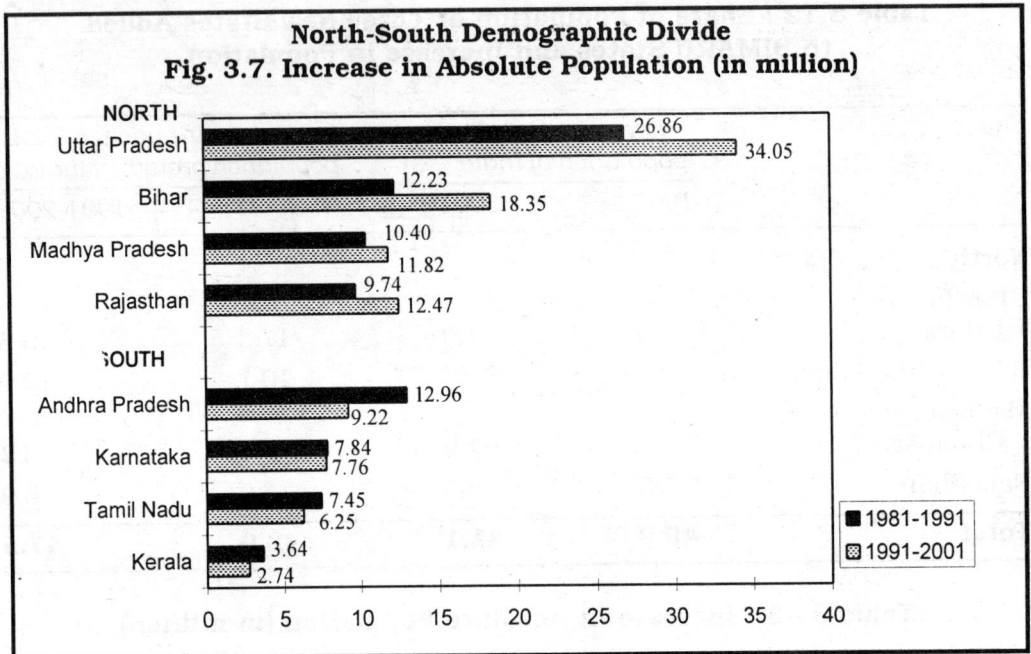

Table 3.14 : Increase in Absolute Population of Three New States and BIMARU States (in million)

State	1981-91	1991-2001
North		
Uttar Pradesh + Uttaranchal	28.3	35.5
Bihar + Jharkhand	16.4	23.5
Madhya Pradesh + Chhatisgarh	14.0	15.0
Rajasthan	9.7	12.5
Total	**68.4**	**86.5**

Highlights

➢ BIMARU states (4+3 offshoots) account for 41 per cent of India's population, contribute 47 per cent to the decadal growth rate and contain 50 per cent of illiterate population.

➢ The total population of the four BIMARU states as of 2001 was 365 million or 35.7 percent of India's total population, if the population of three new states (Chhatisgarh, Jharkhand and Uttaranchal) are added the total population of BIMARU states as constituted in 1991, it is 421 million in 2001 or 41 per cent of India's population.

➢ In absolute term, the population of seven BIMARU states increased by 86 million during the 1991-2001 decade.

➢ The average annual growth rate for these group of states was 2.29 percent during 1991-2000 decade.

➢ In contrast the four Southern states (Andhra Pradesh, Tamil Nadu, Karnataka, Kerala) had a combined population of 222 million in 2001 or 21.7 per cent of India's population.

➢ In terms of decadal growth rate in Southern states during the 1991-2001 decade it was 13.1 per cent.

➢ It may be noticed that Andhra Pradesh recorded the sharper decline in the decadal growth namely 10 per cent point. In contrast the Bihar growth rate during the decade increased to 28 per cent from 23 per cent in 1991.

➢ Finally it may be noted that in the four BIMARU states Bihar recorded the highest increase in the decadal growth rate compared to previous decade whereas in Uttar Pradesh it marginally increased and in Rajasthan it was almost of the same order, while in Madhya Pradesh there was a perceptible decline from 27 per cent to 24 per cent.

➢ In the absence of migration data it is not possible to disaggregate the data on growth rate in terms of natural increase and migration.

➢ In Andhra Pradesh, Tamil Nadu and Kerala there was a decline in the absolute increase in the population during 1991-2001 compared to the previous decade, while in Karnataka the absolute increase during the decade was of the same order.

4. Increase in Literacy Rates in 2001

Table 3.15 : Literacy Rate in States/UTs by Sex, 2001, Ranked According to Female Literacy Rate

Rank	State	Females	Males	Persons	M-F Gap
	INDIA	**54**	**76**	**65**	**22**
1	Kerala	88	94	91	6
2	Mizoram	86	91	89	5
3	Lakshadweep UT	82	93	88	11
4	Chandigarh UT	77	86	82	9
5	Goa	76	89	82	13
6	Andaman & Nicobar Islands UT	75	86	81	11
7	Delhi NCT	75	87	82	12
8	Pondicherry UT	74	89	81	15
9	Daman & Diu UT	70	88	81	18
10	Himachal Pradesh	68	86	77	18
11	Maharashtra	68	86	77	18
12	Tripura	65	81	74	16
13	Tamil Nadu	65	82	73	17
14	Punjab	64	76	70	12
15	Nagaland	62	72	67	10
16	Sikkim	61	77	70	16
17	Meghalaya	60	66	63	6
18	Uttaranchal	60	84	72	24
19	West Bengal	60	78	69	18
20	Manipur	60	78	69	18
21	Gujarat	59	81	70	22
22	Karnataka	57	76	67	19
23	Haryana	56	79	69	23
24	Assam	56	72	64	16
25	Chhatisgarh	52	78	65	26
26	Andhra Pradesh	51	71	61	20
27	Orissa	51	76	64	25
28	Madhya Pradesh	50	77	64	27
29	Rajasthan	44	76	61	32
30	Arunachal Pradesh	44	64	55	20
31	Dadra & Nagar Haveli UT	43	73	60	30
32	Uttar Pradesh	43	70	57	27
33	Jammu & Kashmir	42	66	54	24
34	Jharkhand	39	68	54	29
35	Bihar	34	60	48	26

Table 3.16 : Literacy Rate in States/UTs by Sex, 1991-2001, Ranked According to Variation in Female Literacy Rate (per cent)

Rank	State	Females			Males			Persons		
		2001	1991	Variation	2001	1991	Variation	2001	1991	Variation
	INDIA	**54.2**	**39.3**	**14.9**	**76.9**	**64.1**	**12.8**	**65.4**	**52.0**	**13.4**
1	Jammu & Kashmir	41.8	NA	—	65.8	NA	—	54.5	NA	—
2	Chhatisgarh	52.4	27.5	24.9	77.9	58.1	19.8	65.2	42.9	22.3
3	Rajasthan	44.3	20.4	23.9	76.5	55.0	21.5	61.0	38.6	22.5
4	Madhya Pradesh	50.3	29.4	20.9	76.8	58.5	18.3	64.1	44.7	19.4
5	Uttaranchal	60.3	41.6	18.6	84.0	72.8	11.2	72.3	57.8	14.5
6	Uttar Pradesh	43.0	24.4	18.6	70.2	54.8	15.4	57.4	40.7	16.7
7	Andhra Pradesh	51.2	32.7	18.5	70.9	55.1	15.7	61.1	44.1	17.0
8	Orissa	51.0	34.7	16.3	76.0	63.1	12.9	63.6	49.1	14.5
9	Dadra & Nagar Haveli UT	43.0	27.0	16.0	73.3	53.6	19.8	60.0	40.7	19.3
10	Haryana	56.3	40.5	15.8	79.3	69.1	10.2	68.6	55.9	12.7
11	Himachal Pradesh	68.1	52.3	15.8	86.0	75.4	10.6	77.1	63.9	13.2
12	Tripura	65.4	49.7	15.8	81.5	70.6	10.9	73.7	60.4	13.2
13	Meghalaya	60.4	44.9	15.6	66.1	53.1	13.0	63.3	49.1	14.2
14	Maharashtra	67.5	52.3	15.2	86.3	76.6	9.7	77.3	64.9	12.4
15	Sikkim	61.5	46.8	14.7	76.7	65.7	11.0	69.7	56.9	12.7
16	Arunachal Pradesh	44.2	29.7	14.6	64.1	51.5	12.6	54.7	41.6	13.2
17	Jharkhand	39.4	25.5	13.9	67.9	55.8	12.1	54.1	41.4	12.7
18	West Bengal	60.2	46.6	13.7	77.6	67.8	9.8	69.2	57.7	11.5
19	Tamil Nadu	64.6	51.3	13.2	82.3	73.8	8.6	73.5	62.7	10.8
20	Punjab	63.6	50.4	13.1	75.6	65.7	10.0	70.0	58.5	11.4
21	Karnataka	57.5	44.3	13.1	76.3	67.3	9.0	67.0	56.0	11.0
22	Assam	56.0	43.0	13.0	71.9	61.9	10.1	64.3	52.9	11.4
23	Manipur	59.7	47.6	12.1	77.9	71.6	6.2	68.9	59.9	9.0
24	Bihar	33.6	22.0	11.6	60.3	51.4	9.0	47.5	37.5	10.0
25	Daman & Diu UT	70.4	59.4	11.0	88.4	82.7	5.7	81.1	71.2	9.9
26	Andaman & Nicobar Islands UT	75.3	65.5	9.8	86.1	79.0	7.1	81.2	73.0	8.2
27	Gujarat	58.6	48.9	9.7	80.5	73.4	7.1	70.0	61.6	8.4
28	Lakshadweep UT	81.6	72.9	8.7	93.2	90.2	3.0	87.5	81.8	5.7
29	Pondicherry UT	74.1	65.6	8.5	88.9	83.7	5.2	81.5	74.7	6.8
30	Goa	75.5	67.1	8.4	88.9	83.6	5.2	82.3	75.5	6.8
31	Delhi NCT	75.0	67.0	8.0	87.4	82.0	5.4	81.8	75.3	6.5
32	Mizoram	86.1	78.6	7.5	90.7	85.6	5.1	88.5	82.3	6.2
33	Nagaland	61.6	54.8	6.9	71.8	67.6	4.1	67.1	61.7	5.5
34	Chandigarh UT	76.7	72.3	4.3	85.7	82.0	3.6	81.8	77.8	4.0
35	Kerala	87.9	86.2	1.7	94.2	93.6	0.0	90.9	89.8	1.1

Highlights

➤ Six out of the 28 states in India have a female literacy rate of less than 50 per cent. These states are Rajasthan (44 per cent), Arunachal Pradesh (44 per cent), Uttar Pradesh (43 per cent), Jammu & Kashmir (42 per cent), Jharkhand (39 per cent) and Bihar (34 per cent). The female literacy rate in Madhya Pradesh is 50 per cent on the border of cut-off point.

➤ Among the three new states, Uttaranchal has the highest literacy rate: 72 per cent for the total population, male literacy rate of 84 per cent and female literacy rate of 60 per cent. Chhatisgarh has an overall literacy rate of 65 per cent (male 78 per cent and female 52 per cent). Jharkhand has an overall literacy rate of 54 per cent (68 per cent male and 39 per cent female).

➤ The gap between male and female literacy rates is highest in Rajasthan (32 per cent points), followed by Uttar Pradesh (27), Madhya Pradesh (27) Jharkhand (27), Chhatisgarh (26) and Bihar (26). These figures confirm that Bihar, Madhya Pradesh, Rajasthan and Uttar Pradesh are indeed BIMARU states. The state of Madhya Pradesh cannot be reversed from the list of BIMARU states just because the literacy rate is 64 percent. The overall figure is misleading and insensitive to gender.

➤ The male-female gap in literacy rates is lower in Mizoram (5 per cent points) followed by Kerala (6 per cent points) and Meghalaya (6 per cent points).

➤ It is distressing to note that the male-female literacy gap is high in industrial states like Gujarat (22 per cent points), Maharashtra (18) and West Bengal (18). This indicates social backwardness. Haryana, an economically prosperous state has a male-female literacy gap of 23 per cent points. In fact, Haryana is one of the most socially backward states in India. In fact Haryana can be classified as a BIMARU state from this point of view. So also Andhra Pradesh in South India with a female literacy rate of only 51 per cent and a male-female literacy gap of 20 per cent points.

➤ In terms of progress on the female literacy front during the last decade, Chhatisgarh has the best record (the increase in the literacy percentage by 25 points between 1991 and 2001), followed by Rajasthan (24 per cent points), Madhya Pradesh (21 percent points). In the case of males, Rajasthan has the best record (increase of 21.5 points), followed by Chhatisgarh (20 points) and Madhya Pradesh (18 points). There is no doubt that special programmes launched by the Government and NGOs in Rajasthan and Madhya Pradesh have succeeded in stepping up literacy rates. However, one must wait for 2001 census data on the level of education before we can take a firm view on the classification of states. As we have already stated, the census and SRS data give no ground for removing Madhya Pradesh and Rajasthan from the list of BIMARU states.

5. Vital Statistics, 1999

Though Census Paper I of 2001 does not give any data on vital statistics, we feel that it is necessary to consider such data while discussing the implications of the first results of the 2001 census. We present below the latest statistics on birth rate, death rate, infant mortality rate and natural growth rate, drawn from the latest *SRS Bulletin* of the Office of Registrar General , India.

Table 3.17 : Birth, Death and Infant Mortality Rates, 1999

State	Birth Rate (per 1,000)	Death Rate (per 1,000)	Infant Mortality Rate (per 1,000)	Natural Growth Rate (per cent)
North				
Bihar				
Total	30.4	9.1	66	2.13
Rural	31.3	9.3	67	2.20
Urban	22.6	6.6	51	1.60
Madhya Pradesh				
Total	30.7	10.6	91	2.01
Rural	32.1	11.2	96	2.09
Urban	24.9	7.4	55	1.60
Rajasthan				
Total	31.1	8.4	81	2.27
Rural	32.5	8.9	85	2.36
Urban	24.9	6.4	59	1.85
Uttar Pradesh				
Total	32.1	10.5	84	2.16
Rural	33.1	11.0	87	2.21
Urban	26.7	7.7	64	1.90
South				
Andhra Pradesh				
Total	21.7	8.2	66	1.35
Rural	22.0	9.0	75	1.31
Urban	20.6	5.7	37	1.50
Karnataka				
Total	22.3	7.7	58	1.46
Rural	23.7	8.7	69	1.50
Urban	19.2	5.5	24	1.37
Kerala				
Total	18.0	6.4	14	1.16
Rural	18.1	6.5	14	1.16
Urban	17.7	6.3	16	1.14
Tamil Nadu				
Total	19.3	8.0	52	1.13
Rural	19.8	8.7	58	1.11
Urban	18.2	6.6	39	1.16

Highlights

➤ The latest vital statistics (as per the Registrar General's *Sample Registration Systems Bulletin*, October, 1999) bring out the sharp contrast between North and South.

➤ The BIMARU States are the only states in India where the Birth Rate was over 30 per thousand in 1999. The rural Birth Rates were even higher.

➤ In contrast the Birth Rates in Kerala and Tamil Nadu are below 20 per thousand and in Andhra Pradesh and Karnataka around 22 per thousand.

➤ In Orissa the Birth Rate is moderate (24 per thousand) which is below the natural average of 26 per thousand.

➤ The Death Rates are highest in Orissa (10.6), Madhya Pradesh (10.6) and Uttar Pradesh (10.5).

➤ The natural growth rates are highest in BIMARU States : Rajasthan (2.27 per cent), Uttar Pradesh (2.16 per cent), Bihar (2.13 per cent) and Madhya Pradesh (2.01). In Orissa the growth rate is low (1.34). Therefore, we do not include Orissa in our list of BIMARU States.

➤ In the Southern states the growth rates are very low : Tamil Nadu (1.13), Kerala (1.16), Andhra Pradesh (1.35) and Karnataka (1.46).

➤ The infant mortality rates are shockingly high in Orissa (97 per thousand) and Madhya Pradesh (91). In Kerala it is as low as 14 per thousand.

➤ To sum up, the North-South disparities in terms of the birth rate, death rate, infant mortality rate and natural growth rate are striking. This indicates demographic imbalance and should be a cause for concern for politicians and policymakers, planners and administrators.

Table 3.18 : Distribution of Illiterate Population in BIMARU States, 2001

States	Per cent Illiterate population			Per cent of total population		
	Persons	Male	Female	Persons	Male	Female
Bihar	11.8	12.9	11.2	8.1	8.1	8.0
Madhya Pradesh	6.0	5.6	6.2	5.9	5.9	5.8
Rajasthan	6.1	5.3	6.5	5.5	5.5	5.5
Uttar Pradesh	19.5	20.0	19.3	16.2	16.5	15.9
Total	**43.4**	**43.8**	**43.2**	**35.6**	**36.0**	**35.2**
Chhatisgarh	2.0	1.8	2.2	2.0	2.0	2.1
Jharkhand	3.4	3.4	3.4	2.6	2.6	2.6
Uttaranchal	0.7	0.5	0.7	0.8	0.8	0.8
Total	6.1	5.8	6.3	5.5	5.4	5.6
Bihar + Jharkhand	15.2	16.4	14.6	10.7	10.7	10.6
Madhya Pradesh + Chhatisgarh	8.1	7.4	8.4	7.9	7.9	7.9
Rajasthan	6.1	5.3	6.5	5.5	5.5	5.5
Uttar Pradesh + Uttáranchal	20.2	20.5	20.0	17.0	17.3	16.7
Total	49.5	49.6	49.5	41.1	41.4	40.7
Southern States						
Andhra Pradesh	8.7	9.1	8.4	7.4	7.2	7.6
Karnataka	5.1	5.2	5.1	5.1	5.1	5.2
Kerala	0.9	0.7	0.9	3.1	2.9	3.3
Tamil Nadu	5.0	4.6	5.2	6.0	5.9	6.2
Total	19.6	19.6	19.6	21.7	21.1	22.3

Highlights

➤ Bihar is the most illiterate state in India, with a female literacy rate of 34 percent, male literacy rate of 60 per cent and an overall literacy rate of 48 percent. This is the only state in India where the majority of persons are illiterate. It is also the only state in India where, in absolute terms, the number of illiterate persons has increased from 32 million in 1991 to 35 million in 2001.

➤ The four BIMARU states alongwith three offshoots account for 49.5 per cent of India's illiterate female population, 49.6 per cent of India's illiterate male population and 49.5 per cent of India's total illiterate population.

PART FOUR

2001 CENSUS METHODOLOGY: DEFINITIONS & CLASSIFICATIONS

INSTRUCTION MANUAL FOR FILLING UP THE HOUSEHOLD SCHEDULE

issued by the Office of Registrar General and Census Commissioner, New Delhi, 2000

I. ECONOMIC QUESTIONS : CHARACTERISTICS OF WORKERS AND NON-WORKERS (Qs. 16 TO 20)

76. *A set of five questions will enable you to complete the inquiry on Workers and Non-Workers in the household. These are Questions 16 to 20 with their sub-parts and are almost similar in nature as canvassed in 1991 Census. However, the wordings have been simplified to make these questions easy to understand. During the Census of India 2001, a new question on the commutation of specified category of workers to their work place has been introduced for the first time and the question on seeking/available for work earlier restricted to Non-Workers, will now be canvassed among the Marginal Workers also.*

77. **Every person irrespective of age and sex must be asked Question 16, including the very young or the very old and the answer to this question must be filled in after careful probing.** *The other questions in this series will have to be canvassed to whom these are applicable and appropriate responses recorded accordingly.*

78. **The purpose of these questions is to obtain details of the work (economic activity) done by each person with reference to last one year.** *We may, thereofore, first consider what is meant by 'work' and the 'reference period'. The questions on economoc and non-economic activities and the definitions and concepts therein have to be fully and clearly understood by you so as to correctly probe and obtain proper response from the respondent.*

Definition of Work (Economic Activity)

79. **Work may be defined as participation in any economically productive activity with or without compensation, wages or profit.** *Such participation may be physical and/or mental in nature. Work involves not only actual work but also includes effective supervision and direction of work.* **It**

even includes part time help or unpaid work on farm, family enterprise or in any other economic activity.

80. **For all Questions on Workers and Non-Workers, the reference period is one year preceding the date of enumeration.** *Certain types of work such as agriculture, household industry like, gur making, etc., etc are carried on either throughout the year or only during certain seasons or parts of the year, depending on the local circumstances. In such cases what we are concerned with is the broad time-span of the agricultural seasons preceding the enumeration.* **Therefore, we are not only interested in the current status in relation to economic activity but all the economic activities pursued by the person during the entire reference period of the preceding one year.**

A brief overview of Questions on Workers and Non-Workers

81. *Question 16 seeks to find out if a person is a Worker or a Non-Worker.* **In census, a person is categorised as 'Worker' when she/he has participated in any economically productive activity at any time during the reference period. Having found out that a person is a worker, it has to be ascertained whether she or he has worked for 6 months or more or less than 6 months. A person who has worked for 6 months or more during the last one year is termed as 'Main Worker' otherwise she/he is a 'Marginal Worker'.**

81.1 *If a person is categorised as worker in Question 16, whether Main or Marginal, the economic activity pursued by her/him during the reference period will be recorded in codes under Question 17 (i).* **Her/his work will be classified into one of the four categories of economic activity namely Cultivator (C), Agricultural Labourer (AL), Worker in Household Industry (HHI) and Other Worker (OW). These categories have been explained in the later part of the manual. Please note that if a person has pursued more than one economic activity during the reference period, the economic activity in which she/he was engaged during the major part of the period, determines her/his economic activity for the purpose of this question.**

81.2 *If a worker (whether Main or Marginal) has been classified under the category HHI or OW in Question 17(I), the occupation of this worker, and the nature of industry, trade or service or of self employment, she/he was engaged in will be recorded under Question 17(ii) and 17(iii), respectively.*

81.3 *In Question 17(iv), the 'Worker in Household industry' or the 'Other Worker', will be classified into one of the four categories of class of workers namely; Employer, Employee, Single Worker and Family Worker.*

81.4 *Questions 18 and 19 are meant for only Marginal Workers and Non-Workers. Please note that the major part of the year spent, by a Non-Worker or*

Marginal Worker during the reference period, would be in non-economic activity. The non-economic activities of Marginal Worekrs and Non-Workers will be recorded in codes under Question 18. The non-economic activities for which codes have been provided under this question are Student, Household duties, Dependent, Pensioner, Beggar and Other. In Question 19, it would be ascertained fo.· every Marginal Worker of Non-Worker as to whether she/he was seeking/available for work during the reference period. Questions 20 (i) and 20(ii) are to be canvassed for only those workers (Main as well as Marginal) who have been classified as 'Other Workers' in Question 18(I). Question 20 seeks to elicit information on the distance from residence to the place of work and the mode of travel. **Please note that if the responses to any of these questions are not to be filled in for a person, put a dash (-). Do not leave these blank.**

82. *Certain points that need particular emphasis and should be remembered are listed below for your benefit:*

(i) **Women and children may often be classified as Non-Workers because of non-reporting of their work. It also happens that women and children who work for six months or more are sometimes reported as working for less than six months. You should, therefore, make special efforts for listing women's and children's work by asking probing questions.**

(ii) *A person who normally works may be absent from work any time during the reference period on account of illness, holiday, temporary closure, strike, etc. Such period of absence should not be excluded while deciding whether she/he is Main or Marginal Worker and she/he must be treated as engaged in the work she/he would otheriwse have been doing, but for her/his temporary absence.*

(iii) *Persons under training such as apprentices, with or without stipends or wages, should be treated as workers.*

(iv) *A person who is a Non-Worker throughout the reference period and has been offered work but not actually joined yet, should not be treated as a Worker.*

(v) **If a person is engaged in some economic activity but at the same time also attends to some household chores or attends a school/college, etc., she or he would be treated basically as a worker.**

(vi) *A person, who merely receives an income, such as a rent receiver or a pensioner, but does not have to work for receiving the income, will not be treated as worker unless the person is also engaged for part of the year in some economic activity. Similarly, receivers of agricultural or non-agricultural royalty or of rents or dividends who may be earning an income but are not participating in any productive work should not be treated as workers unless they also work in agriculture, industry, trade, profession, business or commerce, etc.*

(vii) Beggars are to be treated as Non-Workers. In this connection it may be noted that musicians, dancers, rope-dancers, acrobats, snake charmers, jugglers, etc., who entertain people in public places and earn livelihood are to be recorded as workers. Prostitutes and persons engaged in illicit work such as drug trafficking, smuggling, etc. should not be treated as workers even if they identify themselves as engaged in these activities.

(viii) A person who engages herself/himself in work such as rice pounding for sale or wages, or in domestic services for wages for others or minding cattle or selling firewood or making and selling cowdung cakes or selling grass, etc., or any other work like cultivation, etc., she/he should be treated as worker under Question 16. However, any person who is engaged in household duties in her or his own house but does no other productive work should not be considered as worker for the purpose of census.

*(ix) A person may be providing some services or producing goods only for domestic consumption of the household and the services or products are not for sale. Such a person is not a worker, even though from her or his point of view the activity is productive. **However, persons engaged in cultivation and growing of crops (except plantation crops) solely for domestic consumption and persons engaged in rearing of animal for production of milk for their own use will be treated as workers.** There may be a situation where the household has a small kitchen garden in the rear or front portion of the house where some vegetables, flowers, fruits, etc. are grown purely for domestic consumption. The person working in this kitchen garden should not be treated as a worker unless she/he is also engaged in some other economic productive work.*

(x) For an undertrial prisoner enumerated in a jail, record the work she/ he doing before she/he was apprehended. Similarly, for a person temporarily in a hospital or similar institution. record the kind of work she/he was doing before she/he was admitted into hospital or institution. But for convicts in a prison or for long-term inmates of penal or charitable or mental institutions, the persons' previous work should not be recorded. For census purposes, inmates of penal or charitable or mental institutions, if detained for six months or more, should be treated as long term and if they are not engaged in any economic activity. code '3' under Question 16 and code '6' under Question 18 will be entered for such persons. However, if convicts in jails or inmates of charitable or mental institutions, etc. are engaged in economic activities such as carpentry , carpet weaving, stitching clothes, making of baskets and other articles of bamboo, vegetable growing, etc. and are paid for the work they are doing in these institutions, record them as workers.

(xi) A public or social worker engaged in a public service activity or a political worker who is also engaged in furthering the political activity of her/his party will be recorded as a worker and entered accordingly. Such person will also include Members of Parliament, State Legislatures, Local Authorities, Village Panchayat, etc.

Women, children and aged also work

83. It has been the experience of the census organisation that the workers among females, children and the aged are not always properly identified. **A large number of farm and non-farm activities in our country are family based. Many male and female members of the cultivating households, irrespective of their age, work in the peak season of ploughing, sowing, harvesting and collection of farm produce. Some of them, particularly women, children and the aged withdraw themselves from the labour force in the slack season. But not all of them are enumerated as workers during the census.** Similarly, members of the household who work in the household industry intermittently and [according to census concept of Work] qualify to be treated as workers, some of them are omitted as workers. Members of the household also participate in other seasonal economic activities such as gur making, gathering of tendu leaves and collection of other wild growing forest materials, etc.; women and children giving tuition classes or attending to the family shop; tending cattle for the production of milk, etc. **These Women and children are likely to be missed as workers during the enumeration. Therefore, whenever any person, especially children, women and the older persons in the household inform that they did not work at all during last year, never record her/him as Non-Worker straightaway. You must make probing enquiries, if she/he was engaged in any such economic activities to elicit the correct information regarding her/his economic activity in which she/he might have been directly engaged.**

83.1 **Elderly persons are often found to be working even after retirement. Therefore, if any such person says that she/he is retired, you must ask how she/he has engaged herself/himself after retirement. This may bring out her/his economic activity.**

83.2 **Sometimes from the respondent's point of view unpaid work in family cultivation or in family enterprise or in any other work may not be an economic activity. But for the purpose of census, participation of family workers in such activities is to be reckoned as an economic, activity.** Certain economic activities in which children, women and the aged work but may not be reported as such either due to lack of proper probing on the part of enumerator or as a result of respondent's bias are listed below by way of illustrations:

(a) **Help given by women, children and aged during ploughing, sowing, harvesting and collection of farm produce,**

(b) **Women and children working as agricultural labourer for wages in cash or in kind,**

(c) **Women and children self employed or engaged as unpaid family workers in industries that can be conducted on Household Industry basis e.g. cattle rearing for production of milk and milk produce.**

GLIMPSES OF PAID AND UNPAID WOMEN'S WORK

Occasionally not reported, work in family farm, sale of coconut, collection of tendu leaves, beedi rolling, milching, making cowdung cakes for sale, agricultural activities-labour, assistance in apple orchards, tea garden worker, rearing of goat, sheep, preparation of milk products for sale, sale of fish, sale of vegetables & fruits, making pottery & clay objects, rice dehusking, collection of sea shell, making sea-shell (conch) products, assisting in blacksmithy, making & sale of bangles, manufacturing of bamboo & cane products, grinding wheat and masala for sale, assisting in making puppets, toys etc., knitting woolen garments for sale, preparation of papad, pickles & jams etc., at home for sale, preparation of snacks (gole-gappa, chat papri etc.) at home, for sale, weaving dari, carpet, sani, spining, embroidery & sari falls, tailoring on contract/piece work at home, preparation of paper bags, kites & book binding, tution in the home, beautician/beauty parlour, traditional painting & motifs for sale, raising of poultry birds, help in managing family shops, rag pickers, construction labour.

83.3 Obviously, probing questions will have to be asked specially in the case of those who are not full time workers. **It is particularly important to ask such probing questions regarding any work done last year or in any of the seasons during the reference period in the case of women, children and aged in rural and urban areas.** As stated above, women and children in rural areas work in the fields in the sowing, harvesting or other seasons and this may be on their own land or as labourers on someone else's land. **Unless probing questions are asked about such work, the usual answer may be that they do not.**

83.4 A few illustrative sketches of the economic activities pursued by women or children or aged are given in this manual. Carefully glance through these sketches. This would help you in understanding the nature of work carried out by women or children or aged but is quite often missed due to incomplete understanding or probing. You should also show these sketches to the respondent to help her/him in recalling if the women/children members of the household were engaged in a similar economic activity any time during the last year.

83.5 Each of the questions on Workers and Non-Workers can now be described in detail. Please study these instructions carefully. It will help if you read the general introduction given above and those that follow more than once so that the concepts and the scope of the questions are familiar to you.

Q. 16: Did the person work any time last year?

(includes even part time help or unpaid work on farm, family enterprise or in any other economic activity)

Yes: If worked for 6 months or more (Main Worker), write '1' and proceed to Q.17

or

If worked for less than 6 months (Marginal Worker), write '2' and proceed to Q. 17

or

No: If not worked at all (Non-Worker), write '3' and proceed to Qs. 18 & 19

84. **This question is intended to classify the population into three broad streams on the basis of a liberal definition of work. These are the 'Main Workers' who worked for 6 months or more, the 'Marginal Workers' who worked for less than 6 months and the 'Non-Workers' who did not work at all during the last year preceding the date of enumeration.**

84.1. *You must enquire for each person already listed, whether she or he did any work any time last year. Even if the person has worked only for one day, you have to record her/him as a worker against this question.* **Please note that part time helpers or unpaid workers on farm, family enterprise or in any other economic activity, however, insignificant their monetary contribution may appear, should be treated, as workers.** *But the workers under this question will not include those who provide services or produce goods for self-consumption of the members of the household like persons fetching water, collecting firewood, preparing cow-dung cakes, stitching clothes, making flour, etc. Thus, the term 'unpaid worker' may not be confused with those who produce or make goods for domestic consumption. The latter category is to be taken as Non-Worker..*

Note: Please note that persons who are engaged in cultivation or milk production even solely for domestic consumption will also be treated as workers.

84.2 *Find out for the person whom you are enumerating whether she/he did any work any time last year. Obviously, the answer will be either 'Yes' or 'No'. If the answer is 'Yes', you should then ascertain whether the person worked for 6 months or more. If the answer to this question is again in the affirmative, you should record code 'l' (Main Worker) in the appropriate column under this question. You will then proceed to ask Question 17 to record further details on the work done by her/him. Questions 18 and 19 will not be applicable in this situation and therefore simply dashes (-) will be put under these questions. But if the person has worked for less than 6 months during the last year, you should record code '2' (Marginal Worker) in the appropriate column for males or females, as the case may be. Thereafter proceed to fill in appropriate responses against Qs. 17 to 20 for marginal workers.*

84.3 *If the person has not worked at all during the last year, enter code '3' (Non-Worker) in the appropriate column for males or females, as the case* may be. In case of such persons, sub-parts of Question 17 and Question 20 will not be applicable and dashes (-) will be recorded under these questions.

84.4 The entries for males will be made under column 18 and that for females under column 19. It is important to mention here that the appropriate codes for males and females will be entered in the separate columns as provided, failing which it will be difficult for you to work out separate 'Page Totals' for Main Workers, Marginal Workers and Non-Workers for males and females in Items 6, 7 and 8.

84.5 A person may have worked in different capacities during last year. For example, she/he may have worked as a construction labourer (roads) for four months, as an agricultural labourer for one month and as a cultivator for two months. There could even be breaks in between the different types of work performed by her/him. **In computing whether this person worked for 6 months or more, you should include all the three spells of economic activity and if it satisfies the condition of working for 6 months or more, treat her/him as 'Yes: worked for 6 months or more' for Question 16 and record '1' (Main Worker) under column 18 or column 19, as the case may be.** Similarly, if the total period of work falls short of six months, treat her/him as 'Yes: worked for less than 6 months' and record '2' (Marginal Worker) in the appropriate column.

84.6 The reference period is one year preceding the date of enumeration and this includes the agricultural seasons also. A person may have worked as a cultivator or as an agricultural labourer throughout the year or in an agricultural season such as only kharif or rabi or only for a few days. Sometimes non-agricultural activities are also carried out only during a part of the year or in a particular season. Such activities include preparation of sweetmeat and other eatables for sale during specific fairs or festivals, selling of various items in a particular season such as ice cream, roasted groundnut, etc. You will have to make special enquiries to elicit such seasonal activities and their duration to help you in classifying the person correctly as a 'Main' or 'Marginal' Worker. A person may have been a cultivator, an agricultural labourer, or engaged in a household industry or any other work. The definitions of these terms are given later, but the important point is that we are determining the fact that one has done some economically productive work some time during the last one year and the total duration of work in which she/he remain engaged.

84.7 If any member of household is engaged in rearing of cattle for the production of milk for domestic consumption and/or for sale she/he will be treated as workers. On the other hand, if the person is engaged in the production of milk products for domestic consumption out of the milk purchased from -others, they will not be treated as a Worker until a part of it is sold in the market.

84.8 It must be remembered that a man or a woman who is engaged only in household duties or producing items only for domestic consumption (and not for sale) except referred to in the note to para 84 is not a 'Worker' in the census terminology.

Important

84.9 Sometimes women and children who have actually worked for 6 months or more during the last year are recorded or reported as having worked for less than six months. You should, therefore, ask probing questions, in this regard to elicit the correct information.

Q. 17: *Economic activity of the Main or Marginal Worker*

Q. 17 *(i): Category of the economic activity of the Main or Marginal Worker: C -1/ AL -2/ HHI -3/ OW-4*

85. You may recall that under Question 16 you have classified all people into three broad streams namely Main Workers, Marginal Workers and Non-Workers. **This question is only applicable to Main Workers and Marginal Workers** *i.e., for whom you have recorded code '1' or code '2' in reply to Question 16. The person who did not work at all and for whom you have entered code '3' under Question 16, this question will not apply. For them put dash (-) below this question.*

85.1 **For each person classified as Main Worker or Marginal Worker under Question 16, you will be required to ascertain her/his economic activity and enter it appropriately under this question. The economic activity of such workers will be shown in codes.** *For your ready reference, the four categories of economic activities in suitable abbreviations together with their codes are given below Question 17(i) in the Household Schedule. You will have to choose the appropriate code under which the person's economic activity is classified and enter the same under this question.*

85.2 In connection with the entry under this question, it is important to note that it is absolutely essential that appropriate code for male workers are recorded under column 20 and that for females this is entered under column 21. Any mistake in making these entries under the appropriate columns will put you in difficulty in arriving at the 'Page Totals' separately for males and females in respect of Item-9 to Item-12.

85.3 It is also possible that a person who is classified as a Main Worker or a Marginal Worker might have been engaged in more than one economic activity during last year prior to the date of enumeration. **In such a situation you will have to find out the economic activity in which she or he was mostly engaged for the greater part of the year and the code of that main activity is to be recorded accordingly under this question. Main activity of a person who was engaged in more than one activity will be**

reckoned in terms of time disposition. *For example, if a person has worked as a daily wage labourer for four months, as an agricultural labourer for one month and as cultivator for two months, then that person will be considered as daily wage labourer for Question 17(;) and you will have to classify her/him as 'OW' and record code '4' under this question. Similarly for a person who worked for three months as an agricultural labourer and one month in a restaurant, you will have to classify the person as 'AL'.*

85.4 **It is re-emphasised that all those who have answered 'Yes: worked for less than 6 months' under Question 16 and for whom you have recorded code '2', this question should be asked necessarily.**

85.5 *A person who has not worked for the major part of the last year, might have done some work occasionally. For her/him you have already entered code '2' under Question 16. Many such unpaid family workers participating in farm or household enterprises whose main engagement otherwise would have been in household duties or student or pensioner or any other non-economic activity, will be netted here for their part time involvement in any economic activity. Except in cultivation and milk production, mere rendering of service for one's own home or production of goods for purely domestic consumption are not to be treated as economic activity. For example, a servant who works as a cook in her or his employer's home for wages will be considered economically active but a person even if she/he may work much more than a paid servant in having to cook for the family or looking after the household will not be treated as economically active for the purposes of this classification. Similarly, persons who may produce pickles, papad, etc., at home for domestic consumption only will not be treated as economically active unless at least a part of the product is sold. A boy or a girl who is otherwise mainly a student can have a marginal work, say, cultivation, if she/he helped the household in the family cultivation during some parts of the season. But if a student, who also helped in stitching clothes or knitting woollens purely for domestic consumption, or helped in attending to household chores, she/he will not be treated as having any marginal work.*

85.6 *The economic activity of the Marginal Workers which you will enter under this column will be restricted to a period for less than 6 months of the last year. They must have spent major part of the year as a student or doing household duties or as a dependent or as a pensioner or beggar or any other non-economic activity such as rentier, seeking job, etc. This non-economic activity i.e., the manner in which she/he spent most of her/his time as a Non-Worker will be later depicted under Question 18.*

85.7 **Workers are classified into four categories, viz., Cultivators, Agricultural Labourers, those engaged in Household Industry and Other Workers.** *The codes that should be used to indicate these economic activities are given below:*

(I)	*Cultivator: C*	*1*
(ii)	*Agricultural Labourer: AL*	*2*
(iii)	*Worker in Household Industry: HHI*	*3*
(iv)	*Other Worker: OW*	*4*

85.8 The definitions of the four categories of workers are given in the following paragraphs:

Cultivator: C -1

86. For purposes of the census a person is classified as cultivator if he or she is engaged in cultivation of land owned or held from Government or held from private persons or institutions for payment in money, kind or share. Cultivation includes effective supervision or direction in cultivation.

86.1 A person who has given out her/his land "to another person or persons or institution(s) for cultivation for money, kind or share of crop and who does not even supervise or direct cultivation of land, will not be treated as cultivator. Similarly, a person working on "another person's land for wages in cash or kind or a combination of both (agricultural labourer)" will not be treated as cultivator for this question.

86.2 cultivation involves ploughing, sowing, harvesting and production of cereals and millet crops such as wheat, paddy, jowar; bajra, ragi, etc., and other crops such as sugarcane, tobacco, groundnuts, tapioca, etc., and pulses, raw jute and kindred fiber crop, cotton, cinchona and other medicinal plants, fruit growing, vegetable growing or keeping orchards or groves, etc. **Cultivation will not include plantation crops like tea, coffee, rubber, coconut and betel-nuts (areca).** *For a person who is a cultivator, record code '1' under this question.*

Agricultural Labourer: AL -2

87. A person who works on another person's land for wages in money or kind or share will be regarded as an agricultural labourer. She or he has no risk in the cultivation, but merely works on another person's land for wages An agricultural labourer has no right of lease or contract on land on which she/he works.

87.1 For a person who returns her/his economic activity as agricultural labourer, assign code '2' under this question.

88. You must remember that a person can be classified as a cultivator or as an agricultural labourer only on the basis of the crops grown. The growing of the following crops is considered as cultivation. Therefore, only a person who grows these crops or works on land on which these crops are grown can be classified either as a cultivator or an agricultural labourer as the case may be.

(i) Cereal and millet crops: **Paddy, wheat, jowar, bajra, maize, ragi, barley, etc.**

(ii) Pulses: **Arhar, gram; khesari, moong, masur, urd, etc.**

(iii) Fibre crops: **Raw cotton, jute, mesta, sunhemp and kindred fibre crops**

(iv) Oil seeds: **Sesamum, sunflower, soyabean, groundnut, rapeseed, mustard, linseed, castor, etc.**

(v) Cash crops: **Sugarcane, tobacco, betel leaves, etc**

(vi) Edible nuts (other than groundnut): **Walnut, almond, cashew nut, etc.**

(vii) Fruits: **Bananas, apples, grapes, guava, jamun, mangoes, oranges, etc.**

(viii) Ganja, cinchona, opium and medicinal plants.

(ix) All types of flowers.

(x) Roots and tubers, potatoes, sweet potatoes, chillies and turmeric, pepper, cardamom.

(xi) All types of vegetables and singharas.

(xii) Fodder crops.

Important

88.1 The growing of plantation crops as described in para 86.2 is not considered as agriculture. If a person is engaged in the growing of such crops she or he will not be considered as a cultivator or agricultural labourer but recorded as 'Other Worker (OW)'.

88.2 Please remember that you must use the codes given in the Household Schedule, i.e., '1' for Cultivator or '2' for Agricultural Labourer. **It is evident that you will have to ask a specific question regarding the crops grown in all cases where one merely says that she/he is a cultivator or an agricultural labourer** ;

Worker in Household Industry: HHI -3

89. Household Industry is defined as an industry conducted by one or more members of the household at home or within the village in rural areas and only within the precincts of the house where the household lives in urban areas. The larger proportion of workers in the household industry should consist of members of the household. The industry should not be run on the scale of a registered factory which would qualify or has to be registered under the Indian Factories Act.

89.1 For a person who returns her/his main activity as engaged in some production, processing, servicing or repair of articles or goods such as handloom weaving, dyeing, carpentry, bidi rolling, pottery manufacture, bicycle repairing, blacksmithy, tailoring, etc., it has to be ascertained if it is a household industry, and if so, indicate it by the code '3' under this question.

89.2 There may be an industry which is being run by a large joint family of more than 10 persons where power is used or more than 20 persons where power is not used. In such cases, though only family members are involved. this will not be treated as 'Household Industry'. Thus, the meaning of the term 'run on the scale of a registered factory' refers to such cases even if these are not registered as such.

89.3 The main criterion of a Household Industry even in urban areas is the participation of one or more members of a household. Even if the industry is not actually located at home in rural areas there is a greater possibility of the members of the household participating even if it is located anywhere within the village limits. In the urban areas where organised industry takes greater prominence, the Household Industry should be confined to the precincts of the house where the participants live. In urban areas, even if the members of the household run an industry by themselves but at a place away from the precincts of their home, it will not be considered as a Household Industry. It should be located within the precincts of the house where the members live in the case of urban areas.

89.4 **Household Industry relates to production, processing, servicing, repairing or making and selling (but not merely selling) of goods**. It does not include professions such as a Pleader, Doctor, Musician, Dancer, Waterman, Astrologer, Dhobi. Barber, etc., or merely trade or business, even if such professions, trade or services are run at home by members of the household. A list of a few typical industries that can be conducted on a household industry basis is appended to this Instruction Manual as **Annexure-III**.

89.5 Sometimes it is likely that the person who may not be working in her/his own Household Industry may be working in another Household Industry. You should, therefore, enquire whether the person who is not working in her/his own Household Industry is working in any other Household Industry and record as per instructions given above.

89.6 **As mentioned earlier, Household Industry should relate to production, processing, servicing, repairing or making and selling of goods**. However, a household can be engaged in certain other activities collectively but these may not qualify for being considered as Household Industries. For example, a grocery shop which is run solely by the family members will not qualify to be treated as Household Industry, because its nature of activity is trade.

89.7 **Certain activities even though conducted by members of the same household will not constitute a Household Industry**. These are indicated below and therefore the members of the family working in such industries will be classified as 'OW' and not 'HHI'.

(i)   Plantation work.

(ii)   Livestock maintenance and production such as cattle, goats, sheep breeding, poultry farms, bee-keeping; rearing of silk worm and production of cocoons and raw silk, production of milk, eggs, honey, wax, bones, etc.

(iii)   Hunting, trapping and selling of the catch.

(iv)   Forestry and logging: log, fuel, charcoal production, gathering and selling of fodder and other forest produce, etc.

(v)   Fishing including rearing of fish, collection of pearls, shells, sea products, etc.

(vi)   Mining and quarrying.

89.8 The information on Household Industries is much needed by various government and non-government agencies. We should, therefore, get accurate data regarding those engaged in 'HHI'. You must carefully read these instructions and understand them. The main points are again indicated below.

89.9 'HHI' stands for Worker in Household Industry. The main characteristics of the Household Industry are the following:

(a) **One or more members of the household must participate and the component of hired labour should be minimum.**

(b) The activity should relate to production, processing, servicing, repairing or making and selling of goods.

(c) The goods produced should not be for consumption by the household itself but should be wholly or partly for sale.

(d) **In an urban area the industry must be carried out in the precincts of the house in which the household lives. In the rural areas, the industry may be carried out anywhere within the limits of the village.**

(e) The activity should not be on the scale of a Registered Factory.

Other Worker: OW - 4

90. **All workers, i.e., those who have been engaged in some economic activity during the last one year, but are not cultivators or agricultural labourers or in Household Industry , are 'Other Workers (OW)'.** The type of workers that come under this category of 'OW' include all government servants, municipal employees, teachers, factory workers, plantation workers, those engaged in trade, commerce, business, transport, banking, mining, construction, political or social work, priests, entertainment artists, etc. In effect, all those workers other than cultivators or agricultural labourers or household industry workers, are 'Other Workers'. They will be represented by code '4' under Question 17(i).

90.1 **You will recall that it was mentioned that growing of plantation crops is not agriculture. Those engaged in this activity would have to be classified as 'OW'.**

Important

91. *Certain situations would call for some explanation so that you are clear in your mind regarding classifying such activities. A few typical cases are indicated below:*

(a) *If a sweet-meat maker, i.e., a Halwai makes sweets and sells them too, she/he would be classified as 'OW'. However, this person can be classified under 'HHI' also in appropriate cases under Question 17(i).*

(b) *If a person only sells sweets, having brought them from some other place, he would be carrying on a trade and this would <u>not</u> be covered under 'HHI',*

(c) *In many cases such as tea shops, udipis, dhabas, chat shops, etc., eatables are prepared and sold. For example, in dhaba, substantial meals such as chapatties, cooked vegetables, dal, etc., are prepared and sold. This will not be an industry. It will be classified as service, namely, running eating place. Therefore, even if a household carried on this activity it will not be classified as 'HHI', but only as 'OW' under Question 17(i).*

(d) *In many places, there are persons who keep small electrical or hand-mixers or fruit crushers and crush fruits to sell the juice. In such cases since the juice is produced for consumption on the spot and is not bottled as such for sale, such units are carrying on trade and <u>not</u> manufacturing. Therefore, even if a household carries on this business this would not be 'HHI', but 'OW'. On the other hand, if there are manufacturing units, whether big or small, which bottle juice and sell it as bottled, this would be manufacturing and should be classified as 'OW' or 'HHI', as the case may be.*

(e) *Tailoring is an industry and a member of household that carries on tailoring on household industry basis can be classified as 'HHI' under Question 17(i).*

(f) *There may be a person who sells cloth and also provides tailoring services; 'In such cases, the person maybe asked which activity she/he considers more important, i.e., the one on which she/he spends more time. If the person considers selling of cloth is more important then she/he is carrying on a trade. On the other hand, if the tailoring business is more important than the sale. of cloth, such a person should then be considered engaged in manufacturing. If a household carries on a business of this kind, the household members will be classified under 'HHI' or non-HHI depending on whether the household is involved mainly in trade or manufacturing and taking into consideration the definition of 'HHI'.*

Filling up of Questions 17(ii) to 17(iv):
If Code '3' (HHI) or Code '4' (OW) in column 20 or 21

92. In the case of Main Workers or Marginal Workers whose economic activity is identified as Household Industry: HHI or as Other Workers: OW and recorded code '3' or code '4' under Question 17(i), you will have to further ask a set of following three questions i.e., (a) Occupation of the person, (b) Details of nature of industry, trade or service in which engaged and (c) Class of Worker. These details will have to be filled under Questions 17(ii) to 17(iv).

92.1 As you will see from the question itself, these parts are applicable to persons for whom you have recorded code '3' (HHI) or code '4' (OW) under column 20 or 21. If the economic activity has been shown as 'C' or' AL ' under Question 17(i), there is no need to fill in the parts (ii) to (iv) of this question. In such cases dash (-) has to be recorded under each of these parts.

Q, 17(1i): Occupation of the person (describe the actual work of the person)

93. **The nature of occupation or the actual work that a person did during the last one year prior to the date of enumeration is to be ascertained and recorded under this question.** This description of work would be irrespective of the type of industry, trade or service, etc., in which she/he may be working in, the details of which will be incorporated under part (iii) of Question 17. **In case of persons who are self employed, the description of the actual work in which they are engaged will be recorded.**

93.1 **The actual work or occupation of workers, main or marginal should always be given in sufficient detail.** If, for example, a person is merely recorded as 'clerk' with no other details, it will be impossible to properly categorise her/him by the type of work she/he does. She/he may be a clerk attending to correspondence or book-keeping or accounting. Similarly, if a person were merely to be recorded as a technician, it will not help to determine what type of technician/mechanic she/he is, whether computer-technician or a motor-mechanic or a locomotive-mechanic, etc. If a person is recorded as doing leather work, it will not be sufficient for census purposes. It should be clearly stated whether she or he is a carcass lifter, skinner of dead animals, tanner, etc. Similarly, if a person says she/he is a sweeper, you should find out whether she/he is a sweeper, dry; or a sweeper, wet; or a sweeper, sewer. Similarly, in a trading establishment there could be a proprietor, cashier, book-keeper, salesman, etc. **The description of the actual work done by a person should be ascertained in adequate detail and recorded under this question.**

93.2 It is necessary to describe the actual occupation adequately. It is not enough to say that one is a Government official. Whether one is a Bill-clerk or Section Officer, Tehsildar, Police Constable, Chowkidar or Research Officer, etc.

has to be spelt out. There may be Assistant Directors, Deputy Directors, etc., doing different functions. It is necessary to describe the occupation adequately in their case for proper classification, e.g., Assistant Director (Agriculture), Deputy Director (Census), Sub-Inspector (Excise), Panchayat Secretary, Traffic Inspector (Transport Department), etc. For teachers please state if they are university teachers or secondary school teachers, middle school teachers, primary school teachers or kindergarten teachers. Similarly, Engineers can be described as Sales Engineer, Chemical Engineer, Computer Engineer (Software or Hardware), etc. **For those in defence and similar service, it is enough if it is merely noted as 'Service'. Other details need not be given.**

93.3 **It has been found in the past that a very large number of persons are recorded merely as 'general labourers'. It is necessary to probe and find out in which type of work the person is mostly engaged as a labourer, such as a construction labourer (road), a loader or an unloader in a market, a construction labourer (residential building), etc.**

93.4 In case of those who are self employed and working with or without any premises or in the open on road side or pavements such as rope makers, manufacturer of bamboo products, blacksmiths, persons engaged in painting, earth digging, selling fruits or vegetables or groundnut and such other items, newspaper and ice-cream vendors, cobblers, bicycle repairers, hawkers, itinerant vendors, dhobies etc., the work particulars of the person is to be provided in detail. For example, for a person engaged as a labourer in brick laying in the construction of house, 'brick layerer in house construction' will be the work of the person; for a barber 'Barber' will be recorded as his work, 'Fisherman' will be the work of a person if she/he is engaged in fishing in inland waters or in ocean, sea, etc.

93.5 To guide you in answering Question 17(ii) the type of particulars that need to be ascertained in respect of a few typical occupations are given in **Annexure-IV**. Annexure-IV is by no means exhaustive. This just helps in bringing home the need to ascertain the full details of the particulars of work performed by an individual for being recorded, under Question 17(ii).

Q. 17(iii): Describe in detail the nature of industry, trade or service where the person works/worked or of self employment

94. For Main Workers or Marginal Workers whose economic activity is classified as 'HHI' (code '3') or 'OW' (code '4') under Question 17(i); the nature of industry, trade or service where they are engaged is to be recorded here. For self employed, the nature of the industry, trade or service will be the one to which her/his actual work recorded under Question 17(ii) relates.

94.1 **For the purpose of this question, the work place of the person is where she/he is engaged in some economic activity.** It may be an office, factory, firm, workshop; business house, bank, school, insurance company,

*hospital, company, shop, etc. or for that purpose any place even in the open
where some economically productive activity taking place. We are not concerned
with the size of the work place. It can be in a small room having a space to sit
for a person or two, or a big building in which a number of persons can sit or an
open place where the person works.*

94.2 **Since the information recorded against this question will be
utilised to enable proper classification of the sector of economy in which
the person is working, the exact details of activity being carried out in
the work place is to be recorded here.** *The sector of economy in which a
person works may relate to (A) Plantations, Hunting and Forestry; (B) Fishing;
(C) Mining and Quarrying; (D) Manufacturing; (E) Electricity, Gas and Water
Supply; (F) Construction; (G) Wholesale and Retail Trade; Repair of Motor
Vehicles, Motorcycles and Personal and Household Goods; (H) Hotels and
Restaurants; (I) Transport, Storage and Communications; (J) Financial
Intermediation; (K) Real Estate, Renting and Business Activities; (L) Public
Administration and Defence; Compulsory Social Security; (M) Education; (N)
Health and Social Work; (O) Other Community, Social and Personal Service
Activities; (P) Private Households with Employed Persons and (Q) Extra-
Territorial Organisations and Bodies.* **In order to enable us to classify a
person properly, full details of the type of industry, trade or service in
which the person is engaged will have to be recorded here. Please
avoid recording of vague answers. It would be helpful if the name of
establishment/ institution is also recorded in brackets. It is not enough
to record 'plantation' or 'livestock'. You should record whether it is tea
plantation or rubber plantation or sheep rearing or cattle breeding.
Similarly, it is not enough to record 'manufacturing' or 'textile
manufacturing'. You should record to indicate whether it is
manufacturing of cotton textile in handloom or manufacturing khadi
textile or manufacturing silk textile. In the case of industries, the
articles which are produced or serviced or processed should be given.
Likewise recording mere 'trade' is not enough. It should be recorded as
wholesale trading in foodgrains or pulses or retail trading in spices or
grocery and so on. For those in services, the details such as whether
the service belongs to public administration, central government, state
government, quasi-government bodies, etc., as well as nature of service
such as police service, sanitary services, health services, education
services, scientific and research, etc., may be recorded.** *It is further
clarified that in case of persons who are working in institutions which are
directly providing services such as health, education, social and cultural
services, etc., under the control of central government, state government, local
bodies, etc., you have to record the activity of these institutions in detail. In
such cases, you are not to record 'Central Govt. Services', 'State Govt. Services',
'Local Body Services', etc., as these are to be recorded for those persons who*

are working in the administrative offices of the Central or State or Local Bodies who provide such regulatory services. For example, if an accounts clerk is working in a state government primary school, the entry for her/him under Question 17(iii) should be recorded as 'Primary School Education (Govt. Primary School)'. In case this accounts clerk is working in the Office of the Director of Education, his nature of services will be recorded as 'State Govt. Services (Directorate of Education)'. **For defence and similar personnel, write 'Service' only.**

94.3 An *illustrative description of various economic activities are furnished in **Annexure-V** to help you in properly providing the details of the nature of industry, trade or service, etc. It should, however, be noted that the illustrations in **Annexure-V** are by no means exhaustive.*

Important

95. There need not be any confusion as to the scope of Questions 17(ii) and 17(iii). **Question 17(ii) represents the occupation or the actual work the person performs at the work place in which she/he is engaged and Question 17(iii) represents the nature of industry, trade, profession or service, i.e., the sector of economy in which the person is engaged.** Thus, for example, if the answer to Question 17(ii) is 'chemical engineer' or 'bill clerk' or 'accountant' or 'labourer (loader)' or 'truck driver' or 'managing director' and so on, the answer to Question 17(iii) could be 'cotton textile manufacture in mill'. Similarly, under Question 17(ii) the occupation of the person may be 'bill clerk' or 'accountant', 'director (administration)', 'jeep driver', etc., the entry in Question 17(iii) could be State Government Service (Directorate of Animal Husbandry). Again, under Question 17(ii) the answer may be 'orthopaedic surgeon', or 'nurse' or 'sweeper (wet)', etc." and 'under Question 17(iii) the answer could be 'private medical practice'. But in case of those Main or Marginal Workers who are self employed, the entry under Question 17(ii) i.e., actual work of the person could be 'barber' or 'tending cattle' or 'tutor-middle classes' and the entry under Question 17(iii) would be accordingly 'hair cutting' or 'livestock raising' or 'private tuition (middle classes)'. This has been further illustrated as hereunder: -

17 (ii)	17(iii)
Occupation of the person (Describe the actual work of the person)	Describe in detail the nature of industry trade or service where the person works/ worked or of self employment
22	23

Example-I

Chemical Engineer	*Cotton, Textile Manufacture in Mill*
Bill Clerk	*Cotton, Textile Manufacture in Mill*
Accountant	*Cotton, Textile Manufacture in Mill*
Labourer (loader)	*Cotton, Textile Manufacture in Mill*
Truck Driver	*Cotton, Textile Manufacture in Mill*
Managing Director	*Cotton, Textile Manufacture in Mill*

Example-II

Bill Clerk	*State Government Service (Directorate of Animal Husbandry)*
Accountant	*State Government Service (Directorate of Animal Husbandry)*
Director (Administration)	*State Government Service (Directorate of Animal Husbandry)*
Jeep Driver	*State Government Service (Directorate of Animal Husbandry)*

Example-III

Orthopaedic Surgeon	*Private Medical Practice*
Nurse	*Private Medical Practice*
Sweeper (Wet)	*Private Medical Practice*

Example-IV

Barber	*Haircutting*
Tending Cattle	*Livestock Raising*
Tutor (Middle Classes)	*Private Tuition (Middle Classes)*

Q. 17(iv): Class of Worker: Employer-1/Employee-2/Single Worker-3/Family Worker-4

96. The class of worker will be ascertained and recorded under this question in respect of those Main Workers and Marginal Workers whose economic activity is either classified as 'Household Industry (HHI)' 'i.e., code '4' or under column 20 or column 21. This will, however, exclude the workers who have returned their economic activity as 'Cultivatot' or 'Agricultural Labourer' under column 20 or 21 of Question 17 (i). For them put dash (-) under this question.

96.1 **The class of worker under this question will be recorded in a single column and not for male workers and female workers separately. The workers are divided into four categories for the purpose of this**

question. *These categories, for your convenience, are given with the heading of the Question 17(iv) itself. For a person who is:*

(i) an **Employer**, *that is, who hires one or more persons in her/his work described under Question 17(ii) and does not draw salary, record -1*

(ii) an **Employee**, *that is, who does her/his work described under Question 17(ii) for others for wages or salary in cash or kind, record -2*

(iii) a **Single Worker**, *that is, who does her/his work described under Question 17(ii) by herself/himself without employing others or without the help of family members (except casually) or as a member of co-operative unit, record -3*

(iv) a **Family Worker**, *that is, who does her/his work described under Question 17(ii) in a family enterprise along with other members of the family without wages or salary in cash or kind, record -4*

Explanation

96.2 An Employer is a person who has to employ other persons in order to perform the work mentioned in her/his case under Question 17(ii). Such a person does not draw any salary for the work done by herself/himself. For example, if a manufacturer of Ayurvedic medicines has employed pharmacists, laboratory assistants, sales representatives, accountants, clerks, drivers, etc., for manufacturing and sale of Ayurvedic medicines, in such a situation while the manufacturer will be classified as an employer, all other workers employed in her/his enterprise on wages will be treated as employees. Please note that a person who employs domestic servants for household duties is not an employer . Similarly, a person who has subordinates under her/him in an office where she/he herself/himself is employed by others, is not an employer, even if she/he has the power to appoint another person in her/his office on behalf of her/his own employer. A head of department or a local manager of a company may have the power to appoint people, but being herself/himself an employee of that department/company, the said person cannot be an employer. **A government servant irrespective of the post she/he holds is an 'Employee'.**

96.3 An Employee is a person who works for some other person for salary or wages in cash or kind. There may be persons who are employed as managers, superintendents, agents, etc., and in that capacity employ or control other workers on behalf of their own employers, Such persons are only employees, as explained above, and should not be regarded as employers. Please note that a cook for a domestic servant engaged exclusively by someone is an employee. The fact that the person who has hired her/him may herself/himself is an employee is not relevant.

96.4 Single worker is a person who works by herself/himself. She/he is not employed by anyone else and in her/his turn does not employ anybody else. Cycle repairer, vegetable seller, owner of grocery shop, rickshaw puller, a person engaged in making of agarbattis or earthenware pottery, etc., who do their work without employing others or without the help of family workers will be classified as Single Workers. **This definition of a Single Worker will include a person who works in joint partnership with one or several persons hiring no employees and also includes a member of a co-operative which is involved in trading, production, processing and services. Each one of the partners or members of such co-operative should be recorded as 'Single Worker'. Political workers (Members of Parliament, State Legislatures, Local Authorities, Village Panchayat, etc.) and social workers are to be treated as 'Single Worker'.** *Political workers (Members of Parliament, State Legistatures, Local Authorities, Village Panchayat etc., and social workers are to be treated as 'Single Worker'.*

96.5 A Family Worker is a member of the family who works without receiving wages in cash or kind, in an industry, business, trade of service. For example, the working members in a family of dhobies wheres they all participated and each does not receive wages separately, will be family workers. There may be family workers in industry, trade or professions as well. Family Workers must be related by ties of blood or marriage but such workers can belong to different households. Thus what is important is that such workers must necessarily be related even though they may be living in different households.

The family workers may or may not be entitled to a share of the profits in the work or the business carried on either by the person or head of the household or other relative.

96.6 Please note the following important cases:

(a) For persons engaged in Household Industry, i.e., in the case of persons for whom the answer to Question 17(i) is 'HHI -3', generally there will be three classes of workers, viz. Family Worker, Single Worker and Employee. There may not be a formal 'Employer'. Household Industry by its very definition is conducted by the members of the household, the role of hired workers being secondary. If the head along with the members of the household is working in a Household Industry employing hired workers, the head and other family members who are working should be treated as 'Family Workers'. If the head alone is working with the occasional assistance of hired worker(s), whose role should be secondary as indicated above, she/he should be treated as a 'Single Worker', although one might argue that in effect she/he becomes an employer. The hired workers are of course employees.

(b) Members of the household who help solely in household duties, i.e., non-economic activity, should not be treated as Family Workers. In fact, they are not workers.

(c) Members of a co-operative society engaged in trading, production, processing and services who have no other occupation or work except this, should be categorised as Single Worker-code '3'.

(d) **In the case of partnership in which all the partners are related, treat them as Family workers and record code '4'. The partnership firm may or may not employ others, but this will not change the category of the partners. They would be Family Workers -code '4'.**

(e) **In the case of a partnership firm in which some of the partners are not related, treat all the partners, including those that may be related, as Single Worker and record code '3'.** *The firm may or may not employ others, but this will not change the category of the partners. They will all be Single Workers -code '3'.*

(f) *Political workers and social workers should be treated as Single Workers - code '3'.*

(g) **Doctors and lawyers etc., who do not employ any person should be treated as Single Worker -code '3'. One may come across doctors and lawyers employing certain persons on a regular basis in the doctor's dispensary or clinic or in the lawyer's office or chamber. In this case the doctor or lawyer would become an 'Employer' so code '1' should be recorded.** *However, sometimes lawyers have been found to take the help of clerks who remain attached to them on a regular basis but without being formally employed on wages. The clerk usually earns his remuneration independently from the lawyer's clients. In such a case, both the lawyer and the clerk should be treated as Single Workers and code '3' will be assigned.*

*96.7 Some illustrations for filling up of Question 17 are given in **Annexure -VI**.*

Q.18: If Code '2' (Marginal Worker) or Code '3' (Non-Worker) in Column 18 or 19, record Code of non-economic activity from: Student - 1/ Household duties -2/ Dependent -3/ Pensioner -4/ Beggar -5/ Other -6

97. If a person has returned that she/he worked for less than 6 months or did not work at all during the last year, i.e., if code '2' or code '3' is recorded under Question 16, it will be ascertained how she or he engaged herself or himself mostly. If the person has worked for less than 6 months, it implies that she or he was not engaged in any economically productive activity for most of the time during last year. Thus, under this question we are interested to know how she/he spent her/his time mostly in non-economic activity. If she or he is a Non-Worker throughout the year, ascertain the category of Non-Workers she or he belongs to and record the appropriate code under this question. **The non-economic activities of Marginal Workers and Non-Workers are grouped into six categories and assigned code numbers which will be used to record the responses under this question.** *For your convenience these categories along with their codes are shown with the question itself.*

97.1 A Marginal Worker or Non-Worker can be found engaged in two or more non-economic activities during the reference period. For example, a child may have been dependent for nine months had attended school for only three months or a girl had attended School/College for five months during the reference period and was engaged in household duties for the rest of the period. You will also come across situations where a person was found engaged in two or more non-economic activities simultaneously during the period under reference. For example, a student may also be attending household duties, a pensioner may be doing household duties and also seeking work during the reference period. For the purpose of this question the main non-economic activity will be decided on the basis of precedence as indicated below. This means that a certain non-work category will find priority over others. For example, a person who was attending school was also engaged in household duties at the same time will be categorised as 'Student' even though she/he may have spent more time on household duties than on attending school. Similarly, a pensioner who was attending to household duties regularly but was also looking for work and making efforts for a job will be categorised as 'Pensioner'. The prioritisation of non-economic activity has been indicated in the description of the non-work activities in the following paragraphs.

97.2 The explanation of the six categories of non-economic activities are given in the following paragraphs:

Student -1

98. This category will cover all students including those taking part-time classes, correspondence course, attending literacy centres, etc., who are not engaged in any economically productive work. For such Non-Workers, record code '1' under this question. For Marginal Workers who were mainly students during the major part of last year, their non-economic activity, i.e., 'Student' will be reflected by entering code '1' under this question.

98.1 **If a student participates in some economically productive work, say, by helping sometimes as an unpaid family worker in family cultivation or in household industry, trade or business, you would have already treated such a person as Marginal Worker for the purpose of Question 16. Her/his non-economic activity, i.e., 'Student' (code '1') will be shown under this question.**

98.2 **Please note that in many households, the daughters help in the household work though they are studying full-time. They should be recorded as 'Student' (Code '1') and <u>not</u> as doing 'Household duties' (code '2') under Question 18.**

Please remember that married women normally attending to household duties can also be full-time students and they should be recorded accordingly as students under this question.

Household duties -2

99. A person who is attending to daily household chores like cooking,

cleaning utensils, looking after children, fetching water, collectiing firewood, going to market, etc., will be treated as doing household duties. Such persons should be allotted code '2' under this question. A housewife who is also a pensioner will be classified as 'Pensioner' (code '4') and not under 'Household duties'. A beggar also attending to household duties, will be classified as 'Beggar' (code '5') and not as doing 'Household duties'. Similarly, : a person attending to household duties but is also seeking/available for work would be categorised under 'Other' (code '6').

99.1 A housewife may help as unpaid worker in family cultivation or in family enterprise or make and sell cowdung cakes or prepare papad, achar, etc., at odd times and sell them or occasionally tend cattle for production of milk. She is only a Marginal Worker and for her code '2' would have been already assigned under Question 16 and her economic activity already appropriately reflected under Question 17. Her non-economic activity 'Household duties' will now be shown under Question 18. On the other hand, a woman may be working in a factory or an office or as a labourer or agricultural labourer for six months or more in the preceding year and may also be attending to household duties. For such a woman you have entered code '1' under Question 16 and her economic activity already appropriately recorded under Question 17. In such a case, dash (-) will now be entered under Question 18.

99.2 **It will be necessary for you to ask probing questions, particularly in the case of women, to find out if they are engaged in any economic activity, apart from household duties.**

Dependent -3

100. This category includes all dependents such as infants or children not attending (school or persons permanently disabled from work because of illness or old age.

100.1 Dependents may include even able-bodied persons who cannot be categorised in any other category of Non-Workers but are dependent on others. **However, if such a person who is dependent on others for subsistence but is seeking/available for work, she or he should be categorised as 'Other' and assigned code '6' under this question.**

100.2 **If a girl or an old woman attends to household duties she should be categorised as doing 'Household duties' (code '2') rather than 'Dependent' (code '3').** As you are aware, many persons may be dependents in the general sense of the word but may also be studying or doing household duties or looking for work. **In such cases, they should be entered as student (code '1') or doing household duties (code '2') or other Non-Worker (code '6') as the case may be, and not as dependent (code '3').** It is, therefore, necessary for you to ask whether a person who is said to be a dependent is studying or looking for work, etc., and if so, categorise her or him *accordingly rather than as dependent (code '3'). Such persons would particularly include unemployed sons, daughters, brothers, sisters, aged parents, etc.*

Pensioner-4

101. **A person drawing pension after retirement from service and is doing no other work, i.e., not employed again in some work or not engaged in some other work such as cultivation, business, trade, etc., will come under this category.** Code '4' should be noted under this question for a person coming under this category. Please note that alll persons do not receive pension after retirement. Some retired persons may have received a lump sum amount as retirement benefit and earning income from the interest or dividend on this money that she/he may have invested. Such persons would be classified under the category of 'Other'. However, this category will also include persons who receive 'old age pension' under some social benefit scheme of the government and persons receiving 'freedom fighters pension', etc. Widows receiving pension after their husband's death will also fall under this category.

101.1 However, in such cases also a careful probe is necessary. A retired person may be drawing pension and also doing some work, for example, a retired engineer may be working as a contractor or a part-time consultant. Of course, in such cases, she/he has already been categorised appropriately as a Main Worker or Marginal Worker and entered as such under Question 16. If Marginal Worker, her/his non-economic activity, i.e., code '4' (pensioner) will be entered under this question.

Beggar-5

102. This category will cover beggars and vagrants. Prostitutes and persons having unidentified source of income and those with unspecified sources of subsistence not engaged in any economically productive work will also come under this category. As already stated that if any person in this category is also a student, she/he will be classified as 'Student' (Code '1'). Beggars or other persons in this category may be attending to household duties also, in such cases these persons have to be included under this category and not under 'Household duties'.

102. For such persons, record code '5' under this question

Other-6

103. This category will include all Non-Workers and Marginal Workers who may not come under any of the above five categories. They include rentiers or persons living on remittances, agricultural or non-agricultural royalty, interest or dividend; convicts in jails or inmates of penal, mental or charitable institutions

doing no paid work and persons who are seeking/available for work. For such persons, enter code '6'.

103.1 **Before recording the non-economic activity of the undertrial prisoners and convicts in jails or inmates of penal, mental or charitable institutions, you are advised to go through the instructions already given under para 82 (x) once again.** In a few cases, such persons can also be found engaged in some economically productive work and therefore they will have to be categorised accordingly as Main Workers or Marginal Workers.

103.2 **A boy or girl who has completed education or has stopped studying and is looking for work will also come under this category.** A person who is merely spending her/his time at home as a dependent and is not doing any work and is also not seeking or available for work will come under dependent (code '3') rather than code '6'. **A person irrespective of age and whether educated or not, if she or he reports that she or he is not engaged in any other activity but is seeking or available for work will come under this category.**

103.3 For a person who is a rentier or living on agricultural or non-agricultural royalty, interest or dividend, remittances or any other person (other than pensioner) who secure income for which she/he does not have to work, will also come under this category.

103.4. **It must be noted that this category includes only those who do not fall into any of the non-work categories discussed earlier.** There may be cases of students who may be seeking work/employment and quite prepared to give up studies if they got a job. Such persons are students, code '1', for Question 18. The fact that they are seeking jobs will be reflected under Question 19.

Important

104. It must particularly be noted that if there is an entry 'Yes: worked for less than 6 months', i.e., code '2' under Question 16 and also entries or entry under sub-parts of Question 17, there must be an entry under Question 18 and there cannot be dash (-). This is because the non-economic activity of a person who has worked for less than 6 months during last year, must be reflected under Question 18.

Qs. 16, 17(i) and 18- Further Explanation

105. **It is advisable to ask Questions 16 to 18 together for each person and then fill up the requisite details, otherwise, the full and precise answers will not be available and you may have to make corrections.**

105.1 What is meant by economic productive activity that a person has been doing mostly can be easily understood from the following examples:

(a) A person who is mainly a cultivator but during the non-agricultural season works as a construction worker or as a loader. For her/him code '1' will be recorded in the appropriate column under Question 16 and her/his main economic activity, i.e., cultivation (code '1') will be recorded under Question 17(i).

(b) A person may have worked for less than six months as a cultivator. For the major part of the year, this person may have been doing household duties. For this person, code '2', i.e., Marginal Worker will be recorded under Question 16. Her/his economic activity, i.e., Cultivation (code '1') will be reflected under Question 17(i) and her/his engagement mostly during the last year i.e., doing household duties (code '2'), will be shown under Question 18.

(c) A person may be mainly an agricultural labourer for over 8 months but may have worked, say for one or two months, in a Khandsari sugar factory during the lean season. She/he would be treated as Main Worker (code '1') for the purpose of Question 16 and her/his main economic activity i.e., agricultural labourer (code '2') will be entered under Question 17(i).

(d) A person may have worked as salesman for less than six months in a retail grocery shop. For the major part of the year, this person might have been a student. This person will be categorised as Marginal Worker (code '2') under Question 16 and her/his economic activity i.e., Other Worker (code '4') will be reflected under Question 17(i). Her or his non-economic activity in which she or he was mainly engaged i.e., code '1' (Student) would be entered under Question 18.

(e) A person who is mainly a cultivator, also keeps cows and produces milk for use in the household and/or for sale. This person will be categorised as Main Worker (code '1') under Question 16 and his main economic activity i.e., cultivation (code '1') will be shown under Question 17(I).

Q. 19: If Marginal Worker or Non-Worker, is the person seeking/ available for work? Yes-1/No-2

106. This question is to be replied for only those who are returned as Marginal workers or Non-Workers under Question 16. **If an individual in reply to Question 16 has replied that she/he has worked for less than 6 months or did not work at all and you have recorded code '2' or code '3' under this question, you have to ask from her or him whether she or he is seeking work or available for work.** *Seeking work means that the person may have got herself/himself registered in the employment exchange or she/he may be applying for jobs or she/he may have made other efforts for a job, such as looking in the newspaper advertisements with a view to applying for a job with the intention to offer herself/himself for employment.* **It may be remembered that seeking work is more applicable in urban areas where there are facilities of employment exchanges and greater awareness about availability of jobs. In rural areas, there may be no facilities of** *employment exchanges. The person may be available for work but not actually seeking work either because of lack of knowledge of work being available or absence of employment exchanges. Thus, for rural areas where there is no formal mechanism of seeking employment, any Marginal Worker or Non-Worker, if available when offered work, should be considered as seeking work.* However in urban areas, all such Marginal Workers or Non-Workers who are actually making some efforts for employment will be recorded as seeking work.

106.1 You may come across people who already hold jobs or do not normally want to take up employment but may give you general answers that they would not mind taking up work if the salary is attractive enough. We are not interested in such persons since they obviously are already employed or are not really job seekers. You will have to make a probe to get the facts. However, if in answer to this question, a Marginal Worker or Non-Worker says that she or he is seeking work or available for work, you must enter code '1' under this question. In case her/his reply is 'No', you have to record code '2' under this question.

Q. 20: Travel to place of work
If Code '4' (OW) in column 20 or 21

107. Question 20 is applicable to only those Main Workers and the Marginal Workers who have been classified as Other Workers (OW), i.e., for whom code '4' has been entered under Question 17(i). Thus, Question 20 is not applicable to the persons who have returned their economic productive activity as Cultivator or Agricultural Labourer or Household Industry in reply to Question 17(i) and for whom you have entered codes '1' or '2' or '3' under this question. Similarly, if the person is reported to have not worked at all (code '3') during last year in reply to Question 16, this question will also not apply. **In addition, for defence and similar paramilitary personnel, these questions are also not applicable.** In all such cases dashes (-) will be put under Questions 20(i) and 20(ii).

107.1 If the person was engaged in more than one economic activity during the last year, this question will obviously be asked with reference to the main economic activity entered under Question

17(i). **For visitors who qualify to be enumerated in the household in terms of the eligibility criteria, this question will be canvassed with reference to the usual place of residence and the place of work from where she/he has come to live with this household.**

Q. 20(i): Distance from residence to place of work in kilometres

108. For workers other than those engaged in cultivation or as agricultural labourer or in household industry, 'place of work' may be defined as premises or an institution or an office or an establishment where the person is engaged

in some economic productive activity. These could be the places where mining and quarrying or manufacturing, processing, servicing or repairs (other than in the household industry) are carried out. The following also are work places where economic activities relating to generation and transmission and distribution of gas, steam, water supply, etc., construction, wholesale or retail trade, hotels and restaurants, transport, storage, warehousing, communication, financing, insurance, real estate and business services, community, social and personal services, public administration, offices such as banks, post offices, police station, court, etc., schools, hospitals, recreation and cultural services, community services such as temples, etc., takes place. In addition, you must note that the places where economic activities such as rearing of cattle and production of milk, rearing of sheep for production of wool, rearing of other animals such as pigs, rearing of bees and production of honey, rearing of silk-worms and production of cocoons and raw silk, hunting, trapping, collection of fuel and other forest products and their sale, gathering of materials such as herbs, resins, etc., catching and selling of fish, etc., are carried on are also work places.

108.1 For such persons whose work place is not fixed, the entire area of operation including the field of her/his economic activity will be treated as her/his place of work.

109. **One way distance from residence to the place of work will be considered for entry under this question. The distance from residence to the place of work will always be recorded in Arabic numerals.** *Three boxes are provided to enter the distance under this column. If the distance is in one digit prefix two 'O's and if it is in two digit, prefix one 'O'. If the distance is returned in three digits, enter one digit in each box. In case the journey is carried out through any mode of land transport, the road distance from the residence to the place of work may be recorded in Kilometre (Km.) rounded to the nearest unit. If the distance of the work place from the residence is less than 0.5 Km., '000' may be noted under Question 20(i). But the distance, if varies from 0.5 Km. to 1.4 Km., '001' will be recorded under this question and so on. In case the journey is performed by any of the modes relating to water transport such as ship, ferry-boat, boat, etc., the aerial distance for the journey performed in waters combined with the road distance, if any, will be indicated under this question. For a person whose place of work is same as the place of residence, '000' will be entered below this question.*

109.1 For peddlers and persons who have no fixed place of work, distance will be reckoned as the distance from residence to the nearest point of the area of operation. If there are two different areas of operation then the area which is farthest will be considered. For persons commuting to more than one place in connection with her/his economic activity, the place which is farthest from the residence will be considered as work place for recording distance under this question. If a person has to commute to differerent places on different days, then the place of work to which she/he goes more frequently will be considered for making entry under this question. If the nature of work of the person is such that she/he has to travel long distances temporarily on tour or ˉshe/he has to make field visits on a few days in a month, then this distance should not be taken into account for recording answer to this question. In such cases the normal distance from his regular place of work should be recorded .

109.2 If a person has to use more than one mode of travel to reach her/ his place of work from her/his place of work from her/his residence, the distance she/he travels by each of these modes will have to be added in order to arrive at the distance to the place of work.

Q.20 (ii): **Mode of travel to place of work**

110. **After you have found out the distance from residence to the place of work, enquire how this distance is covered by the person to reach her or his place of work.** *The appropriate code will be entered below this question to indicate the mode of travel. 'Mode' here refers to the mode of transport normally used for commuting. It is not necessary that the mode of travel used to reach the place of work is owned by the person. Reaching the place of work 'on foot' is also included as a possible mode. The following ten modes with their codes which are self explanatory have been prescribed to record the responses under Question 20(ii):*

On foot	1
Bicycle	2
Moped/Scooter/Motor Cycle	3
Car/Jeep/Van	4
Tempo/Autorickshaw/Taxi	5
Bus	6
Train	7
Water transport	8
Any other	9
No Travel	0

110.1 These codes are provided at the bottom of the Household Schedule. You must enter the appropriate code of the mode of travel to reach the place of work after ascertaining the same from the person concerned. If the person has to use more than one mode of travel to reach her/his work place, the mode accounting for the longest distance will be considered to record the information under this question.

110.2 Code '9', 'Any Other', will include mode of travel not covered by codes '1' to '8'. These could be rickshaw, tonga, cart, tractor trolley, etc., owned or hired to reach the place of work. **If the main economic activity of the person is carried on at her/his own place of residence i.e., she/he has** not to travel to undertake her/his economic activity, code '0' will be entered under this question.

II. MIGRATION CHARACTERISTICS (Qs. 21 and 22)

111. **Questions 21 and 22 are aimed at capturing the details of migration characteristics of the people. For example, rural to urban migration or migration from one part of the country to another.** *In recent years with increased mobility of population the study of migration characteristics has assumed significant importance.* **For Census purposes, there are two types of migrants, namely (i) migrants by place of birth and (ii) migrants by place of last residence.** *While Question 21 captures the details of the number of migrants by place of birth, Question 22 will provide similar details on migrants by place of last residence.*

Q. 21: Birth Place

112. Certain details regarding the place where the person enumerated was born are to be collected and entered under Question 21. **For defence and similar paramilitary personnel, this question is not applicable.** *For them put dash (-) against Questions 21 (i) and 21(ii). The explanation and instructions as to how the information against these questions is to be filled are as follows:*

> **Is the person born in this village/town?**
>
> **If 'Yes', put dash (-) against qs. 21(i) and 21(ii)**
>
> **or**
>
> **If 'No', enter particulars:**

113. **For every person there can be one and only one place of birth. Find out the birth place of each person already listed. For a person who was born in the village or town where she/he is being enumerated, put dashes (-) against Questions 21 (i) and 21 (ii).** *If person is born in some part (hamlet) of the same village or in another locality of the same town where she/he is being enumerated, the village or town of enumeration would be considered as the place of her/his birth. The detailed entries against these questions will be made only if the person says that she/he was born in any place other than the place where she/he is being enumerated.* **Please note that different persons in the same household can have different places of birth.**

Birth place:

Q. 21 (i): State/Country (if birth place within India, write the present name of the state or if birth place outside India, write the present name of the country)

114. **For a person born outside the village or town of enumeration but within the country, find out the present name of the state/union territory where she/he was born and record it against Question 21 (i).** *This could even be the state/union territory, where the person is being enumerated.*

114.1 **For those born outside India, note merely the present name of the country and there is no need to enter the name of the constituent state of the foreign country.** *Where a person cannot name the country, the name of the continent may be noted. In case of persons born outside the country Question 21(ii) will not be applicable and only dash (-) will be put against the question.*

114.2 *For a person born on the high seas, record 'born at sea', against this question and put dash (-) against Question 21(ii).*

Q. 21 (ii): **District [If birth place within India, write the present name of the district or if birth place outside India, put dash (-)]**

115. **The information against this question is to be recorded only if the person was born outside the village or town of enumeration but within the country. Write the present name of the district where the person was born. This could even be the district where the person is being enumerated. If the person cannot name the district, write 'not known'.**

115.1 *For a person born **outside India,** put dash (-) against this question.*

116. *If a person was born in a train or bus or boat or aircraft, etc., within the country, enter the present name of the state/union territory against Question 21 (i) and the present name of the district against Question 21 (ii) where the birth was registered. If not registered, enter the particulars against Questions 21(i) and 21(ii) with reference to the administrative territory where the event occurred.*

Important

117. *Please note that name of the state/union territory or district or country of her/his birth place may have changed since the time of her/his birth. This can be due to two reasons (a) change in the name itself and (b) jurisdictional change as a result of the creation or re-organisation of state/union territory or district or country.* **The present name of the country or state and district has to be entered here and not the name by which they were known at the time of her/his birth.**

Q. 22 Place of Last Residence

118. *Question 22 has five sub-parts i.e., Questions 22(i) to 22(v). Responses to Questions 22(i) and 22(ii) give the details of the place of last residence of the person, namely, the country or the state and the district.*

Response to Question 22(iii) will provide the status of the place of last residence (whether Rural and Urban). Question 22(iv) will elicit information on the reason of migration of the person, while Question 22(v) will bring out the duration of stay since the time of migration from the place of last residence.

119. **Question 22 and its parts will be asked of all persons irrespective of age.** *If a person is living at the place of enumeration since her/his birth and never gone out except on* **temporary visit** *to their relatives, pilgrimage, tour, etc., she/he will be deemed to be a non-migrant by place of last residence and dashes (-) will be entered in Questions 22(i) to 22(v).* **Detailed response in these questions will have to be filled in respect of all those persons who had another place as the place of normal residence (irrespective of her/his place of birth) before she/he came to the present place where she/he is being enumerated.** *Even if a person was born at the place of enumeration but because of her/his work or for studies, etc., she/he had* **shifted** *subsequently to another village or town and had come back again to the place of enumeration, she/he should be deemed to have come from elsewhere to reside in this village/town.*

119.1 *Put dash (-) against Questions 22(i) to 22(v) for* **defence and similar personnel** *as these questions are not applicable for them.*

119.2 *Migration of persons in search of job is high in our country. In many cases such migrations are only seasonal in nature.* **People migrate to other places for work in a particular season and come back to their usual place of residence after three or four months. For the purpose of this question all such workers will be treated as migrants.** *Similarly, if a person moved to any other place for attending a short-term vocational course or for attending particular educational course that lasted for only a few months of a year, she/he too will be recorded as a migrant. Thus, in both these situations, the person will be deemed to have come from other places to live in the village or town of enumeration.*

119.3 *The immediate previous village or town of residence is relevant only if she/he had been outside the village or town of enumeration and not simply in another house or locality in the same place. For example, if a person born in one part of Mumbai City is found residing in another part of Mumbai at the time of enumeration, the change of residence should not be treated as change of place of residence because both the areas are within the same city of Mumbai. Similarly, a person born in hamlet 1 of village Rampur and found in hamlet 2 of the same village at the time of enumeration, is not a migrant. Where a person had merely gone out to another place or had been shifting from place to place purely on tour or pilgrimage or for temporary business purposes, she/ he should not be deemed to have had another residence different from the place where she/he or her/his family normally resides. In case of a visitor who is being enumerated in the household, the place of her/his usual residence will be recorded as the place of last residence. Similarly, if a person is* enumerated at a place other than her or his place of birth and if she or he had no other place of normal residence before coming to the place of enumeration, the place of birth would be the place from where she/he had come to reside in this village/town.

119.4 It would not be possible to specify the duration of stay which will qualify for reckoning the change of residence. The circumstances of each case would have to be taken into consideration in deciding whether a person had come from elsewhere or not. For example, an officer who has been transferred for a short period must be considered as moving from her/his place of previous posting which would become her/his place of last residence, irrespective of her/his stay in the new posting. However, temporary movement like women moving into a hospital for delivery, a person moving into a hospital for treatment, etc., at a place other than their usual residence, will be ignored and these places will not be treated as the last residence. **When a woman temporarily moves into a hospital or to her parents or other relative's house for delivery and if the hospital or the parents/relatives house is in a place different from usual place of residence, the place where the hospital or parents/relative's house is will be the place of last residence of the child but not of the mother.**

Has the person come to this village/town from elsewhere?

If 'No', put dash (-) against Qs. 22(i) to 22(v) or

If 'Yes', give following particulars:

120. For a person who has been in the village or town of enumeration continuously since birth (except for shifting to other place outside the village or town of enumeration for a purely temporary stay), put dash (-) in Questions 22(i) to 22(v) as she/he has never changed her/his residence since birth. **But for a person who had her/his last previous residence at any place outside the village or town of enumeration (irrespective of her/his place of birth), fill-in the requisite details, where applicable, in Questions 22(i) to (v).**

Place of last residence:

Q. 22(i): State/Country (if place of last residence within India, write the present name of the state or if place of last residence outside India, write the present name of the country)

121. For a person whose immediate last residence was outside the village or town of enumeration but **within India,** the present name of the state or union territory in which it is situated will be recorded against Question 22(i). **This could even be the state or the union territory in which the person is being enumerated.**

121.1 For a person whose immediate last residence was **outside the**

country, *write the present name of the country and if name of the country is not forthcoming, write the name of the continent against Question 22(i). In case of such individuals whose immediate place of last residence was outside India, Questions 22(ii) and 22(iii) will not be applicable and dashes (-) will be entered in these questions.*

Q. 22(ii): District **[if place of last residence within India, write the present name of the district or if place of last residence outside India, put dash (-)]**

122. **For a person who has come to reside in the village or town where she/he is being enumerated, from any other place within India, you have to enter the present name of the district against this question where her/his immediate last place of residence is situated. This could even be the district where the person is being enumerated.** *If the person cannot name the district, write 'not known' against this question.*

122.1 *For a person whose last previous residence was* **outside India,** *put dash (-) against this question.*

123. *The present name of the country, state/union territory or district is being insisted upon, because it might be possible that after migrating to the place of enumeration, the name of the country or state/union territory or district to which it belonged earlier might have changed, as already stated in instructions to Question 21.*

Q.22(iii) : At the time of migration, was the place of last residence: Rural -1/ Urban -2

124. *For a person who had previously resided outside the place of enumeration, ascertain if the place of her/his last previous residence from where migrated was rural or urban and record the answer.* **Rural or urban status has to be determined with reference to the status existing at the time of migration.** *Broadly, if the place was city or town and had any local body such as municipality, municipal corporation, cantonment board, notified town area committee, etc., to administer its affairs, this would be treated as urban. If it was a village, this would be treated as rural.*

124.1 *For a person whose immediate last residence was a village, record code '1' under this question, and for 'Urban', enter code '2'.*

124.2 *For a person who last resided in a foreign country, put dash (-) below this question.*

Q.22(iv): Reason for migration of this person

125. *The question will be asked of a person who has come from elsewhere to reside in the village/town where she/he is being enumerated and for whom there is an entry against Question 22(i). This question will not be canvassed in the case of those for whom you may have entered dash (-) against Question 22(i). This is because they have had no change in the place of last residence.*

In all the other cases you must find out the reasons for migration from the place of last residence and note the reasons by entering the appropriate code as given below:

Work/Employment	1
Business	2
Education	3
Marriage	4
Moved after Birth	5
Moved with household	6
Any other reason	7

125.1 *These codes have been printed at the bottom of the Household Schedule. You must enter the appropriate code depending on the reason for migration under this question.* **For defence and similar paramilitary personnel, this question will also not apply,** *since you will not have canvassed the Questions 22(i) to 22(iii) for such personnel. Dash (-) may be put under this question in case the question is not applicable.*

125.2 **The reason for migration will be determined as applicable at the time of migration and not in reference to any point of time after that.** *For example, if a person had moved from the place of her/his last residence for the purpose of education and subsequently at some point of time got employment there only. the reason for migration would be 'education' and not 'work/employment'.*

126. *A person can be said to have moved for work/employment, if she or he has moved into the village/town of enumeration in the following cases:*

(a) *If she or he has moved in search of a job.*

(b) *Because she/he has been offered a job and moved to take up the job.*

(c) **Already having a job, she/he has moved due to a transfer, even if this is on promotion.**

(d) **Due to a change in her/his job.**

126.1 *As regards situation (a) above, this will cover the people who migrate to urban areas in search of employment and take up jobs like rickshaw pullers, coolies, masons, domestic servants, care takers of buildings or to work as labourers for construction of roads and buildings, etc., for their livelihood. A few others migrate to another rural area to earn their livelihood and work as farm labourers, diggers, construction workers, etc. All such persons who migrate to other places in search of work or employment even without receiving any formal offer for a job or for service will be covered in this category .*

126.2 **If a person has moved for any of the above reasons record code '1' under this question.**

127. *A person can be said to have moved for 'business' if she or he has moved to the place of enumeration from her/his place of last residence for joining a business or setting up/running a business. The word 'business' refers to an economic activity involving some risk-taking either on own account or in partnership with others. Please note 'business' is different from work or employment for which wages/salary is received in cash or kind. For 'business' you have to enter code '2' under this question.*

128. *A person can be said to have moved for educational purposes if she or he has moved to the place of enumeration from her/his place of last residence, for joining a school/college or any other type of educational institution either for the first time or for continuing her/his studies. For such a person, code '3' has to be given. However, if a person has moved along with her/his family because the entire household has moved due to any reason and she/he has joined a school/college at the new place of residence, the reason for migration will be 'moved with household' and not 'education'.*

129. *If a person has moved consequent on getting married, record code '4' for that person.*

130. **The reason 'moved after birth' (code '5') is to cover all cases referred to in para 119.4. The important point here is that the person returned within a short period after her/his birth (usually) along with her/his mother (who had temporarily moved for the purpose of delivery) and is living in the place of enumeration ever since.** *Please note for a person born in a place different from the place of enumeration but moved from that place after a longer stay say, a year or more, in such a case the reason for migration cannot be 'moved after birth'.*

131. **The reason 'moved with household', code '6' will refer mainly to cases where the entire household moves.** *Such cases will come up if the head of the household or the person on whom the family is dependent has moved due to any reason such as transfer, shifting of business, etc. There are cases where one or more members of the household move along with the person who has moved in search of employment or education or for other reasons. While the person who has moved for a particular reason will be assigned the appropriate code, the other members who moved as a consequence along with that person will be assigned code '6', i.e., 'moved with household',*

132. *Code '7' 'any other reason' will include all other reasons for migration not covered under codes '1' to '6' i.e., work/employment, business, education, marriage, moved after birth and moved with household. This may include cases like movement due to natural calamities like drought, floods, etc.; medical or health reasons; retirement; displacement; social or political turmoil; etc.*

133. **It is important to note that the reasons for migration are being noted for each person separately. Therefore, in the same household, there may be cases where the reasons for migration are**

different for different members of the household. *For example, if the head of the household is promoted and transferred, in her/his case code '1' will have to be assigned under this question, because her/his movement is consequent on employment while the spouse and other dependants should be assigned code '6' because the household moves. There are also cases of migration, particularly from the rural areas to urban areas, where a girl or a boy moves to a town or city for higher studies and in order to look after her or him an elderly person also moves. In such a case, for the person who moves for higher studies the reason for migration will be 'education' i.e., code '3' while in the case of the elderly person, it will be 'any other reason', code '7'. If in case the entire household has moved along with the student, for all the other members of the household you will have to assign code '6' 'moved with household'. It is, therefore, necessary for you to make careful enquiries and not to get confused with the different reasons that may be applicable to different persons of the same household.*

134. *Some persons move to other places only during certain seasons for work or search of work (seasonal migrants) and return to their usual place of residence during the lean season. This is a common phenomenon in certain parts of our country. For example, agriculture labour migrates from Bihar to Punjab. When such persons return to there usual place of residence in Bihar and enumerated there, the reason of migration for such persons would be 'other', code '7' and not 'work/employment'. However, if such persons are enumerated in Punjab, the reason for migration would be 'work/employment', code '1'.*

135. *In particular, please note that you must make detailed enquiries in the case of any unrelated members of the households, such as cook, servant, etc.* **In their cases, their movement from the place of last residence may have been due to employment.** *Similarly, in the case of those members of the household who are rather distantly related to the head of the household, you must also make such detailed enquiries.*

136. *Please note that in case of every person who has come into village or town of enumeration from any other country as a result of partition or been repatriated, the reasons for migration will be noted as 'any other reason', code '7' and not any other code.*

Q. 22(v) Duration of stay in this village or town since migration (in completed years)

137. **Enquire and note the period in completed years of the continuous residence in the village or town where the person is being enumerated. The duration of stay in this village or town since migration will be entered in the boxes provided under this question.** *Enter one digit in each box. If the number of years of continuous stay in the village or town of enumeration is in single digit, you have to prefix '0'.*

137.1 This question will apply even to a person born at the place of enumeration who had subsequently shifted to some other place because of the reason noted against Question 22(iv) and come back again to reside in this village or town. **But this question does not apply to defence and similar personnel.** *For them put dash (-) under this question.*

137.2 **If the person had left this village or town and lived elsewhere for sometime and has come back to this village or town, then the duration of residence to be noted under this question is the period of the latest continuous residence.** *But if a person had been away on a temporary visit or tour, etc., that should not be taken as a break in the period of her/his continuous residence here.*

137.3 If the person was born at the place of enumeration and also had no other place of residence, i.e., for whom dash (-) has been noted under Question 22(i), then dash (-) will also be put under Question 22(v).

137.4 For a person whose duration of continuous residence at the place of enumeration is less than one year, put '00' in the boxes under this question. The duration of residence for visitors would generally be '00'.

137.5 Seasonal migrants who move to other places to earn their livelihood and also those who go to other places to attend short term educational or vocational courses and come back to their usual place of residence, the duration of their continuous stay at the place of enumeration will necessarily be recorded as '00'.

III. HOUSELESS POPULATION

162 The enumeration of the houseless population will have to be carried out in the block assigned to you The houseless population can be found in any place and they should be necessarily covered during the Population Enumeration.

163. You will be required to enumerate the houseless population in your enumeration block(s) on the night of 28th February, 2001. In order to do this, it would be necessary for you to complete the enumeration of all the persons in all the normal and institutional households in your jurisdiction between 9th February and 28th February, 2001. During this period, you will have also taken note of the places where houseless population was found living, such as on the roadside, pavements, in hume pipes, under fly-overs, bridges and staircases, or in the open, in temples, mandaps, railway platforms and the like. You must have entered the particulars of all these places in Section 4 of the Abridged Houselist while canvassing the Household Schedules in respect of Normal and Institutional households. On the night of 28th February but before 00:00 hrs. of 1st March, 2001, you will have to quickly cover these and all other such places where houseless population is likely to live and enumerate them. In case a very large number of houseless persons have been identified in your jurisdiction whom you may not be able to enumerate single-handedly in one night, make a report to your Supervisor in advance, so that one or more extra enumerators can be deputed to assist you in the one-night enumeration of such houseless persons. You should keep particular watch on the nomadic population living in the open within the boundaries of your enumeration block. These people will have to be covered on the night of 28th February, 2001. You should, of course, make sure that these persons' have not been enumerated elsewhere.

IV. HOW ACCURATE IS THE CENSUS?

Highlights of the post census enumeration check — 1991 census

Excerpts from

CENSUS PAPER 1 OF 1994, REPORT ON POST ENUMERATION CHECK

Census of India 1991, Series 1, India Issued by Registrar General and Census Commissioner

From the 1951 Census onwards, a Post Enumeration Check PEC has been conducted immediately after the Census to assess the coverage of Census enumeration. The objective of PEC was to quantify the likely omission or duplication in Census enumeration. In recent Census, its scope has been expanded to include a check on the contents. The 1991 PEC in particular provides a check on quality of information on items collected in the Census like age, literacy, whether worked any time during last one year, whether main or marginal worker, main activity in case of main workers, the industrial and occupational distribution of main workers as well as the data on ever born and surviving children of ever married women. In simpler terms, the survey envisages answers to the following two questions:

(a) *How accurately has every individual been enumerated (Coverage Error) in the Census?*

(b) *How precisely have the particulars of individuals been recorded (Content Error) in the Census?*

For any Census to provide reliable information to users it is essential that such errors are kept at the minimum possible level. Study of such errors is useful in understanding the source of these errors and taking corrective measures in the design of questionnaire and operational procedures in future Censuses. This will also help the data users to come to the right conclusions based on Census data.

The coverage error investigated in PEC consists of two components:

(i) *Omission or duplication of persons due to omission or duplication of households.*

(ii) *Omission or duplication of individuals in enumerated households.*

These are called Type I and Type II errors respectively.

The content error arises from the way in which the enumerator canvasses the question or from the way the respondents understand the question or both. Further in a mass operation like Census, it is not always the concerned individual who provides data. Errors may also arise because the person who answers the question may not know all the particulars of a person about whom the information is being reported in the Census. Thus, for example, the head of the household may not know the correct age of his daughter-in-law or some other person who stays with him at the time of Census. Errors can also occur because of difficulty in understanding the concepts. For example, one may give his running age instead of the completed age that is required.

To study the coverage and content errors in the 1991 Census, it was decided to conduct the Post Enumeration Check survey in all the states and Union Territories with a population of two million and above.

For any study on coverage error, the instructions given to enumerators on whom to enumerate are very important. The Census defines certain persons only as eligible for enumeration in a particular household. These are:

(i)   persons who normally stay and are present in the household during the entire period of enumeration i.e. 9th to 28th February, 1991, both days inclusive.

(ii)   persons who are known to be usual residents of the household and have stayed there for part of the enumeration period but are not present at the time of enumeration.

(iii)   persons who are usual residents but are away at the time of visit of the Census enumerator but are expected to return to the household before the 28th February, 1991.

(iv)   Visitors who may be present in the household during the entire enumeration period.

A person who has been away from his normal or usual place of residence throughout the enumeration period will not be eligible for enumeration as a member of the household in which he is a normal resident. He/she will be enumerated wherever he/she is actually found during the enumeration period. Such persons were cautioned that they should not get themselves enumerated in case they move from the place where they were enumerated.

The coverage error arises mainly because the instructions are not strictly followed in the field by the enumerator or by the respondent. For example, a housewife may have a tendency to include her husband's name in the household, even when he is away for a short duration covering the entire Census enumeration period unless the enumerator asks probing questions to bring out the correct picture. There may also be cases of persons who are living at one place but have come to visit their family during the weekend. Such persons may also be included in the household unless probed by the enumerator. On the other hand, some people may be omitted from the Census inadvertently by the respondent himself. This may occur in case of children as the respondent may feel that the child is too young to be included in the Census.

Visitors and domestic servants who may be living with the household are also likely to be omitted as the respondent may not be aware that they are also to be enumerated. It is the aim of the Post Enumeration Check to find out such cases of omission and duplication.

The 1991 Post Enumeration Check used a different approach in the manner of reckoning normal residents in a given household from the practice adopted in the Census enumeration. The Post Enumeration Check covered only the de jure population, i.e., persons who are usual or normal residents of the household. All visitors were excluded. Since the group of normal residents absent throughout the Census enumeration period from their normal place of residence is the same as the group of visitors who are present at their places of visit during the Census enumeration period, the study attempted to cover these persons at one place only where they are more likely to be present at the time of Post Enumeration Check. The Census covered the visitors present throughout because they were physically present at the time of Census at a particular household and, therefore, were easy to contact. However, in the Post Enumeration Check, normal residents absent throughout have been included in the study and visitors present throughout were excluded. This is because, at the time of visit of the PEC enumerator, visitors need not be continuing to stay there and hence may not be available, while normal residents who were away during Census are more likely to be available in the household. The instructions also emphasised that in PEC, to the extent possible, information should be collected from the persons concerned directly. This will not be possible in case of visitors who may not be living with the household at the time of PEC. There is also another reason why normal residents absent throughout the enumeration period, rather than visitors were included. There may be a few cases in which a visitor may not be known at the place of visit. For example, an officer going on tour to another place for 20 days in February and staying in a guest house may be enumerated at the guest house but may not be available at the time of PEC enumerator's visit. Getting the details of such persons will be difficult. However, at his/her normal place of residence it may be possible to find out details of the whereabouts of the person during the Census period. Questions have been included in the schedules on the correct residential status of each individual to determine whether he/she has been enumerated elsewhere or not. In short, all normal residents including those who may have been absent throughout the Census enumeration period were listed in Post Enumeration Check in preference to visitors.

As will be noticed, the results of PEC indicate that the proportion of persons who were away from their normal place of residence throughout the Census enumeration period is very small, being of the order of 0.27 percent of total population. Though their proportion is very small the coverage error rates are very high for this category of persons.

Organisation of Post Enumeration Check

Taking into consideration the operational aspects like the available resources and trained manpower that can be spared for the survey it was finally decided to fix the sample size at 4,200 enumeration blocks at national level. It was also decided to use stratified systematic sampling to select the enumeration blocks.

The sample selection was independently done for the rural areas, non city urban areas and the cities of the each state where PEC was conducted.

For estimating the content error in the Census, it was necessary to have well trained and dedicated enumerators. They were needed immediately after the Census, when a lot of post Census activities were on hand. Considering these aspects it was decided to conduct the survey to estimate the content error in a 20 per cent sub sample of the blocks selected for studying coverage error. Thus the total sample size at national level for studying coverage error was 840 enumeration blocks.

Sampling frame and sample selection

To prepare the sampling frame, the concerned Census directorates were asked to provide in prescribed proforma the number of enumeration blocks in each Census charge. This information was collected separately for cities, non city urban and rural areas.

For selecting the sample, all the Census charges in a state in a particular stratum were arranged in the order of their location code. The required number of enumeration blocks were selected linear systematically after keeping all the strata together. This procedure gave the number of blocks allocated to each stratum in proportion to total number of enumeration blocks in that stratum. A 20 per cent sub sample of the enumeration blocks selected above was taken linear systematically for the survey on content error. The sample selection was completely done at the headquarters of the office of the Registrar General, India, New Delhi and the list of selected blocks was communicated to the states so as to reach them by March 1, 1991.

Procedure for the survey

Three main schedules were canvassed in the field. The forms used and their purpose were as follows:

Form I - to identify the households which have been omitted or duplicated; in other words, to determine Type I error;

Form II - to find out persons omitted or duplicated in households which have been enumerated in the Census; in other words to determine Type II error;

Form III - to determine content error in selected Census questions. This form was to be canvassed only in a sub-sample of the PEC blocks.

Detailed instructions issued for filling up the different forms may be seen in appendix.

All houses and households in the selected blocks were listed for the study of Type I error. This list was compared with the Abridged House list updated at the time of Census using certain criteria for matching households and wherever necessary field reconciliation was done to identify the omitted/duplicated households. The members of such households were then listed along with certain particulars.

For estimating Type II error, a 10 per cent sub sample of households enumerated in Census was selected from each block. These households were selected linear systematically in the Regional Tabulation Offices from the updated Abridged house list, after excluding the institutional and houseless households. In the selected households all the usual residents were listed and this list was compared with the Household Schedule using a few criteria for matching persons. All the unmatched and partially matched cases were further investigated by the enumerator to determine the enumeration status.

The same sample of households selected above was used for canvassing the Form III meant for assessing the content error. The information collected in this form was matched with the corresponding information in the Household Schedule and the unmatched cases were reconciled in the field to arrive at correct responses.

Selected Tables

The composition of the zones is as follows:

Southern Zone: Andhra Pradesh, Karnataka, Kerala and Tamil Nadu.

Eastern Zone: Assam, Bihar, Orissa, Tripura and West Bengal.

Central Zone: Madhya Pradesh and Uttar Pradesh.

Western Zone: Maharashtra and Gujarat

Northern Zone: Haryana, Himachal Pradesh, Punjab, Rajasthan and Delhi.

Coverage Error

Table 4.1: Net Omission Rates (per thousand) by Sex and Residence, India and Zones

Based on Dual Estimation

India/Zone	Total			Rural			Urban		
	Persons	Males	Females	Persons	Males	Females	Persons	Males	Females
1	2	3.	4	5	6	7	8	9	10
India	**17.6**	**17.3**	**17.9**	**16.8**	**16.0**	**17.7**	**19.8**	**21.1**	**18.3**
Southern Zone	19.4	20.0	17.9	19.8	20.4	19.2	18.5	22.2	14.7
Eastern Zone	14.7	13.7	15.7	14.5	13.3	15.8	15.7	16.0	15.4
Central Zone	21.5	20.2	22.9	21.0	19.7	22.5	23.2	22.3	24.1
Western Zone	14.9	16.1	13.5	11.2	11.1	11.3	21.3	24.5	17.6
Northern Zone	15.2	13.3	17.3	13.1	11.0	15.5	20.0	18.6	21.6

Table 4.2: Rates of Gross Omission, Duplication and Net Omission

		Rates per 1000	*Rates per 1000*
Zone	Gross omission	Duplication	Net omission
India	**21.1**	**3.5**	**17.6**
Southern Zone	22.6	3.2	19.4
Eastern Zone	15.8	1.1	14.7
Central Zone	27.8	6.3	21.5
Western Zone	20.6	5.4	15.2
Northern Zone	17.0	2.1	14.9

Table 4.3: Net Omission Rates by Sex and Residence 1981-1991

Sex	Total		Rural		Urban	
	1981	*1991*	*1981*	*1991*	*1981*	*1991*
Persons	18.0	16.9	15.0	16.2	27.6	19.0
Males	17.1	16.7	13.8	15.4	27.7	20.3
Females	18.8	17.1	16.3	16.9	27.5	17.5

Table 4.4: Net Omission Rates by Type of Error, Sex and Residence, India

Resid-ence	Type I			Type II			Total		
	Persons	Males	Females	Persons	Males	Females	Persons	Males	Females
1	2	3	4	5	6	7	8	9	10
Total	1.9	2.4	1.3	15.0	14.2	15.8	16.9	16.7	17.1
Rural	1.3	1.5	1.0	14.9	14.0	15.9	16.2	15.4	16.9
Urban	3.7	5.3	2.0	15.3	15.1	15.5	19.0	20.3	17.5

Table 4.5: Net Omission Rates by Age and Sex, India

Age Group	Persons	Males	Females
All ages	**17.6**	**17.3**	**17.9**
0-4	23.8	24.0	23.5
5-9	17.6	17.5	17.6
10-14	19.3	20.0	18.5
15-19	19.2	16.3	22.6
20-24	24.1	26.5	21.7
25-29	18.6	19.7	17.6
30-34	14.8	14.7	14.8
35-39	11.7	12.7	10.6
40-44	9.9	10.9	8.8
45-49	10.6	9.2	12.2
50-54	10.3	8.8	12.2
55-59	8.9	7.5	10.5
60+	14.9	10.8	19.6

Table 4.6: Net Omission Rates for those Aged 7 Years and above by Literacy and Sex, India

Literacy	Persons	Males	Females
1	2	3	4
Total	16.3	16.0	16.5
Literate	16.1	16.8	14.9
Illiterate	16.4	14.7	17.5

Table 4.7: Net Omission Rates by Marital Status and Sex, India

Marital Status	Persons	Males	Females
1	2	3	4
Total (aged 10+)	15.7	15.4	16.1
Never married	19.5	21.1	16.9
Married	14.1	12.8	15.5
Widowed/Divorced/Separated	17.8	10.9	20.6

Table 4.8: Net Omission Rates by Sex and Relationship to Head

Relationship	Persons	Males	Females
1	*2*	*3*	*4*
Total	17.6	17.3	17.9
Head	7.5	7.4	9.1
Spouse	10.3	104.1	9.5
Parents	40.8	73.6	34.1
Children	16.8	16.4	17.5
Other relatives	28.7	32.8	25.7
Unrelated	115.9	111.3	125.0
Members of nuclear family	13.3	13.1	18.3
Others	29.9	34.4	24.8

Table 4.9: Net Omission Rates (Type II) and Distribution of Persons Enumerated in PEC by Residential Status

Residential status	Net omission rates (per 1000 population)		
	Total	Rural	Urban
Total	17.9 (1000.0)	18.2 (1000.0)	17.1 (1000.0)
Present throughout	17.5 (996.6)	17.7 (996.3)	16.8 (997.4)
Absent throughout	110.0 (2.7)	117.3 (3.0)	78.7 (2.0)
Present partly	147.2 (0.7)	142.6 (0.7)	164.0 (0.7)

Note: Figures in bracket indicate the proportion (per 1,000) of the population in that category

Table 4.10: Distribution of Persons Counted in Census by their Enumeration status

Enumeration status	Total	Rural	Urban
Total census count	1000.0	1000.0	1000.0
Enumerated correctly	991.7	991.6	991.8
Enumerated once only but at wrong place	4.7	4.7	4.9
Duplicated	3.6	3.6	3.3
Out of scope	Neg.	Neg.	Neg.

Table 4.11: Age Distribution of Population Adjustment for Omission

| Age group | Total | | | Rural | Urban |
| | Persons | Males | Females | Persons | Persons |
1	2	3	4	5	6
All ages	**100.00**	**100.00**	**100.00**	**100.00**	**100.00**
0-4	12.31	12.12	12.52	12.80	10.83
5-9	13.80	13.70	13.91	14.28	12.37
10-14	12.08	12.43	11.69	12.10	12.01
15-19	9.54	9.67	9.40	9.38	10.02
20-24	8.95	8.64	9.29	8.56	10.15
25-29	8.14	7.78	8.52	7.88	8.90
30-34	6.81	6.67	6.95	6.60	7.44
35-39	6.18	6.31	6.04	5.95	6.88
40-44	4.85	5.07	4.60	4.74	5.18
45-49	4.19	4.23	4.16	4.17	4.27
50-54	3.66	3.91	3.38	3.74	3.41
55-59	2.57	2.49	2.66	2.61	2.45
60+	6.87	6.90	6.84	7.15	6.03
0-14	26.11	25.82	26.43	26.08	23.20
15-44	44.46	44.15	44.80	43.10	48.56
15-59	54.88	54.78	54.98	53.62	58.68

PART FIVE

MEDIA AND THE 2001 CENSUS

Excerpts from Print Media

Acknowledgements

We have taken excerpts from news items, articles and editorials from the following newspapers, magazines and journals and given credit to the authors concerned/reporters/correspondents and also given the publication details.

Decan Herald
Economic and Political Weekly
Frontline
Grassroots
The Hindu
Hindustan Times
Indian Express
Outlook
People
Pioneer
Statesman
Times of India
Tribune
Week

We have presented the material in italics in double columns keeping in tune with the newspaper formats. We have given the names of authors, special correspondents, reporters and others and the date of publication.

We have tried to capture the interest taken by the print media before and after the census enumeration of 2001 and the publication of the first results of the census. Time did not permit us to make systematic and comprehensive scanning; we must have missed out many important news items, articles and editorials, for which we express regret.

We have also not commented on the material presented here as the focus of the book is on census methodology and census data. Interpretations differ. We have however referred to some material from part five in the Overview and in part three on implications.

The material for this part has been ably prepared by Anita Haldar and she deserves special thanks.

Contents

I.   Census Publicity

II.   General

III.   Census Enumeration

IV.   Caste

V.   Sex Workers

VI.   Reporting the First Results of the 2001 Census

VII.   Unborn Daughters : Decline in sex ratio of the child population (0-6 years)

I

CENSUS PUBLICITY

All News Papers
Friday, February 9, 2001

PRESIDENT
REPUBLIC OF INDIA

MESSAGE

The fourteenth Population Census of India will be carried out between February 9-28, 2001. This would be one of the biggest administrative exercises undertaken by any government in the world leading to enumeration of about a billion-strong population of our country.

Census is no longer a mere academic exercise, of interest only to the scholar and the researcher. It has become a major planning tool in the hands of the policy maker and the development planner, making it all the more necessary that the data collected is accurate and authentic. It is, therefore, in the interest of each person that information about him or her and the family is rightly recorded and properly incorporated in the Census data.

I invite and urge every person to actively participate in this decennial exercise and make the task a complete success. I also extend my greetings and best wishes to all those involved in this nation-wide operation.

K. R. NARAYANAN

New Delhi
February 6, 2001

Friday, February 9, 2001

PRIME MINISTER

MESSAGE

The fourteenth decennial Population Census of India will take place between 9 and 28 February, 2001. This 20-day exercise followed by a 5-day revisional round from 1 to 5 March, 2001 will be a gigantic operation of immense national significance in which every single person will be enumerated.

Over 2 million trained enumerators and supervisors will go from door to door to collect vital information on the demographic, social and economic characteristics of each individual. The information so gathered will be of immense use to plan socio-economic development of the country. It is, therefore, critical that the data collected in the course of this Census is reliable and authentic and does not suffer from inaccuracies. This cannot be ensured by the Government machinery alone. For a Census to be successful, active participation of all persons is essential.

I, therefore, appeal to everyone to join hands and extend the fullest cooperation to the Census staff. It is only through such concerted efforts that the goals of Census of India - 2001 will be fully accomplished.

A. B. VAJPAYEE

New Delhi
February 6, 2001

The Times of India, February 23, 2001

History of Census in India

— *Aniruddha Tripathi*

After Independence, the Census Act was passed in 1948. In 1949, the government of India took two important decisions:1. to initiate steps for improvement of registration of vital statistics, and 2. to establish a single organisation at the Centre under the Registrar General to deal with vital statistics and census. The first post-Independence census was taken in 1951. Its report attempted to interpret the past changes in the size and structure of the population and to point out their implications for the standard of living of the people. For the first time, an attempt was made in the history of Indian Census to recheck the Census count.

The Times of India, February 23, 2001

Enumerator No. 1

As Census Commissioner, J.K. Banthia is overseeing the mammoth counting exercise currently underway. He talks to Bisheshwar Mishra about the tasks involved and the problems encountered.

Q. What special measures are being undertaken this time to obtain accurate data?

A. Census questionnaires are being published in all major newspapers....to make the public aware of the questions they will be asked so that they can come out with correct answers.... informed public about the confidentiality of the information given by them.

Q. How far do you think you have succeeded in involving the public?

A. One simple measure introduced was requesting the people to put their signatures in the form. ....they are given an opportunity to go through the entire form and see what has been recorded and point out if any inaccuracy has crept in.

Q. But don't you think by asking them to attest their signatures, people may be apprehensive in disclosing their identity and would prefer to withhold information?

A. We are not asking people about their income. Neither are we asking questions of citizenship of nationality.

Q. .... But then, how do you know that people you have counted are Indian nationals?

A. The Census is for the people living in India. It is not for Indians in India only.

Q. So what exactly are you trying to find from the Census?

A. We are trying to find out the size of India's population. How it is distributed geographically, etc. So many characteristics like the literacy status of the population, the highest education qualification, mother tongue, the age at marriage, the marital status, their occupation. There is a question also on disability. We would like to know the migration stream, whether it is from rural to urban, urban to rural or urban to urban. Whether the number of women in India per thousand men is increasing or decreasing.

Q.   Other backward castes (OBCs) say they should be counted.

A.   Since independence we have been only asking questions on Scheduled Castes and Scheduled Tribes status. The 2001 Census is the same thing.

Q.   What is the margin of error in your data collection?

A.   As far as coverage is concerned, it is more than 98 per cent. But as the urbanisation process increases the margin of error is expected to increase. In urban areas the coverage is a more complex problem because of the mobility of the population, living at odd hours, difficult areas and all sorts of things. So the urbanisation process is making the Census more and more difficult. Another problem is that getting urban people involved in the Census process is really difficult and challenging.

Q.   Why is this so?

A.   For rural people it is some sort of festivity. In urban areas, people think half an hour's Census is an interference, some even feel it is intruding on their privacy. But in urban slums, people welcome enumerators. But in elite colonies there is a security guard, there are plaques showing 'beware of dogs'. It is often impossible.

Q.   By when will the census information be ready and available to the public?

A.   .... the provisional results will be produced very quickly, say in about four to six weeks time.

Q.   What about the final version?

A.   It will take a longer time. It's a long drawn process. Several things have to be checked and rechecked. The credibility of the census depends on the scrutiny. It has long-term implications.

The Times of India, February 9, 2001

From today, stand up and be counted

— By Staff Reporter

....Over 20 lakh government employees and teachers will set out on Friday to start the largest ever Census operations held in the country. ....This Census apart from being a mammoth operation, will include a number of new features. Questions on the distance between home and work place and kind of transportation have been added.

At the moment, nobody even has as much as an estimate on these. This data will be specially helpful in framing programmes and policies for the improvement of transport services. Slums will be treated as a separate entity and as a result the government will be able to get all details on slums and also know what percentage of a city's population resided in these areas. Information and data on physically and mentally challenged persons will be collected and presented separately. Five broad categories of disability have been formed — disability in seeing, speech, hearing, movement and mental.

When it came to fertility, till now only women had been taken into account so far. But in the Census this time a decision has been taken to ask men their age at marriage. In this Census the definition of work has been expanded. Even if a woman tends to a cow whose milk is consumed within the household, the woman will be considered to be a worker.

Similarly if cultivation is being done and the product is not sold outside but consumed by the cultivator and his or her family, this will be taken to be work.

Since the Census Act of 1948 makes it obligatory for each and every person to answer all the Census questions truthfully and correctly, this time, a provision for the respondent's signature has been made on the Census form.

The Pioneer, February 10, 2001

Census 2001 Begins Today
Enumerators told to be sensitive to respondents

— Karuna M John

"SO HOW fertile have you been this year?" The Census 2001 wants to know. The curious enumerators have begun doing what they do best — count. But trained by specialists after attending a staggering 1000 classes (per day) all over the country, these men and women promise to be more sensitive this time.

According to Deputy Registrar General (Census) Mr. D. G. Mitra, "The respondent is supreme and all information gathered is confidential," as per the Census Act (1948).

However, the respondents are sure to be amused by some of the questions.

The 'Household Schedule' : Part one, deals with the general and socio-cultural statistics. The fertility question itself is only addressed to the women respondents. However, the men should not be too offended as a senior Census official put it, "Well the woman is the one who gives birth, it is assumed that a fertile man was involved".

The Department has tried to be careful when dealing with sensitive issues like religion.

Hindus, Muslims, Christians, Sikhs, Buddhists and Jains all have a code number. Any remaining faiths will be written down in full, instructs the questionnaire. "In case the respondent has no religion, even that has to be recorded," said Mr. Mitra.

What may generate debate amongst Women's Rights organisations is perhaps the last question. Question 23 is titled 'Fertility' with sub-clauses like 'for ever married women only," - of course including divorced, widowed or separated, explains the instructions.

The sub clauses in the fertility section are also addressed to the women only. "Number of children ever born alive?" asks question number 23(1), but adds that it includes both living and dead sons and daughters.

The sub-clause for "currently married women only" asks for the "number of children born alive in the past one year (After 9th February)."

While it is still early days for a debate on the Census to begin the Disabled Rights activists have already hailed the Census of India 2001 as 'path breaking'.

The 14th Census has taken in to account the disabled were counted was in 1981 (also the International Year of Disabled) and had only three categories - 'totally dumb'. This, said activist Javed Abidi, "left out the mental challenged and all the hearing impaired".

The Times of India, February 12, 2001

Census 2001: More than just the numbers game

— *Divya Vasisth*

....the nature of the questions which find a place in the first Census of the new millennium take the form of distance of the workplace from one's residence; the mode of transportation used;

According to Samar Sandhu, a resident of Jangpura, "I use different modes of transport to reach my work place in Chandni Chowk, depending on the weather, the conveyance available, the time on my hands and, sometimes, even my mood. Consequently, it could be an autorickshaw, a bus, or even my car which takes me to office. If the questionnaire requires me to pinpoint a single mode of transportation, It gets to be a bit too much,"

The official machinery would like to believe otherwise, "All the questions have been drafted by the Registrar General of India in consensus with various government and semi-government organisations. Information compiled through the questionnaire will be used to frame economic policies and help decide on the amount of funds to be allocated to different sectors. As regards the question on the mode of transport used to reach one's workplace, it will help the government ascertain the quantum of funds to be allocated for public transportation, explains R. Harikrishan, joint director of Delhi's population cell.

In the capital's context, the city's population is expected to jump from the figure of 94.2 lakh (as recorded by the 1991 Census) to 1.43 crore. Incidentally, the projected population will take into account domestic helps irrespective of their native roots. With preparatory work having taken up the better part of two years, the city sarkar appears to be geared up in right earnest to tackle the Census proper. "Keeping in mind that new methods have been employed, officials have been put through intensive training and clear-cut guidelines have been issued to personnel, the Census will throw up highly accurate, unambiguous information which think-tanks can make use of to frame policies," maintains Bimla Jindkar, Director of the Census Operations in the city.

II
GENERAL

The Statesman, February 11, 2001

Union Home Minister's Statement on Population

The Union home minister Mr. L.K. Advani was speaking at a ceremony to unveil a stamp to mark Census 2001. He thanked the communications minister, Mr. Ram Vilas Paswan, for implementing his suggestion of bringing out such a stamp.

Mr. Paswan, who unveiled the stamp, said "population explosion" is a dampner on the developmental policies and it is important to stabilise in human growth.

The census stamp symbolises the 'hum do hamaare do' slogan - the digit '2' of 2001 on the stamp is depicted in the form of a woman, while the two zeroes are in the form of children and 1 in the form of a man.

The first time a census Bill was introduced in Britain in 1753, it was opposed in the fear that enemy nations would come to know the population of the country.

In countries like Britain and USA, the population has almost been the same in the last 20 years and so, unlike in India, there has been no need to build new schools or hospitals," Mr. Advani said.

"In India, the mushrooming population marginalises our achievement. If we make a school for 500 students, we find there are already 5,000 students waiting to get admitted. The same is the case with hospitals," he said.

Education of the masses is crucial in creating awareness about population control, Mr. Advani said, but there is also a need for "legal incentives and disincentive".

"I think using force (for population control) , as the executive did in 1975 and 1976, was not correct.... A law offering incentives and disincentives to control the country's population is a better idea than the method of 'force' adopted by the Congress government during emergency, Mr. L. K. Advani said today.

The Sunday Times of India, February 25, 2001

Census 2001: It's about people, not population

— Lalita Panicker

Census 2001 will reveal quite a few new figures but on the population front, there will be no surprises. It's a billion plus, a number which almost always sends a frisson of horror down our collective spine. Experts across the board agree that at present levels of development, there's no cause for cheer that we will soon be the most populous country in the world.

Dr. Ashish Bose, professor emeritus at Institute of Economic Growth, has been one of the harshest critics of the government's family planning efforts, "Simply by calling it reproductive health instead of family planning is not going to solve anything. This is just playing to the international galleries," he says. The real effort has to be made not at the national level but at the block level. The Census data ought to equip leaders at the grassroots level with the information they need to provide the services that truly empower people, he feels.

Eminent demographer Mari Bhat, professor at the Institute of Economic Growth, concurs with Bose, 'You cannot have quality without sacrificing quantity. Only a reduced population can improve the quality of life," he says.

But does the billion plus figure really cause concern among people? No, very few people ever think of the big picture and this is where the government has been going wrong each time. So what use is a National Population Commission (NPC) comprising 140 members who gather in New Delhi from time to time to deliberate on how to reduce the numbers.

As Nina Puri, president of Family Planning Association of India puts it, "People have families, nations have populations". It is precisely because we have missed the people for population that no national effort has ever paid off.

Dr. Saroj Pachauri, regional director, Population Council, feels that the key to effective family planning is to target India's growing youth population. "Even if fertility declines, the fact that there is such a big youth population will keep up population momentum," she says.

India's family planning programme has so far been premised on the myth that the poor want to have large families. This has been conclusively disproved. People have more children because they have no access to reversible contraception or health services. The focus on sterilisation has been a major deterrent for those seeking to limit their family size.

No one wants to give up the choice to have children, irrespective of socio-economic circumstances. The public health system is simply not geared either to reduce maternal and infant mortality – the key determinants to reducing fertility – or offering couples a choice of reversible contraceptives. But instead of focusing on these details, the government is still stuck with commission and policy mode.

Neither has worked and neither will. First we had the slogan hum do hamare do. No one paid the slightest attention. Then came Sanjay Gandhi who proclaimed that the disadvantaged cease all reproductive activity forthwith. We all know where that got his party. Since then, not one politician has dared to tackle the subject seriously. Witness Renuka Choudhary's flip sloganeering: ek bacha acha hai.

Outlook, March 5, 2001

Sensus and Sensibility

— Soma Wadhwa

The Great Indian Headcount is on, under heads which are refreshingly new. A user-friendly, *gender-sensitive questionnaire is doing the rounds of over 152 million households to count a billion Indian people and map the changes in their lives in twentieth century's last decade. Carrying out a 19-day census in the world's largest democracy are 20 lakh enumerators, trudging through every city, town, village and hamlet in India with 23 questions in their bags – some of which never asked before.*

These ambitious new queries are designed as much to assess the needs of modern-day India as they are to show up the invisible, and the forgotten among our people. Ergo, questions ranging from mode of travel and distance to workplace, to those pertaining to the disabled members in one's families find new mention in Census 2001.

But there are some reservations about expanding the original brief of a census; a faithful headcount of the population. "Yes, they've been brave introducing many new questions this time around. But I do believe that a task of such mammoth proportions should remain as basic and simple as possible," says demographer Ashish Bose, "Too many questions only complicate matters and should be left for smaller surveys. A lot of bogus data might get collected." Saraswati Raju, professor of social geography at the Jawaharlal Nehru University, voices similar sentiments: "A Census is as good as its responses are. Public awareness of the census is anyway low. Include demands for new information, however, forward-looking in their purpose, and they usually make people suspicious, tight-lipped."

The family's changing lifestyle, meanwhile, is going to be gauged by a series of questions regarding specifics about educational qualification and how far its members have to travel to work. "On the basic level, such statistics help urban planning and structuring of employment schemes better. At yet another level, cross-interpretation of this data might throw up significant facts about how intense the issue of rural unemployment is, even linkages between, say for example, how more educated women travel farther to work," explains Raju.

The Hindustan Times, February 25, 2001

New Features of 2001 Census

— Chetan Chauhan

❀ *Collection of information about type of ailments regarding the physical challenged.*

❀ *Age at which the males got married.*

❀ *Educational qualifications of the citizens expanded to attending school, college, vocational institutes and literacy centres.*

❀ *Marginal labourers being asked if they are available for work. (Women helping their husbands in the business considered main workers, as contributing to Gross Domestic Product. Those working for less than six months during the preceding year considered marginal workers).*

❀ *Mode of transport, and the distance of work from residence.*

❀ *A 100-year 'ready reckoner' to*

calculate age of persons unable to give data of birth vis-à-vis Christian Calendar.

● A 100-year chart listing national and regional important events, as many relate their birth dates with such events.

Times of India, March 29, 2001
China's population growth slows

— Harvey Stockwin

Hong Kong: As Beijing announced on Wednesday that its latest Census has detailed a population of 1.265 billion, China remains by far the largest nation in the world and it may be even larger than it admits, when doubts about the accuracy of these statistics are taken into account. China's population is now 238 million larger than India's. But the figures are not strictly comparable since India's census figure of 1.027 billion was taken this month whereas China's was taken last year.

Also at first sight, the Chinese census shows that China has been remarkably successful in reducing its population growth. The population increased by only 132.2 million since the last census in 1990. The annual rate of population growth has been further reduced to 1.07 per cent, or by 11.7 percent in the decade under review.

These figures compare with the 1991-2001 increase in India of 181 million people at a population growth rate of 21.34 percent. So on present trends India still looks likely to overtake China in total population at

some point between 2025 and 2050, depending on which projection is accepted as valid.

But the Chinese statistics (and perhaps India's too) have to be treated with a degree of skepticism. There are several reasons for assuming that the figures announced in Beijing today could represent a considerable underestimate. Various unofficial estimates suggest the total could be between 1.4 and 1.6 billion.

First, the official Chinese target was to keep the total population under 2.3 billion for this census. That target has been met, even when the population of Hong Kong, Macau and Taiwan (which China claims but does not control) is also added in. The total all-china population is given as 1,295,300,000. As official Chinese statistics so often do, this meets the Chinese Communist party imposed target. Second, as a result of the CCP's effort to impose a one-child-per-couple limitation, there is almost certainly a good deal of under-reporting. Those who have transgressed and had more than one child may well conceal that information from census-takers.

Third, census-takers also have a reason to under-report family size. The local administration, which provide the census takers, all have their strict birth control quotas to meet. Only in some poorer rural areas is the one-child per couple stricture relaxed. The government stresses that census statistics are strictly confidential but may local officials may not be prepared to take the risk that this is actually so. Fourthly, there is the undoubted fact that China's economic reforms have helped to create a huge "floating" population of people who seek work far from their place of official domicile. Guesstimates put the number of internal migrants as high as 200 million. On the other hand it is possible that in some cases this phenomenon leads to some inadvertent double counting.

People

Population & Development Newsletter April 2001

Population on Back Burner

— *Usha Rai*

It is almost a year since the National Population Policy was announced and a National Population Commission set up. Several states have also announced population policies. Since the billionth baby Aastha was born in May, over 1.52 million more babies have come into the world without fuss.

Alas, after all the public pronouncements and setting up of umpteen groups to look at various aspects of population growth, the gargantuan machinery of the government has not really moved. Whatever happened to the Rs 100 crore population fund? Whatever happened to the empowered committee that was to zero in on the BIMARU states? What has happened to the fervour with which the Commission was set up?

Bihar, one of the BIMARU states, has still not announced a population policy. Now we have Jharkhand, Chhatisgarh and Uttaranchal, states carved out of the BIMARU block, that have not even begun thinking of population problems. In UP, as the last issue of People pointed out, the progress has been slow. The USAID funded States Innovations in Family Planning Strategies Agency (SIFPSA) is working in a limited area of the state.

On March 29 the Family Welfare Secretary, Mr A.R. Nanda, launched our website (www.reportingpeople.org). We hope to now reach out to more people who share our concerns on population and development issues.

III

CENSUS ENUMERATION

The Hindustan Times, February 16, 2001

At Rabri's house, one form wouldn't do

— A. K. Mishra
Patna, February 15

The enumeration job was an altogether different proposition at 1 Aney Marg, the official residence of the Bihar Chief Minister. The officials had to use two forms to fit in the details of all the 11 members of the family. On the contrary, the job was done in a jiffy at Raj Bhawan where Governor Vinod Chandra Pande, a bachelor, lives in solitude.

In fact, the time spent at Rabri Devi's residence extended far beyond the time routinely spent on the exercise. This did not come as a surprise considering the size of her family. As Laloo remarked, "Our list is rather long. But you all will have to bear with us."

Not surprisingly, two forms were required for recording the Census details of all the 11 members of the family. Only 10 names can be accommodated in one Census form. Even one form would have served the purpose had the Chief Minister's eldest daughter Misa Bharti who is married not been present when enumeration officials came visiting.

Interestingly, when the question as to who was the mukhiya (head) of the family was posed, Laloo replied, "She (Rabri) may be running the affairs of the State but at home I call the shots". Rabri chose to remain silent.

Laloo was, however, stumped when the enumerators sought to know his mother-tongue. Pat came the reply - Hindi. But when the enumerators sought to correct him the former Chief Minister mulled and said it was Bhojhpuri. He added that he was equally at ease with Maghi.

When asked about his educational qualification, Laloo said he had a law degree, and as a rejoinder added, "I could have argued my case but chose not to do so."

Sources said that the Yadav couple was quite forthcoming in its replies. They answered a total of 253 questions, 23 for each member of the family.

The Hindustan Times, February 16, 2001

Close encounter of the third kind

— Vikas Bhargava
Lucknow, February 15

Sex does matter, especially for an enumerator, who now has to have a preconceived idea of sexes for keeping government files free of anomaly. On day one of Census, when an enumerator in Lucknow, declared Tara the first 'man' among the eunuchs. "he" flew into a rage. For Tara, one thing was clear: her existence should not be linked to either of the sexes.

When the enumerator addressed the 52 year-old Tara as 'he', (s)he was shooed away. That's what Tara had to say: *Who are you to give me that status? We are no ordinary citizens. We are the watchdogs of the society and report to God about the human activities on the Earth.*

As if that was not enough, (s)he served the men on Census duty with a warning: *"Don't dare think of us to be ordinary citizens. We are the descendants of Shikhandi, the man responsible for the death of Bhishma Pitamah."*

Tara obdurately struck to the point: *"Has your government ever bothered to find out how I fend for myself despite being disabled?"* For the past 50 years, I have been struggling for survival. And you dare not talk about putting me on par with a man.*

Tara's belligerence had a telling effect on the counting process. The enumerator forgot to counting process. The enumerator forgot to ask all the questions (s)he has been trained to ask. The question that he had learnt during the training for Census work disappeared. So the enumerator barely managed to blurt out four questions against the total 23. *Q. How long have you been residing here? A. By birth. Q. What is your name? A. Tara. Q. What's your age? A. Between 50-54 years. Q. What is the method for earning? A. I have rented my house to a dry-cleaner who pays me a paltry sum as rent.*

The horrified enumerator wound up: *"Thank you, Mr. Tara! Please give your thumb impression on the Census sheet."* Tara kept complaining to the by-standers. And hurling choicest of abuses for being called a man. But, the poor enumerator was hardly at fault. *"We have been told during our training sessions to address the eunuchs as "Mr",* he explains. But, Tara's not convinced, and (s)he keeps mumbling as they pack up their stationery in the long cloth bag that the government has provided them with.

The Hindustan Times, February 10, 2001

Census begins, but elite 'cold - shoulder' enumerators

— HT Correspondent

Many enumerators, who got on their job with the beginning of Census 2001 today, had a tough time because of the alleged non-cooperative attitude of Delhi'ites. They were given a cold shoulder, specially by those staying in posh areas like Golf Links, Defence Colony and DLF Qutab Enclave.

Even as Delhi Lieutenant Governor Vijay Kapoor, who was enumerated at his residence today, appealed to the people to fully participate in this exercise of great importance, enumerators were turned away by people on flimsy grounds.

The Hindustan Times received calls from Census officials who claimed to have been "humiliated" by the public during the course of discharge of their duty. A woman enumerator said: "People said that they did not have the time to answer the questions and were too busy. We were turned away from several houses in Golf Links as we had 'disturbed' their afternoon nap. They said that we should come back later as they were having their lunch. It was a harassing experience. It will be really difficult to work if people continue to behave in such an arrogant manner throughout the remaining 19 day period of the Census operation".

Another official on condition of anonymity said that people did not cooperate even in filling up the two-page questionnaire. "When I asked a family if they were Hindu, the lady of the house rudely replied, 'dikhta nahin bindi lagai hai toh Hindu hi honge (Can't you see I am wearing a bindi so it's obvious that we are a Hindu family)."

Though people have been very helpful, but in certain areas, mostly upmarket localities, the response to the exercise was negative due to the high-handed attitude of the people, he added.

The Hindustan Times, February 16, 2001

Census enumerators face strange situations, yet go on

Locked flats greet officials at high-rise

— Rathin Das
Gandhinagar, February 15

....while the census operations are going on smoothly all over the State, the enumerators in certain areas of Ahmedabad are finding it difficult to go on with their job. With the 'prediction' of another round of earthquake between February 15 and 19 again gaining currency, many people from the high-rise buildings have abandoned their flats and gone elsewhere.

"We can enumerate people any day up to the official date of March 5", clarified State Census Commissioner Jayant Parimal, adding that it would not be a major problem. But, then, many of the multi-storeyed residents, who have gone to their native villages and towns, may get themselves counted there too.

Such double counting would be avoided as the enumerators have been telling the people not to register themselves at two places, he added.

Another problem for the Census operation in the quake-hit areas is the moving out of many migrant labourers to their native States like Bihar, Orissa and Uttar Pradesh. They would be either counted in their native villages or would be left out if they do not return here by the first week of March.

While no one is likely to gain or lose by undercounting or over-counting, some Government and public sector undertaking employees have a vested interest in Ahmedabad city population registering upwards of 50 lakh as this would give it the status of a mega city. This magic figure would entitle them to a higher House Rent Allowance and City Compensatory Allowance in the future.

The Times of India, February 23, 2001

Of won't-take-hubby's-name syndrome and other perils

— Abhijit Majumdar

The veterans and newcomers agree that while census work is a lot easier this time because of a better awareness campaign, there are still certain quirks. For instance, it is *easier to work faster in the slums than in upper class localities, where carrying out census work can be tedious and sometimes even perilous. "First, the watchman stops you at the gate. Then, you encounter the watchdog." says a supervisor. "A man in Chennai was recently arrested for setting his dog on the census staff."....Assistant charge officer P. S. Pawar narrates the next quirk. "Most Indian women simply refuse to utter their husband's name. And that can take the census for a toss, unless you are extremely persuasive or come back when the husband is around."*

New parameters in the census form this year, like disability and fertility, have shattered the rules of routine query. Since categories like 'lula pagla' are downright insensitive and are unlikely to elicit a response, skilled enumerators adopt a circuitous conversation technique.

Parents who have breached the hum-do-hamare-do benchmark are often extremely defensive and hostile to queries on the number of children they have. "The highest I have come across this time is a couple with 12 children," says an enumerator.

Meanwhile, Dr. Khergamkar's team has moved onto the next house. A census staffer says proudly, "Yesterday, we interviewed Amitabh Bachchan. Tomorrow's Sunil Gavaskar house. The Arthur Road jail next."

The Hindustan Times, February 25, 2001

Woes of an honorary duty
Not everyone's forthcoming about their domestic arrangements, find the census officials

— *Chetan Chauhan and Sridhar Krishnaswamy*

A woman is not willing to disclose whether her son was born to her or was adopted. The enumerator insists. She rings up the Census Control Room to complain. Another Census enumerator argues in vain with a senior citizen, who wants the harassment meted out to him by his sons to be recorded. The senior citizen flies into a rage and tells the enumerator to leave. Then, he calls the Control Room. A retired Army officer shoots several posers at a hapless enumerator. How will the Census operations help a common man? Has it provided relief in the past? If yes, how? The retired officer laughs and rings up the control room, asking the census official to first educate the enumerator. and bangs the phone down.

Of course, some are genuine calls to dispel a misinterpretation.

Sometimes, the landlords are not even willing to give us the exact number of people residing in his building," said the Director of Delhi Census, Bimla Jingdar.

Slum clusters were another problem area for some enumerators. "We have a tough time telling them we are not from MCD's Slum Department. Fear of being uprooted makes them clam on basic questions like the year of their arrival in Delhi, and places where they have resided earlier," an enumerator said.

There are other problems as well. Subletting of flats is illegal in government colonies. Obviously, the reception is hostile in such cases. *"But this sort of behaviour is not just limited to one type of residential area. In many places, we're not allowed to enter because the head of the family has left for work,"* said an exasperated teacher of a government school in South Delhi.

Many others also treat us as a nuisance and talk to us rudely. They ask us either to come later or tell us bluntly not to disturb them," added another teacher.

"There's no way of checking what we're being told. So, we write whatever data is given," was the wry comment of most of the teacher-enumerators.

The Week, February 25, 2001

Census: Taking Stock

It's more than just a head count

— Palash Kumar

Mr. Raj Kumar Kaushik, a school teacher who is part of the Census India 2001 team, went to the Green Park residence of M. D. Sharma, a security guard told him to wait. *"Saab's children are leaving for school,"* he said. For the next 20 minutes, Kaushik watched as the children were driven off in different cars. The guard then returned to tell Kaushik that the children's grandmother had asked him to return the next day as everybody was *"very busy"*. *"This was my second visit to this house,"* said

Kaushik, *"On my first, I was just told to get lost. This is the problem we face in some areas particularly in south Delhi."*

If some find locked doors and uncooperative occupants, others recount stories of how they were chased by dogs and shooed away by gardeners and security guards. *"But some people are nice and even offer us tea,"* said Harinder Toor, a supervisor with six enumerators working under her, covering south Delhi.

The exercise has been particularly tough for women, who form a major chunk of the census team. Many are already complaining about the rigorous schedule. Saroj Sahrawat, a teacher, leaves home at 7.45 a.m. and often returns late in the evening. *"I have small children and it is difficult to manage the census work, school and household work,"* she said. *"It is not such a good idea to involve a large number of women, who have their commitments home,"* said Harinder Toor. *"Also if someone asks them to come in the night, they have to take their husbands along."*

The Hindustan Times, March 2, 2001

Counted at last in India's bursting billion

— Chetan Chauhan

There is something for the 70 year-old homeless Ranpal Singh of Uttar Pradesh to cheer about. For the first time after Independence he was counted as part of the over 1 billion population of the country. So has been the 48 year old Ramesh Hanumanth Rao Kadam of Hyderabad.

They are among the thousands of people for whom Delhi's streets have been the abode for years. Of different hues and colours, they live together irrespective of the Capital's swinging weather. On the nights of February 27 and 28, the enumerators took pains to get them enlisted in the 2001 Census.

Vagabond Ranpal Singh reached Delhi about 45 years ago, after being thrown out of his house for his bad habits. "Since then I have been putting up on the streets near Kashmere Gate and Chandni Chowk. I don't remember whether someone ever approached me for my personal details," he said, adding he has no clue about his wife and children.

When the enumerators woke him up last night, it was a shock for him. "I thought they will throw me out of this place," he commented. But in the end, he slept at peace.

Kamla Devi, a Nepali, believes that her adopted family may find mention in the Census even though her children threw her into the wilderness five years ago. Mohammad Latif of Hardoi, UP who now looks after her....was very happy for getting a mother, officially. "I have just bought her bangles," Latif said, as the enumerators questioned his 'adopted' mother.

Like the others, Hanumanth Rao was being enumerated for the first time. He reached Delhi in 1970 looking for work. An year later, he lost both his legs in a rail accident while saving a

girl. And since then Delhi streets are his first home. He has no clue about his family back home though he remembers them often.

However, unlike the rich, the homeless believe that the Census can bring a sea change for them. "Atalji may frame a policy for our betterment and we may get houses," Rao said. An enthusiasm which is shared by many.

At midnight, it was a job well done by the enumerators. "We have to convince them first that the Census will not evict them and a lot of probing has to be done. Some of them want to be enumerated twice and some want to evade it. Dealing with them is a tough job," an enumerator said.

Another enumerator learnt this, when his pocket was picked at Chandni Chowk.

The Times of India, March 2, 2001

Census 2001 ignores the homeless ...or prefers to treat them roughly

— Radhika D Srivastava

A survey by a Times of India team in the wee hours of Thursday revealed that many of the homeless had not been visited by an enumerator. What was worse was that many spots which serve as a shelter for such persons were missed altogether.

Despite Banthia's instruction the fact of the matter was that after midnight, there was hardly any enumerator out on the job. If a spot was not covered till 1 pm, there was not much chance of anybody arriving there later. For, each enumerator had been allotted only one area where he was supposed to begin work by 9 pm.

Some main areas left out are Shraddhanand Marg which has been covered only partly and Subhash Park opposite Red Fort.

In this park close to 100 persons sleep in the open. Around 11 pm. rickshaw-puller Raju sat in the park, with a quilt around him. "*Koi janganna wale aye the (did any Census person come here)?*" he was asked. Raju was quiet for a moment and then he said, "*Janganna, woh kya hota hai (what is Census)?*" he asked blankly.

Just outside Jama Masjid, which was still a hub of activity late in the night, sat Salim. This 40 year old man huddled near a big *patila* (utensil) placed on three bricks. "*I am boiling mutton. I will do this all night,*" he said.

Salim said he sells biryani (a preparation of cooked rice and mutton) through the day and as a result he gets time to prepare it only during the night.

"*I normally cook three kg of mutton and then boil the rice in the early hours of the morning. You see, I have been sitting here all the time. But no enumerator has come,*" he said.

Salim is not happy that the enumerators have not come to him, "*I could have given them all the correct answers as I am not a angootha chaap (illiterate),*" he said wryly.

....or prefers to treat them roughly

Under the Hanuman temple flyover behind Red Fort Netai sleeps with a dirty sheet wrapped around him from head to toe. He is a leper and his right hand has no fingers. Home for him is the traffic triangle under the flyover.

Around midnight, a census official walks up to the sleeping figures and gives Netai a kick. Netai wakes up and pulls down the sheet from his face. "*What is your name? how old are you?*" the questions come fast. Another official grimaced, "*Bahut ganda hai, saala*" (the idiot is very dirty). Netai is confused, he is still rubbing his eyes. After a while he begins to answer, the voice no more than a whisper.

In Chawri Bazaar, Chandni Chowk, pushcarts are lined on both sides of the road. On each one there is a man sleeping, curled up, covered completely. There are a couple of enumerators who have emerged on the scene after being told that journalists were taking stock of the Census work.

None of the labourers sleeping on the carts have been enumerated. The officials quickly begin work, "*Oye uth, khara ho ja (wake up, stand up).*" shouts an enumerator as he rudely pulls back the sheet from one sleeping figure.

Torches are flashed on his face and Rehman wakes up, blinking "*Nam bata apna, hum police wale hain (tell us your name, we are from the police),*" the official says as others around him laugh loudly. The poor man is speechless.

In the municipal corporation night shelter at Delhi Gate, none of this rudeness will do as senior officials from the government are present.

But the attitude prevails. Even though shoes are not allowed inside the area where the homeless men sleep on the floor, the entire entourage goes in, footwear in place.

The Hindustan Times, March 3, 2001
Row over Census officials' claim

— HT Correspondent
Ghaziabad

Controversy has arisen over the Nagar Nigam's claim for having completed the process of census successfully within the stipulated time.

The Nagar Nigam officials claim that they have completed almost 99 per cent of the census task. But the truth is that none of these officials has till date visited several areas. They have, in fact, submitted cooked up figure to the census office.

Keeping in view of complaints, the District Magistrate has announced that necessary inquiry would be made in all the wards of the city.

But it has come to notice that the staff deputed to collect data in Lajjapuri did not visit the area. A similar complaint has come from Valmiki Kunj. Besides, the residents of Lohia Nagar, Vivekanand Nagar, Kavi Nagar, Raj Nagar, Vijay Nagar, Shastri Nagar and Lajpat Nagar say that the Census staff has filled in the required data according to the list prepared by them earlier.

In Hapur also, the census staff did not reach more than five dozen houses in Ward No. 25. The cases in Modi Nagar are no different. The District Magistrate Indrajit Verma told mediapersons today that five special squads had been constituted for verifying the complaints.

Outlook, March 5, 2001
Sensus and Sensibility

— Soma Wadhwa

Many who have faced the enumerators allege that they are in a clumsy rush to finish with the job and are generally disinterested. When single Delhi-based public relations manager Amrita Sengupta told an enumerator that she shared a flat with an unmarried friend, an embarrassed enumerator avoided any further questions and left. Chennai-born advertising professional Ravi Venkataraman was asked by another headcounter whether his birthplace was located in West Bengal. People have also found many enumerators ignorant and insensitive while asking questions. Mostly full time government school teachers saddled with this side assignment, the enumerators crib about the travails of having to perform a task they are so ill-prepared for. "I've had people refusing to tell me how many sons they have saying 'Nazar lag jayegi' (I'll cast an evil eye on them)." protests Renu Kumar, a teacher who has the difficult task of counting villagers in Pasonda village in Ghaziabad. With not more than six hours of training, she barely manages to cope with the aggression that she meets with when she asks people how many dead children they've had. "Women don't come out and men don't care. The majority don't know and don't want to know about the census. They ask why the government is so interested in counting them and their children suddenly?" Because they are the critical numbers in the arithmetic of welfare.

The Pioneer, February 19, 2001

A night time Census

— Karuna M John

The two million enumerators walking the country will soon look under staircases, flyovers, temples, mandaps, railway platforms and huge pipes for the 'houseless households' in the dead of the night on Feb. 28.

Even those who are not Indian citizens, including the approximate 16 lakh Bangladeshis in the capital alone, will be counted as part of the Indian population.

The Pioneer, February 22, 2001

Army will have its own Census

— Karuna M John

"The Army itself assists in the enumeration of those posted at the fronts," said Mr. Banthia. The men and women in uniform will be enumerated at the place they are stationed. However, the civilian enumerators will keep away.

The Hindustan Times, March 10, 2001

Car, Cellphone owners on homeless list

— Rathin Das

The findings of the first census of the millennium are likely to surprise many as far as Gujarat is concerned.

This is because many middle and upper middle class people have been rendered homeless after the January 26 earthquake.

"Census rules stipulate who-so-ever is found homeless at the time of enumeration should be counted as such, irrespective of whatever assets he might have elsewhere," State Census Commissioner Jayant Parimal told the Hindustan Times.

The migrant labourers living at construction sites are also counted among the homeless, although they might have a house at their native place, Parimal said.

The Census has been suspended in the worst-hit Kutch, three talukas of Rajkot and one taluka of Jamnagar districts. Otherwise, the figures for homeless would have shown an extraordinary increase as thousand continue to live in temporary shelters in Kutch.

The Census form has three categories - house, institution and homeless - for enumeration.

The Times of India, February 23, 2001

Headcount rendered partial by quake

— Aniruddha Tripathi

January 26 Gujarat earthquake has not only devastated thousands of families in the state, it has also rendered a setback to the Census operations now underway in the country. The districts of Kutch, Rajkot and Jamnagar have been left out, making the exercise less than comprehensive for the third time in the 130 year history of the Great Indian Census.

In an unbroken series since 1872, only twice before have Census operations been suspended in parts of the country; Assam in 1981 and Jammu and Kashmir in 1991. The operations were not suspended even in 1941, in the midst of World War -II, or for that matter in 1951, soon after Partition.

IV

CASTE

The Indian Express, February 16, 2001

First victim of census caste anomalies is country's First Citizen

Gaping holes in format will affect data

— Sankarshan Thakur

....Narayanan is a Scheduled Caste (SC) from the Paravan community in Kerala which is unlisted in SC lists in the Capital for the simple reason that Paravans, like many other SC communities in various parts of the country have no recorded social history in or around Delhi.

A senior Census official said...."quite apart from his own case, President Narayanan appears worried about the larger implications of insufficient methods. He appeared disturbed about the possibility of the current enumeration process ending up offering grossly erroneous data about caste categories and their location."

One way, Census Office sources said, of finding way around the problem with identifying SCs is that enumerators should carry comprehensive all-India lists of communities available with the Union Public Service Commission (UPSC) which conducts recruitment examination with special reservation for SCs and STs on an all-India basis.

In the "People of India" report of Anthropological Survey of India, probably the most comprehensive study of the country's sociological structure, there are 751 Scheduled Caste communities in India spread over all states other than Arunachal Pradesh, Nagaland, Mizoram and Meghalaya. Among the states that have the highest number of SC communities are Uttar Pradesh (88), Orissa (67), Madhya Pradesh (53) and West Bengal (49). The four major southern states together have 191 SC communities.

However, few of these are static communities. With political empowerment and social emancipation (access to education, in particular) mobility has been on the increase; there has been substantial, though unregistered and uncharted, migration of Scheduled Caste away from traditional roots.

....The Nonias, an SC community peculiar to Bihar and parts of Uttar Pradesh, have migrated to urban centres like Delhi in large numbers in search of employment but are not listed. All these could now face the possibility of their caste identities being thrown into anonymity by Census 2001.

The Indian Express, February 27, 2001

Castes and religions out of the box

There are serious problems over enumerating SCs and STs in the Census

— B. K. Roy Burman

The Indian Express had reported that President K. R. Narayanan, who belongs to the Scheduled Caste (Paravan) of Kerala, could not record his caste status in Delhi during the current Census operations (February 16).

Under Article 341 of the Indian Constitution, specific SCs are notified in respect of specific states and no fresh inclusion or exclusion can be made except through invoking the authority of Parliament. As Paravan is not notified as SC in Delhi, a person belonging to the Paravan caste cannot enjoy the benefits or rights due to SCs provided by the government of Delhi, just as Naga from Nagaland cannot enjoy similar benefits.

The Director of Census of the National Capital Territory of Delhi is apparently under a legal constraint to enumerate a Paravan as a SC or a Naga as a ST in Delhi. But it requires to be considered whether a Paravan loses his SC or a Naga his ST status, during his sojourn in Delhi and can be denied claims to benefits provided by the government for such categories. As far as I remember, in 1952 to 1953, the issue was examined by the ministry of law and it was held that a SC or ST person did not lose the status conferred by the Constitution during his sojourn in some other state where his caste or tribe was not scheduled.

There is a practical side to the issue. In the fifties and sixties, the number of SC, ST persons sojourning outside their respective states was presumably insignificant. For policy decisions at the all-India level, it perhaps did not matter much if a small number was enumerated in the category of the general population. But, today with the spread of education, the green revolution, the displacement of large population in the wake of hydel and other projects, and so on, the number of sojourners has gone up sharply.

For instance, it is reported that a few hundred thousand tribal workers from Jharkhand are sojourning in Punjab, Haryana and western Uttar Pradesh as agricultural labourers. Similarly, migrations of SC communities of Chhatisgarh, parts of Uttar Pradesh and Rajasthan to industries in Maharashtra and Gujarat is reported. If such sojourners are not enumerated as ST or SC, as the case may be there will be a substantial undercount of such categories of the population at the all India level.

For instance, while according to the 1991 Census, the SCs and STs are 16 per cent and 8 percent of the population, reservations for them in government jobs is to the tune of 15 per cent and 7.5 per cent respectively. But if, on enumeration of the sojourners, the percentages of SC and ST go up by one or two per cent, more adjustments will have to be made.

It may be argued that by allowing enumeration of persons as SCs and STs in the states where the respective communities are not listed under the provision of the Constitution, the Census Commissioner would be overstepping his authority. This can be avoided by including a column in the Census slip indicating the state or UT where the caste or tribe to which the person belongs is an SC or ST.

The Indian Express, February 14, 2001

Christian Council Smells politics in Census Operations

The All India Christian Council has decided to take legal action over what it calls "a blatant attempt to communalise the entire Census operation".

The council has said it is apprehensive about the Schedule Caste category where a person has only three choices: Hinduism, Sikhism and Buddhism. "A Scheduled Caste.... is not allowed to claim that he belongs to the Muslim, Christian, animist, indigenous, agnostic or no-faith categories," said council.

According to the council, to deny a Scheduled Caste person the religion of their choice violated the Constitutional provision of Freedom of Faith.

"The punishment of caste transcends religion. The government took away all religion except Hinduism, Sikhism and Buddhism," said John Dayal, secretary-general of the council. "Ideally a person should be given the freedom to chose the religion." he added and said that since the Census had already started they would settle for Schedule Castes not being asked their religion at all.

When asked about the controversy, director, Census operations for Delhi, Bimla Jindgar said, "Only these three religions have a caste system."

Dayal says that they have received complaints from different parts of the country over the way the Census was being carried out. In Madhya Pradesh allegedly there are cases where tribals are not being allowed to register themselves as Christians. While in Tamil Nadu and Andhra Pradesh, Dalits are not being allowed to register their religion. In the form under Q9 it says that Scheduled Tribes can be from any religion, while under Q8 it says "Schedule Castes can be only among Hindus, Sikhs and Buddhists".

The council has served a legal notice to the registrar general over the Census. They also might move the Supreme Court over the issue. The council has already made a formal complaint to the National Commission for Minorities and has written to the president, prime minister, chief election commissioner and the National Human Rights Commission.

The Indian Express, February 27

Risk of losing ST sops fails to lure Dangs tribals away from their faith

— Tanushree Chatterjee

The Kukna tribesmen of the Dangs turned Christians a decade ago and no privileges assured them as members of scheduled tribes (STs) by the Constitution will make them change their mind.

They are determined to be counted as christie in the ongoing census. This would mean forfeiting the privileges given to them for being scheduled tribe members.

Till the last census, these

tribesmen were unconcerned about which religious category they were put under. But the attacks on missionaries about two years ago have prompted them to show their loyalty for those who risked their lives for the tribals' welfare.

Raisinh Puar, a Dangs tribal, said: "Amme Hindu christie chiye (we are Hindu Christians)." He converted about 27 years ago. Raisinh proudly said: "Both my daughters are married to Hindu Christies and they are happy."

Tell him there is no Hindu Christian category in the Census form and Puar looks least bothered. "If there is no such category, then we will prefer to be counted as Christians."

He adds: "There is sudden concern about which religion I want to belong to. It's simple. As I follow Christianity, I will be counted as one. Earlier, I would not have cared much about which religion they put me under. But since the missionaries were attacked sometime ago, and they have withstood that bravely, it is time for me to show my loyalty towards them."

Gulabbhai Motiabhai Puar too voices a similar opinion. He said: "These missionary people came to us when none of the government agencies thought about us. We were leading a life of abysmal poverty.

"But with the missionaries educating our children and working for our welfare, our lives have changed for the better. So how can we deny all that the faith has given us."

Motiabhai added: "We now have pucca houses. Until 10 years ago, all we had were thatched houses of dried leaves and twigs. All this prosperity is recently acquired and all with Lord Jesus's blessings."

Ramsinh Puar, another tribal, said: "These so-called benefits (for STs) that are supposed to be given us have never reached us. So why should we leave what we have in anticipation of what will never reach us. The state never bothered to find out about our welfare or work towards it."

The residents of the area hail from the kukna tribe but now a large number have left behind the animism faith they followed and have not joined the folds of Christianity.

Jesus' and Virgin Mary's calendars and posters on the walls of the tribal households show their belief in Christianity. Sureshbhai Gavit, a driver at Jeevan Jot, the local missionary school, said: "We are Christians and there is no denying that. Even if we are denied privileges like reservations in government jobs and higher education, it means nothing to us." Gavit's family adopted the faith some 15 years ago.

It is at Gavit's sprawling courtyard in front of his brick house that the Sunday mass is held for all villagers and the sevak who conducts it comes from Ahwa.

The entire affair of loyalty to a faith here resembles a football fan's devotedness to a club. One brother may be a staunch Christian and the other a devout Hindu. Religion, however, does not come in the way of a cordial relationship because a tribal's religion here is a matter of choice and not of force.

The Hindustan Times, February 15, 2001

Christian tribals being denied ST tag

— *Udayan Namboodiri*

India's 24 million Christians – about one-third of whom are tribals – already sense discrimination against them with the country's census process underway.

There are widespread anger over the census' exclusion of converted Christians from the category of Scheduled Castes (SCs). And according to latest reports, tribals are not being included in the Scheduled Tribe (ST) category, despite the fact that there's no religion bar.

The Christian community's angst at being excluded from the SC group is an old one. The demand for inclusion of Christian Dalits in it is also an old one.

The Census form, in its eighth question, asks whether a citizen is in the SC category and puts in parenthesis the clause that only Hindus, Sikhs and Buddhists can be recognised as such. But in the ninth question – whether a person belongs to the ST category – it is clearly spelt out that "ST can be from any religion".

Says John Dayal, president of the All-India Christian Council, "There are ambiguities in the Census Enumerators' Manual, which are either being exploited intentionally or quite by accident".

Each enumerator is given lists of recognised STs. If a person does not belong to a tribe on the list, he cannot be included. Also, an enumerator has the discretion to "investigate" when he has doubts of misrepresentation.

Quite often, says Father William of Jhabua district of Madhya Pradesh, the poor tribal is never asked whether he is from the ST or not. This may be widespread across many of the "mixed" regions of the country where tribals and non-tribals are present in more or less equal measure.

In "endemic" areas like the northeastern States, Chhattisgarh, Jharkhand and parts of Orissa, West Bengal, Bihar and Himachal Pradesh, it would be difficult for enumerators to hedge the fact that a person is a tribal.

The heart of the matter is the bias against Christian Mundas, Oraos, Kharias, Santhals and other tribals. Because they are generally better educated and their standard of living is relatively higher than non-Christians, the same discrimination which works against Christian Dalits is applied to them too.

Also, the tendency to brand all non-Christians as Hindus is also perceived as objectionable by the Church since most of them practice indigenous faiths without the involvement of scriptures.

Father Anand Jojo, assistant secretary of Catholic Bishops Conference of India (CBCI), says the community has a long-standing dispute with the Government over identification of Christians as tribals. John Dayal says, "A blatant attempt has been made to communalise the entire Census operation".

The Hindustan Times, February 16, 2001

Jats sore over exclusion from OBC category

— Chetan Chauhan

Delhi's 10 lakh strong Jat community is fuming over not being granted the status of Other Backward Classes in the ongoing Census enumeration. .....Jats constitute majority of the population in Rajasthan and Haryana apart from having a considerable presence in Punjab. The inclusion of Jats in the OBC category was the main election issue during the last Assembly elections in Delhi and Rajasthan. Irrespective of the party, the Jats had vowed to vote for the party, which accepted their demand. The Congress won the election in both the states. Finally, they succeeded in getting themselves in the OBC category.

Delhi Minister for Development Dr. Yoganand Shastri was caught totally unaware on the issue. "I will speak to the officials about it. We have given them the status of OBCs and they should not be deprived of this by the Census officials," he said.

The Tribune, February 26, 2001

Census sees change of heart among Bagris

— Gurpreet Singh

The ongoing census has witnessed a change of heart among the Hindi speaking population of Punjab villages along the Haryana border where anti-Punjab sentiments had prevailed on account of Sikh militancy.

Earlier, the Hindi population of this village wanted the villages to be merged with Haryana as it is just a kilometre away. Political parties of Haryana had tried to exploit their sentiments.

Kandu Khera, which was supposed to serve as a corridor between Haryana and Abohar-Fazilka towns of Punjab, has 500 houses, including 150 belonging to "Bagri" families. The Bagri population now prefers staying in Punjab on account of free power facility and adequate irrigation waters.

Mr. Hanuman Parshad said that Sikh militancy was the reason why most Bagris wanted to go to Haryana. "Our outlook has changed now. We prefer staying in Punjab that offers free power for farming." "Moreover, being a part of the Punjab Chief Minister's Assembly constituency, Kandu Khera is being well looked after," he added.

V

SEX WORKERS?

The Hindustan Times, February 16, 2001

Thieves, sex workers labelled beggars

— *Chetan Chauhan*

Smugglers may politely describe their vocation as 'import-export business'. Thieves, petty or otherwise, may say they are for a more equitable distribution of wealth. Commercial sex workers may claim that the world's oldest profession is also a noble profession. But Census authorities, who are categorising them as beggars, obviously think otherwise.

But there's discrimination here too. While petty thieves, robbers, cheats and smugglers are being dismissed as beggars, the big guns – those accused or convicted of heinous crimes like murder and rape – are being counted as criminals. Only newcomers, who have been in Tihar for just a few days, are being exempted from the beggar category.

Enumerators tasked with counting the Tihar's 11,000 inmates have been directed by the Directorate of Census to list them as beggars, which in official parlance means they are 'non-workers'.

When asked why criminals and commercial sex workers were being termed 'beggars', Delhi Census Director Ms. Bimla Jangdar said that it was because their method of making money was not legitimate. "It is because of their illegal activities that they are being listed as beggars. Same is the case with prostitutes. If we list them as members of the 'working class', it will mean a blow to those who earn money by hard labour," she added.

Identifying criminals and prostitutes under the general category of beggars may not serve the purpose of conducting Census, which provides a wide database for various government and non-government departments. "At the end of the day, we may find that India has no criminals but a large force of beggars," quipped one official.

The Hindustan Times, March 6, 2001

Sex workers protest Government move of enlisting them as beggars

— *HT Correspondent*

For the 30 odd sex workers who assembled outside the Census Commissioner's office, this afternoon's protest rally was tagged as a 'fight for identity'.

The government had, the sex workers said, "wrongfully and illogically" categorised them as beggars in the new census.

"It is not fair. Yes I am a sex worker. But that is no excuse to ignore me and everyone else like me," said Nasreen, a sex worker originally hailing from Karnataka. "We sell our body for a living. We do not, repeat do not, beg."

Nasreen and the rest of the group got a taste of government apathy when a couple of Census workers visited GB Road kothas six days ago, many of whom, allege the sex workers, had never even bothered to walk up stairs to the kothas and speak to them.

"Those who bothered to meet us for the census were driven away as they spend more time asking us awkward questions. Why should any of us answer these questions when they were anyway treating us as beggars," added Mumtaz, who has been living in Delhi for the past 14 years.

Accompanying the sex workers in their protest were activists of the All India Shakti Vahini Foundation and activist Nafisa Ali, both of whom are credited with having extensively worked for the uplift of these women. "This year has been declared as the year of the women by our Prime Minister. Meaning no woman should be discriminated on the basis of her caste, creed or kind of work she does. Then what kind of a label is this (beggar)? For a progressive nation like ours, the Census work undertaken should be intelligent and rationale in its approach. It is fair if these sex-workers were called workers, instead of demeaning them so," Ms. Ali said. "They must have an identity of their own."

"Please do not disclose our identity," a sex worker was heard pleading with a photographer. "We hide our faces because our children back in the villages do not know about our work. But do give us a chance to better ourselves. We do not want anybody to deride us as the government has in

this census." They wanted to be heard and understood. Not exposed.

The Hindustan Times, April 18, 2001
Sex workers come out to prove their artistic talent

Singing and dancing has been their way of life for generations. Labelled simply as sex workers today, tawaifs and artists from several states came together in the Capital to participate in an annual festival where they showcased their talents.

The two-day Guria Mahotsav organised over the weekend sought to promote the talent of these women handed down over generations. "We are artistes and want to be appreciated for our talent. But today we are often referred to as common sex workers which pains us very deeply," said Roshanara, a singer from Jaunpur, in Uttar Pradesh.

Most of them seemed to be reluctant to admit that they had to service their "patrons" and "fans" even while being trained artistes. "We may not be able to marry, but we can seek the support and patronage of a respectable person. That person may not lend his name to my children and may leave me after a while but that still does not mean that I am akin to a sex worker," said Aruna from Muzzafarpur in Bihar.

However, Neelam and several other women admitted that the men who married them often left them after a few years, burdened with children, and they were forced to return to the kothas where they resumed their singing and dancing.

"Guria is an NGO which organi-

ses this annual festival in the Capital to encourage the artiste in these women. We want them to take pride in their art and build their confidence to participate in such performances which could become their financial mainstay. That way they would be less dependent on prostitution for their livelihood," explained Ajit Singh of Guria.

"The popularity of traditional music and folk songs is fast dwindling. These women are the keepers of folk music that has evolved over centuries. Encouraging the artiste in them ensures that this music survives," felt Ajit Singh.

Not only women from Madhya Pradesh, Karnataka, Maharashtra, Gujarat and Bihar participated, but even children of sex workers took part in the festival. The programme included, dadra, ghazal, qawwali, Rai dance, nautanki, dramas and other folk dances. Some of the dramas they put up dealt with the problems of their everyday life such as harassment of the police, poverty, religious oppression and health problems.

Having got a chance to perform in the Capital, most of the artistes want to come back, and many do, swelling the number of the artistes in the festival every successive year.

The Tribune, February 26, 2001

Female work figures 'puzzling'

— PPS Gill

When did women in Punjab not record their participation as "workers" in economically productive activities on either farms or in family enterprises during Census 1991? The official definition of "work" was any physical or mental activity, including supervision or direction, paid or unpaid. One could be either the "main" or "marginal" worker.

In a state like Punjab, where agriculture is the mainstay of the economy and the lifeline of the people, the low participation of women is puzzling. In fact, besides playing a major role as "workers" supervising home and farm work, females in Punjab villages, as per Punjab Agricultural University studies, have been playing an increasingly important role even in "decision making" at home. Therefore, their contribution can neither be ignored nor denied. It was, however, for the enumerators to extract information from village women who are "workers", though unpaid but acting as key operators.

....at least 1,300 odd villages (out of a total of 12,428) not a single woman was reported to be a worker. Out of these in 900 villages, where the total female population was up to 100, not a single female worker, main or marginal, was reported. A similar trend was witnessed in scores of other villages despite a high percentage of female population.

Punjabi men and women are known for their entrepreneurial spirit, hard work and resilience. Yet the low female work participation rate remains a puzzle. Will Census 2001 solve the riddle?

VI

REPORTING THE FIRST RESULTS
OF THE 2001 CENSUS
(Provisional Figures)

The Indian Express, March 29, 2001

Census: You are living in a city of 13.8 million

The provisional results of Census in the Capital indicates more people, higher literacy rate and the highest density of population in the country. The city now is home to 1.34 per cent of the country's population: 13,782,976.

In absolute terms, the population of Delhi has increased by 4.36 million since the 1991 census. Among the nine districts, North-East has the highest population growth rate of 62.52 per cent in the last decade. South-West district recorded a growth rate of 61.29 per cent. The population growth in the North, East and New Delhi districts has been less than that of Delhi while Central district registered negative growth.

Delhi tops the charts in the density of population for category. The density has been calculated at 9,294 per square kilometre. At last count, in the 1991 census, it was 6,352 per sq. km. At the national level, the density of population is 324 persons per square kilometre, much lower than the Delhi number. Among the nine districts, the highest density has been recorded in the North East district (29,395 per sq. km). South-West district had the lowest at 4,165 per sq. km.

The literate percentage has gone up from 75.29 in the 1991 census to 81.82 per cent. On the whole, the literacy rate in Delhi has gone up by 6.53 per cent. The literacy rate of males has risen by 5.36 per cent, from 82.01 in 1991 to 87.37 this census. Female literacy rate has shown a growth rate of 8.01 per cent. The sex ratio is the only disappointing statistic. The number of females per 1000 males has dropped to 821 as against 827 in 1991. The sex ratio at the national level is 933 women for 1000 men.

Outlook, April 9, 2001

Stasis behind Statistic

— Soma Wadhwa

The first round of results by the Census Commission makes for a very optimistic picture. But halt the celebrations for a moment

We've known we are a billion people for some time now. Now we know for sure. At the last count on March 1, 2001, we were 1,027,015,247. So says the first round of results released by India's Census Commission last week.

And the 184 page long Provisional Population Totals does more than just record this humongous headcount of the second most populous nation on earth. It notches up many more numbers; numbers that speak of the quality of our life, our achievements and failures. Snapshot statistics that bring us heartening news of India's declining population growth rate, her growing literacy, improving sex ratio. Along with disturbingly dwindling numbers that point to the continuing decline in our girl child's fortunes. Also, the spectre of a free fall in key social indicators accompanied by a continuing rise in population in some north Indian states.

All this, however, is at a glance. Demographic arithmetic is already adding up these fresh census numbers to draw quite another picture from them.

Even as the Census Commission flashes the good news of a fall in the decadal growth rate in our population by 2.5 per cent points – the sharpest decline since Independence – experts are wary of giving it their unqualified approval. "The census count is 14.63 million people more than we had projected for the year 2000. So actually we have grown more than we expected to," says Delhi-based demographer Mahendra Premi, who was a member of the Technical Group of Population Projection appointed by the Planning Commission in 1996. Besides, the current annual rate is still too high to expect early stabilisation of population.

Had the family welfare programme been as successful as expected, observes demographer Ashish Bose, the growth rate should have been even lower than it is. Says he: "We're adding about 50,000 people to our population every day. There's little sense in celebrating a decline in growth rate, and that too one that falls short of expectation."

The narrowing gap in the country's sex ratio may be good tidings, but it is also tempered by some sobering facts. The number of women per 1,000 men has gone up to 933 from 927 over the last decade. "But this is no reason for complacency. There is sufficient reason to be sceptical about this improvement in figures," says Rameshwar Prasad Tyagi, managing editor of Demography India, a publication brought out by the Indian Association for the Study of Population. Pointing out that the '81 Census had recorded 934 women per 1,000 men, Tyagi says that the '91 census most likely undercounted women at 927: "We are quite probably comparing this decade's figures with artificially low numbers of the 1991 census and overemphasising an improvement in gender balance. Compare this time's 933 with 1981's 934 and we have, in fact, lost some women."

Premi agrees and points out that the latest figure actually remains far below even what it was a century ago - 972 in 1902. The current increase in the numbers of women to men, he says, might also be because life expectancy for women has been edging ahead of that for men in the 1990s. So, because women are living longer now, there are more of them to be counted this time. "But for the real story of gender imbalance in India," says Premi, "look at the figures that speak of our vanishing girl child."

This census has indeed registered an alarming decline in the number of girl children in the below-seven year age group. Only 927 girls per 1,000 boys against 945 girls in 1991. "Sex determination tests, gender selective abortions, amniocentesis, foeticide, infanticide... all seems to have taken their toll," says Saraswati Raju, professor of social geography at the Jawaharlal Nehru University. Take away social malices and there should be more women than men in the overall sex ratio, she contends. "Statistically, in most parts of the world, more boys are born than girls," says Raju. "But it evens out because boys have a higher mortality rate, plus women usually have higher longevity. The new number in the 2001 census speak of horrific prejudices that aren't giving our girls a chance to survive and that is a matter of great concern."

Significantly, and paradoxically, experts like Raju are finding an "uncomfortable fit" between growing literacy and diminishing girl children. Himachal Pradesh, for instance, has made an impressive improvement in literacy rates but has also seen a decline in its sex ratio. "This speculative, but education could be even teaching us how to access modern methods of foeticide," says Raju.

Some statistical succour, though, is provided by the considerable leap in the number of literates in the country. At 65.3 per cent, the literacy level has never been better. According to the 2001 census figures, three-fourths of our male population (75.85 per cent) and over half our female population (54.16 per cent) is lettered now.

However, most demographers do make the point that enumerators often tot up literacy figures without checking whether the 'literates' in question fit the census definition of "persons with the ability to read and write a simple letter." Nor do enumerators factor in the reality of "relapse into illiteracy" when, for instance, a 45 year old who remembers nothing of what he was taught in the two years he attended school in childhood says he is literate.

"Having accounted for all these errors in enumeration, however, one must concede that these mistakes couldn't have been peculiar only to the present census," says Premi, "So if these figures are inflated, then all the past figures would have been too."

There seems little doubt that the country is better educated than before. Two National Family Health Surveys and a National Sample Survey conducted over the last decade did indicate a trend towards higher literacy levels much before the census presented the new literacy figures. Says Tyagi: "The increase in numbers of government and private schools, teachers, education schemes would have all contributed towards an increase in literacy."

Also, for the first time since independence, the number of "absolute" illiterates has shown a decline. And yet, we do still have a whopping 31.96 million people who aren't acquainted at all with the written word. Moreover, as Raju says, "Average mean little. It doesn't help that nearly all of Mizoram is literate and most of Bihar isn't. More than rejoicing at these figures, we should be using them to home in on the regions that need urgent help."

The theory doing the rounds currently suggests that the provisional results have highlighted yet again the gaping divide between the North and the South. "Uttar Pradesh, Bihar, Rajasthan have some of the highest growth rates and lowest literacy levels; Kerala, Tamil Nadu, Andhra Pradesh, Karnataka, have done so much better," says Bose. "Development in our country seems to be so lopsided."

Jayant Kumar Banthia, Registrar General and Census Commissioner of India, advises that we wait some more before making any such demographic conclusions. "Let the district level data come and then we'll see many areas in the South mimicking the prejudices of the North," he says. "Meanwhile, let us talk of the disturbingly increasing masculinity of our population and, more importantly, our growth rate that is more than most countries in the world. A broader perspective would help us comprehend what our burgeoning populace is doing to the earth's resources." Because, any which way we look at it, every sixth person in the world is an Indian. And it's official now.

The Hindu, March 31, 2001
India's population

— C. Rammanohar Reddy

More than the decline in the population growth rate it is the spurt in literacy rates that makes this Census stand out from the others in post-independence India

India's Census of 2001 has already received a fair degree of comment, including questions on its reliability. One must wait for the results of the post-enumeration survey to have an idea of the extent of the under-count. But instead of carping about the statistics it is more important to understand what the Census, which has always had a reputation for more than reasonable accuracy, says through the provisional results about population, literacy and the sex ratio (the number of females for every 1,000 males).

A lot has been made of the decline in the rate of growth of the population during 1991-2001, which, at an average annual growth or 1.95 per cent, is the lowest in the past four decades. More recent annual yearly growth, based on the Sample Registration Scheme, suggests an even slower rate of increase. The Economic Survey of 2000-01 reports a yearly population growth of around 1.6 per cent between 1997 and 1999. If this is a pointer to the future then the slow-down may be even more rapid than that suggested by the Census data.

In analysing the variations in population growth across States, the impressive slow-down of population growth in the four Southern States (especially in Andhra Pradesh) has been compared with the increase in Bihar and the near stagnancy in Uttar Pradesh. But the bigger story of Census 2001 is that even states with no history of a slowing population growth rate have turned in fairly dramatic performances. The four examples in this respect are Assam, West Bengal, Orissa and Chhatisgarh, all of which have seen their decadal population growth rates decline from 20 to 25 per cent to between 15 and 18 per cent. Out-migration is unlikely to be the larger cause for this deceleration. And while the population growth rate depends on the movement in both fertility and mortality, the complete Census data will hopefully show that the decline in 1991-2001 was not on account of death rates falling at a slower pace than birth rates.

More than the decline in the population growth rate it is the spurt in literacy rates that make this Census stand out from the others in post-independence India. The Census confirms what a number of surveys and field reports have been indicating in recent years - there is now a strong emphasis on education. Perhaps on account of the literacy campaigns but more likely because of a parental thirst for education of their children, the Indian population is finally moving towards a reasonable level of literacy. There is of course a very long distance yet to travel and the "achievements" of the past decade look impressive only because progress in the previous four decades was abysmal. First, literacy, as defined in the Census, is only the ability to read and write while what even the poorest of parents ideally want for their children is at the bare minimum the completion of elementary education. Second, one-third of all Indians still do not possess even the basic proficiency in literacy. And, third, female literacy rates have only just crossed the 50 per cent mark. But none of this can take away anything from the fact that for the first time since 1951 there has been an absolute decline (32 million) in the number of illiterates in the country and that the gap in literacy rates between males and females is narrowing, even if very

slowly. Here again the bigger story is not that the Southern States are doing well, but that even some of the traditionally "backward" states are showing impressive improvements. The literacy rate in Orissa, for example, is now higher than that in Andhra, and only a little lower than Karnataka's. This is true as well of Madhya Pradesh, Rajasthan, and Chhatisgarh. Bihar and Uttar Pradesh are of course way behind. But what is interesting is that even in these states literacy rates rose fairly sharply in the previous decade. What this means is that in spite of the government schooling system in near collapse in most of the poorer states, parents are yet able to make their children functionally literate. How much more could have been achieved if the Centre and the State Governments had shown a greater commitment to school education in the 1990s?

While being appreciative of the movements in literacy rates one should not be blind to one large dark spot that Census 2001 has thrown up. This is the substantial fall in the child (0-6 years) sex ratio even as the overall sex ratio has improved for the first time in decades. The child sex ratio (the number of girls for every 1,000 boys) has fallen from 945 in 1991 to 927 in 2001 and the Census reports a very sharp decline in some of the northern states as well as in Gujarat and Maharashtra. There is no inconsistency between the two movements in opposite directions. The sharp fall in child sex ratio seem to suggest prima facie that the forces which discriminate against the girl child are getting stronger rather than weaker even as the overall sex ratio has moved a bit in favour of females.

Demographers suggest there could be three reasons why the child sex ratio is declining. Prof. Mari Bhat at the Institute of Economic Growth, Delhi, argues that one reason is better reporting of the ages of both boys and girls in the 0-6 age group. But the two others reasons that Prof. Bhat suggests are very worrisome. One is an adverse sex ratio at birth caused by a growing resort in large and small towns to foeticide - a practice that the media has reported is quite common not just in Punjab and Haryana but in all parts of the country. The other reason is the continuation of higher mortality among girls in the 0-6 age group, even if there are some signs of the gap narrowing. This higher mortality in the extreme takes the form of girl infanticide. If it is the twin phenomenon of son preference and discrimination against the girl child that is more behind the decline in the child sex ratio then voluntary action by Indian couples is leading to the same results as the forced one-child policy in China. This is the bleaker message from Census 2001.

The Times of India, April 1, 2001
Sikhs classified as minority in Punjab

— Ajay Bharadwaj

Even as Shiromani Gurdwara Prabandhak Committee (SGPC) is wrestling with the definition of a Sikh, the Punjab government has opened a Pandora's box by classifying Sikhs as a minority in the state in order to bestow minority status on educational institutions being run by the SGPC.

This according to officials, has been done with the sole purpose of reserving 50 per cent of the total seats for Sikhs in three SGPC educational institutions - a medical college and a dental college in Amritsar and an engineering college in Anandpur Sahib.

The Times of India, April 1, 2001
Mumbai records lowest sex ratio in 100 years

The provisional Census 2001 for Maharashtra shows that the state's population has gone up by 18.41 per cent in the last decade. The decadal growth rate, which has gone down from 25.73 per cent during 1981-91 to 22.57 per cent during 1991-2001, is still monstrous compared to states like Kerala, where the current corresponding growth rate has been only 9 per cent.

While the population of the state has gone up from 1,78,15,060 to 9,67,52,247 the population of Greater Mumbai municipal area has gone up from 99.25 lakhs in 1991 to 1.19 crore in 2001, registering a whopping 20 per cent growth rate. Interestingly, Thane continues to grow at the fastest rate in the past two decades.

And that's not the worst. The proportion of females to males is at an all-time low in the past 100 years - it has dropped from 934 in 1991 to 922 in 2001 - casting a poor reflection on aspects of social development in the state.

Mumbai fares at the bottom of the table with an alarmingly low sex ratio of 774.

The literacy rate is at a all-time high in 100 years at 77.27 per cent, compared with 64.87 per cent in 1991.

State Director of Census operations S K Biswas attributed the state and Mumbai's high growth rate to migration and a high birth rate. "In Mumbai, there are 22 births per 1,000 people while the death rate is only seven per 1,000," he said.

Biswas also expressed serious concern at the low sex ratio in the state. "Kerala and Pondicherry have more than 1,000 females per 1,000 males, which is always the case in progressive countries. A poor sex ratio indicates male bias and other unhealthy trends in the society," he said, adding "There is an immediate need for intervention in this area."

While literacy registered a climb, Maharashtra ranked 10 among the states, failing to improve on the same rank in the 1981 and 1991 Census. However, in 1971 it had ranked second.

The Times of India, March 3, 2001

Delving into the dark side of family planning *

— *Radhika D Srivastava*

As per the provisional census results for 2001, upto the age of six years there are 927 girls for 1,000 boys. In 1991 the ratio was 945 and in 1981 it was 962.

Experts dub this steady decline the "darker side" of family planning.

Families want fewer children and only boys. So female foetuses are aborted illegally.

The preference for a male child is particularly pronounced in Punjab, Haryana, Gujarat and Madhya Pradesh where the ratios have fallen considerably.

Census Commissioner J K Banthia said, "The low child sex ratio is both alarming and disturbing. The government has to take measures to improve the ratio." If nature is allowed to take its own course, there would be as many girls as boys. United Nations Population Fund's representative Francois M Farah said, "The accepted sex ratio at birth is 105 boys per 100 girls. But the life expectancy of girls is higher than the boys so the numbers even out."

That the skewed child sex ratio in India is a clear indication of sex selective abortions has been accepted by the authorities. Union ministry of health and family welfare secretary A.R. Nanda said, "It seems that our laws prohibiting sex determination test and sex based abortions are being hoodwinked as many families want only sons."

The main cause of the low sex ratio is gender discrimination, he said. "Even if girls are born, they are being discriminated against and many die before their sixth birthday. There is some evidence of infanticide as well though the incidence would be low", he said.

Admitting that the government's girl child welfare programmes may not have much of an impact, Nanda said, "We need to start a social movement in the country. Doctors have to stop unethical abortions."

According to demographer Professor Ashish Bose, "There is an unholy alliance between tradition and technology. While tradition demands sons, technology provides the means to ensure only male babies took birth."

Bose said ultrasound machines proliferated in the private sector around 1980 and since then the child sex ratio has fallen steadily. "The son complex is deeply entrenched in Indian society. Though the literacy rate has improved, social evils like the dowry system has remained."

The distorted child sex ratio may have many serious implications in the future, said Farah. "Fewer girls may lead to an imbalance in the nuptial market after 10 to 15 years. Not all men would be able to get married and start a family", he said.

Crime against women may rise, too. He said, "At the very start the act of aborting a female foetus is a gender crime." Women may become even more vulnerable to violence.

The Tribune, April 4, 2001 (Editorial)
Messages from the census

There are both comforting and depressing messages from the census figures. The cheerful development is that the annual population growth rate has come down to 1.93 per cent from 2.14 per cent in 1991, when last census operations were conducted, though the total figure has increased to over 102.70 crore, up by 181 million in 10 years. The second encouraging message is that the literacy rate has improved considerably for both males and females – from 52.2 per cent in 1991 to 65.4 per cent in 2001. It is a different matter that only a little more than half (54.6 per cent) of the female population can read and write. The third good news is that there is some improvement in the sex ratio – for every 1000 men there are 933 women today though 10 years ago the females numbered only 927.

But this is only one side of the picture. The other side so depressing. If the country continues to add to its population at the current rate, or even a little less than this figure, in the next 50 years India will surpass China, earning the dubious distinction of being the most populous country of the world. Already we have added a Brazil to our numbers, which is the fifth largest country in terms of population. Here lies a major challenge for the ruling class. In fact, all political parties have to give a place of primacy to the population issue on their agenda. Unfortunately, the entire political class has been neglecting the problem, especially after the 1975-77 Emergency excesses at the hands of those engaged in implementing the population programme. But it is a serious matter. The country can neglect it at its own peril. Any drive to reduce the number of Indians should concentrate more on Bihar and Uttar Pradesh, the two states whose performance has been the worst. More attractive incentives will have to be offered to the poverty-stricken and illiterate people as they prefer to have as many children as they can because in their case more hands mean more income to the family. The northern states will have to learn a lot from the southern states, which have performed excellently. The sharpest decline has been registered by Mr. Chandrababu Naidu's Andhra Pradesh, from 24.2 per 1000 in 1991 to 13.9 in 2001. All said and done, these achievements – not enough, of course – have been made despite the fact that the population question has remained relegated to the background because of its poor vote catching appeal. The country could have done definitely better had the successive governments accorded it the attention it deserves.

Pioneer, 9 April, 2001 Bhopal

Madhya Pradesh registers 20 per cent jump in literacy rate

Madhay Pradesh government led by Chief Minister Digvijay Singh has accomplished a "mission impossible". The state has registered an unprecedented jump by 20 per cent in literacy rate.

This had been possible by redesigning of initiatives and schemes in the field of literacy. The provisional data on the recently concluded census for the year 2001 speaks for themselves as far as the State Government's literacy drive is concerned.

A jubliant Madhya Pradesh Chief Minister Digvijay Singh said that literacy in Madhya Pradesh had gone up from 44 per cent in 1991 to 64 per cent in 2001.

Thus, Madhya Pradesh is on fast track to get rid of the stigma of being bracketted with "BIMARU" states. The Madhya Pradesh Chief Minister strongly feels that now the Central Government and all concerning authorities will have to coin a new acronym because Madhya Pradesh is out of the club of "BIMARU" states.

Hailing the quantum jump by the state in the field of literacy Chief Minister Digvijay Singh congratulated teachers, volunteers and Government officers, including R. Gopalakrishnan, coordinator for Rajiv Gandhi Shiksha Mission as well as the mission.

Director Mrs Amita Sharma, while addressing a Press conference in Mantralaya here the other day Mr. Singh informed that an estimated jump of about 20 per cent had been possible due to change of strategy of the State Government.

"This impressive rise vindicates the mission mode adopted by the Madhya Pradesh Government," asserted Mr. Digvijay Singh. In the census held during 1991 Madhya Pradesh stood 26th among 32 different states and Union Territories of India whereas now Madhya Pradesh was ranked 24th in 2001 as far as literacy rate was concerned.

Chief Minister Mr Digvijay Singh attributed the quantum jump to state specific initiatives that the state had launched under the umbrella of Rajiv Gandhi Shiksha Mission. Initiatives like the Education Guarantee Scheme (EGS) and "Padhna, Badhna Andolan" were responsible for such a massive increase as those schemes reached out to the poorer communities in remote habitations.

It is all the more creditable said Chief Minister Mr Singh, because largeness of numbers involved (the two states of MP Chhatisgarh together) remoteness of locations and the problems associated with reaching out to poor population in far flung habitations.

This decision had been taken because problem of female literacy continues to be a major challenge, districts like Jhabua where only 25 per cent of females were turned literates, he said. The only matter of satisfaction is female literacy rates in Jhabua is more than the national average.

Apart from this districts of Raisen, Shajapur, Narsinghpur, Jabalpur, Ujjain, Bhopal and Mandsaur have done exceedingly well under the Padhana Badhna Drive, said Mr Singh. The female literacy which stood at 28 per cent in 1991 census had now gone up to 50 per cent stated the MP Chief Minister adding male literacy rate had gone upto 76.80 per cent.

Within Madhya Pradesh 21 out of 45 districts now have a literacy rate above the national average. Significantly, male literacy was now above relatively more developed states like Punjab and Karnataka, said Chief Minister Mr. Digvijay Singh.

Deccan Herald, April 7, 2001

Preliminary Census Results From BIMAROU to BIROUK

— *Vinod Vyasulu*

The Registrar General and Census Commissioner has just released the provisional results of the census completed in February and March, giving provisional details of the Indian population as on March 1, 2001. The census office – and the teachers who collected the data – must be congratulated on a massive job not only well done, but done in record time.

While there will be many analyses of these results, one aspect seems to stand out. The Ashish Bose inspired concept of BIMAROU states – the collection of Bihar, Madhya Pradesh, Rajasthan, Orissa and Uttar Pradesh as being the sick or 'bimar' states of India, backward in crucial ways - may have to be revised. At first glance, it would appear that Madhya Pradesh's performance, especially in education, takes it out of the BIMAROU group. And a new entrant – this time from the progressive South – Karnataka – takes its place. The 'maldevelopment' concept of the twenty-first century then, is, BIROUK – Bihar, Rajasthan, Orissa, Uttar Pradesh, Karnataka. These are the laggard states of India today.

Madhya Pradesh, which had a literacy rate of 44% in the 1991 census, has now recorded a literacy rate of 64% – an increase of 20% in one of the most backward states of the century. Female literacy has gone up from 29% to over 50% – an increase of 21%. MP's achievement is all the more laudable because it started with big disadvantage: a feudal society, a low value for education, a dispersed population that made the organisation and setting up of schools difficult, inequitable gender relations that did not value female achievements and many more qualities typical of Bimarouhood. But in a systematic manner, through the Rajiv Gandhi Missions for the social sector, the state has determinedly worked towards improvement. Of course, there is still much to be done – but is has to be recognised that much has been done.

Starting with the pioneering Human Development Report it released in 1995 – four years before the next state level HDR prepared by Karnataka – Madhya Pradesh has moved to reduce deprivations and improve the quality of life in education, health and the like. The second HDR released in 1998 gave a clear indication of how this was to be done – by bringing the people back in. People were victims of the earlier development policy – they should not be blamed for their plight.

Madhya Pradesh tapped the energies released by the 73rd constitutional amendment to use the Panchayat system to bring in the people in solving their problems through what has come to be known as the Lok Sampark Abhiyan. MP sees people as the source of solutions to problems, not passive recipients of state largesse. The results have been the Education Guarantee Scheme, the Padhna Badhna Andolan, the Rogi Kalyan Samithis, the Gram Sampark Abhiyan and so many other developmental initiatives. With experience, lessons were learned a new step taken. The first clear evidence that these efforts have begun to yield fruit is this census result. Once things begun to happen, the state has no claims to continue as a member of apathetic Bimaroudom.

Equally, by dint of hard work and application, a state can gain admittance to Bimarouness. Karnataka is, perhaps, one such state. Starting from a base of 52% literacy, Karnataka has reached 67% in 2001 – an increase of 15%. This is a tribute to the efforts of those involved in education, both within and without the government. Karnataka was widely recognised as having an enlightened civil service, progressive politicians, and highly qualified professionals. These were its initial advantages.

The difference across districts remains high. The backward districts of Karnataka, from Chamrajanagar to Raichur, from Kolar to Bidar, from Bangalore city to Bangalore (rural), qualified the state for membership of Bimarou in the past decade. But for some reason, Ashish Bose did not accord the state this honour. This denial angered Karnataka so much that in the 1990s, it has made great efforts to rectify this error. It systematically negated its advantages with mindless red-tape.

Karnataka has achieved this with policies logically the opposite of those of Madhya Pradesh – by disenfranchising its Panchayats. Karnataka, which had been a leader in deepening the democratic nature of its polity in the 1980s through its (pre-73rd amendment) Panchayati Raj Act, did all it could to reverse the process. Panchayats were superseded by an Act of the legislature in early 1992. Powers were taken away from panchayats, and entrusted to line departments. The mistakes and excesses of 1980s were rectified. The spin doctors of the state made the process appear as a continuation of the work of the 1980s – thus showing their Gobbelsian abilities. In health, in drinking water – in pretty much about everything that concerned local people, the panchayats were given little role to play.

The state government bureaucracy knew best. In education and other crucial sectors, money allotted to districts often could not be spent. Money is clearly not the problem of the state. The difference between allocations and expenditures increased as the 73rd amendment was gradually implemented. The potential for rapid progress, made possible in the 1980s by people's participation, was systematically reduced. The result: increasing corruption, greater inefficiency, and as a consequence, admission to Bimarouhood as a replacement to the fast-moving Madhya Pradesh. We thus have BIROUK.

Thus success of the IT revolution and the changes in Bangalore – such as the successful self assessment property tax scheme – tend to mask this achieved backward status of Karnataka. The IT revolution took place due the initiative and dynamism of outstanding individuals, not the progressive policies of the state. Now that the state has woken up and arrogated to itself the responsibility of IT and related sectors, the dangers of decline and regression have increased manifold: for the state will not do, and will not let anyone do, anything useful. Its few successes only go to underline the truth: in general,

little will be done. After all, in building the Richmond Circle flyover in Bangalore, delay in completion is measured in years. That is the normal truth that justifies Karnataka's claims to biroukdom.

Karnataka had the opportunity this year to take the lead and show the other states the way to economic progress by introducing a Value Added Tax.

Businesses were clamouring for this change. The Tax Reforms Commission, headed by a former Chief Minister, had provided a road map for the change, and shown that such a change would be revenue neutral. If this VAT had been brought in, Karnataka would have shown the other states how reforms could be pushed ahead. But the complex and mindless procedures that have harassed commerce for years have been continued. This is only a further instance of the state knowing what to do, and resolutely refusing to do the 'right' thing. This is the essential characteristic for conferring Biroukhood on Karnataka. Even Ashish Bose will agree that Karnataka's hard work should be rewarded!

Editorial

Economic and Political Weekly *March 31-April 6, 2001*

Behind the Population Numbers

This last decade India has seen the sharpest decline in the population growth rate since independence. Although in absolute numbers, we have added 181 million people, the decline in growth rate is heartening. It is tempting to view the products of the mammoth Census 2001 exercise as the key to the numbers game. While numbers are certainly important, the Census figures, even these preliminary data, should be read as a comprehensive comment on decadal socio-economic development.

The Census office in its press note has made much of the enormity of adding 181 million people:"... which is more than the estimated population of Brazil, the fifth most populous country". And there is the ominous note sounded on the fact the two of the most populous states, Bihar and Haryana, have actually shown an acceleration in the population growth rate. That the growth rate in the southern states has continued to decline, most sharply in Andhra Pradesh, is to the Census office, demographers and to the newspaper-reading majority cause for celebration. No doubt this will give rise to more enthusiastic dissection of the "Tamil Nadu model" and its replicability. Equally, the fact that Uttar Pradesh continues to be the most populous state, accounting for 16.17 per cent of the population with Maharashtra second a long way behind at 9.42 per cent has been seen as a distress sign.

If we were to drop the coloured glasses we have worn – as per the prescription provided by an international community of population scientists since the 1960s – a very different picture emerges. Let us just take the numbers first. Population growth in the southern region has been the lowest at 16 per cent over the decade, in the west it has been 40 per cent, in the north 30 per cent and in

the east 28 per cent. The fact that roughly half of India's population lives in four states – Uttar Pradesh and Bihar in the north, West Bengal in the east and Maharashtra in the west may be reason for concern, but also some introspection. The fastest growth has taken place in a region of high industrialisation and high employment relatively. Maharashtra's growth is, after all, in spite of its comparatively better health facilities, a well-administratered family welfare programme and an active women's and people's movement but perhaps because of its economic and industrial growth profile. How much has in-migration for employment contributed to this growth? Moreover, given that other socio-economic development indicators are certainly not poor in this region, the numbers in themselves should hardly be a source of distress. A more detailed look at several indices of development as well as migration patterns is indicated.

The single most worrisome feature is the poor improvement in sex ratios all round and particularly in the 0-6 years age-groups. The all-age sex ratio has improved from 927 females per 1,000 males in 1991 to 933 females per 1,000 males in 2001. While the highest sex ratios are for Kerala as in the 1991 Census, Haryana has the lowest with 861. Further, sex ratios have seen the sharpest decline in Haryana, Punjab, Himachal Pradesh, Gujarat and Maharashtra. The decline in the last state needs some explanation, one of which has been in-migration of men looking for employment. But this does not explain the continuing low sex ratios in the 0-6 years age-group.

The number of children in that age-group has gone down from 17.9 per cent of the population to 15.42. And the decrease has been sharper among female than male children. There are today 75.9 million female children and 81.9 million males. In as many as 13 states there has been an absolute decline in the number of children this decade, with the southern states leading the decline. In Punjab and Haryana the sharp decline in the sex ratio in this age group-in Punjab it is a chilling 793 females for every 1,000 males and in Haryana there has been reportedly an even sharper decrease, though the figures are yet to be released – has been attributed to the high incidence of female foeticide that many independent studies have revealed. According to the Indian Medical Association, for instance, five million female foetuses are aborted every year. It may be recalled that these facts and a dynamic and well-organised campaign drawing from the health, science and people's movements pushed through relevant legislation first in Maharashtra. This raises some disturbing issues. First, as every campaigner and social activists will point out, this particular legislation is, for a variety of reasons, being implemented in the breach. Even in states like Maharashtra with its relatively high level of awareness on the issue created through a sustained campaign for over a year at that time, this legislation has been but poorly enforced with hardly any cases of default registered. Secondly, what does this decline of girl children say of the impact of the numerous target programmes? Is this an indicator that such programmes, because of their narrow conceptualisation emphasising physical inputs rather than education and awareness-building, have failed to play a significant role in changing cultural practices? Nor in fact do they appear to have succeeded even in their limited objective, through feeding programmes, of preventing the loss of girl children. And this is disturbing – that in a decade which has seen a wealth of literature, action and movement around issues of women's empowerment and the rights of girl children, there should have been so little improvement in the vital statistics on women.

The glimmer of hope is perhaps in the significant change in literacy levels. The south emerges as the most literate region with 78 per cent literacy, the west with 72 per cent, the north with 69 per cent and east with 65 per cent. For the first time since independence there has been a decline in the absolute number of illiterates. The all-around improvement in the number of literates has come about as a result of a slightly more rapid increase in literacy rates among women resulting in a narrowing of the difference between the respective literacy rates from 28.84 percentage points in 1991 to 21.7 percentage points in 2001. Interestingly, however, the figures do not appear to support the assumption of a direct link between female literacy and women's status and fertility rates – Himachal Pradesh has shown vast improvement in literacy rates, but has registered a decline in the sex ratio from 976 to 970 and the western region, the second most literate region, has shown the sharpest population growth rate. This needs to be explored further.

While the actual decline in fertility is less than predicted, there is not doubt that India has entered the phase of such decline. The 40-odd years of the family planning programme, a marked improvement in the economy notwithstanding the ups and downs and continuing poor employment opportunities, education, expanding access to information, and other modernising features have, however unevenly, generated a sufficient groundswell towards smaller families. All that is needed today perhaps is a good health service network, the economic wherewithal for families to take radical decisions on the size of their families, and the availability of the means for implementing these decisions. The time now is for a change of tack. The patterns of growth over the last decade seem to uncompromisingly point to the significance of social and economic factors in their determination. The declining population growth rates in states like Andhra Pradesh and Tamil Nadu, the sharp decline in sex ratios in states with high economic indices, the rising literacy levels, the continued uneven development facing migration need to be comprehended in their socio-political context and integrated into the planning of intervention programmes.

Frontline April 27, 2001

Census 2001
Some progress, some concern

—Venkatesh Athreya

Excerpts
Sex Ratios
Demographers and policymakers,

especially those with a "population control" mindset, often tend to focus mainly on the "overall numbers" and the growth rate of population as such, and generally celebrate observed declines in fertility. However, as is being increasingly recognised, in a patriarchal society universalisation of the small family norm may bring about a fertility decline that is far from being sex-neutral. It may, in fact, lower the survival chances of female foetuses and infants, in the context of the strong preference for sons in society. It is important, therefore, to look at the sex composition of the population.

The overall population sex ratio – the number of females per 1000 males – has increased from 927 in the 1991 Census to 933 in the 2001 Census. Since 1901, the sex ratio has been showing a secular decline, from 972 in 1901 to 927 in 1991, with a marginal inter-census rise on two occasions: from 945 to 946 between 1941 and 1951, and 930 to 934 between 1971 and 1981. It remains to be seen whether the observed increase in sex ratio between 1991 and 2001 constitutes a reversal of the secular trend of decline or is an ephemeral phenomenon like the 4-point increase between 1971 and 1981, which was followed by a 7-point decline between 1981 and 1991. The sex ratio has improved in a number of major States between 1991 and 2001. These include all the southern States, Orissa, West Bengal, Madhya Pradesh, Chhatisgarh, Bihar, Jharkhand, Uttar Pradesh, Uttaranchal, Rajasthan and Assam. But it is worrying to note that the sex ratio has declined sharply in Maharashtra (from 934 to 922) and Gujarat (from 934 to 921) and has declined from an already low level in Punjab. One also notes declines in Himachal Pradesh and Haryana.

The temptation to ascribe the decline in Maharashtra and Gujarat to sex-selective, male in-migration from other States in search of jobs in these two "rapidly industrialising" States should be resisted. This becomes clear when one looks not at overall population sex ratios, but at sex ratios in the age group of 0 to 6 years, the so-called juvenile sex ratios (JSR), which are not likely to be distorted by sex-selective adult migration.

One finds, for the country as a whole, a sharp decline in JSR from 945 in 1991 to 927 in 2001. The decline is even sharper in several States. Thus, the JSR has declined from 951 to 897 in Himachal Pradesh, 875 to 793 in Punjab, and 879 to 820 in Haryana. In Gujarat, it has declined from 928 to 878 and in Maharashtra, from 946 to 917. In fact, the JSR has declined in every State with a population exceeding 20 million in 2001, with the solitary and honourable exception of Kerala. Only Sikkim, Tripura and Lakshadweep show a significant increase in the JSR and Mizoram, a marginal rise.

The general decline in the JSR practically across the entire country must be viewed with concern. The Census publication concedes, though rather cautiously, that "the data on sex ratio at birth for the past many years as obtained from the Sample Registration System is indicative of a larger than usual shortfall in female birth as compared to male births" (page 91). But it stops short of linking this trend with sex-selective foeticide. However, in its discussion of decline in child sex ratios, or the JSRs, it notes the sharp declines in the States mentioned earlier and raises the question: "Are the sharp declines in child sex ratios indicative of an underlying trend of sex-selective abortions in these areas?" (page 97). Its answer is non-committal: "We may really have to wait for some more data before coming to any definite conclusion in this regard" (page 97).

Leaving aside the question whether such abundant caution may or may not be warranted in an official publication, there is enough evidence from the field to indicate an alarming spread of the practice of female foeticide not only in the contiguous belt of Punjab-Chandigarh-Haryana-Uttaranchal-Himachal Pradesh, but also in Maharashtra and Gujarat; even more worrisome, in the much-vaunted South, where the female foetus and infant were earlier not thought to be at great risk.

In Tamil Nadu, for instance, there is considerable evidence of the practices of female infanticide (Frontline, July 11, 1991; Economic and Political Weekly, April 26, 1997 and December 2, 2000) and of female foeticide (Frontline, December 18, 1998 and November 19, 1999) being spread over a significant part of the State. It is, of course, possible that there may also be factors at work which contribute to a trend decline in sex ratio at birth. But while one may need more data to confirm the presence of such factors, there is already enough confirmation of the spread of the practices of female foeticide and infanticide not as a relic of an atavistic past, but as consequences of a narrowly based, consumerist path of capitalist development within a framework of strong patriarchy and son preference, and an environment of universali- sation of the small family norm and unrealisable aspirations promoted by the unrealisable aspirations promoted by the dominant consumerist ethic. Policy intervention and social mobilisation are urgently needed on this issue.

Literacy rates

Perhaps the most positive piece of news from the 2001 Census is that of a significant increase in both the literacy rates and the number of literate persons. The improvement in literacy status is significant not only for the population as a whole, but also for every category of it, whether by sex or region.

For India as a whole, the proportion of literate persons among the population aged 7 years and above is reported to be 65.38 per cent, which represents a jump of 13.17 percentage points over the actuals of 1991. The female literacy rate has increased even more rapidly, by 14.87 percentage points to reach 54.16 per cent, while male literacy has increased by 11.77 percentage points, to reach 75.85 per cent. Accordingly, the male- female gap in the literacy rate has declined to 21.70 percentage points,

the lowest since the 1951 Census, when both male and female literacy rates were abysmally low. Among the major States, Kerala predictably leads the pack with a literacy rate of 90.92 per cent and a fairly small male-female gap of 6.34 percentage points. Maharashtra's literacy rate, which was ahead of Tamil Nadu's by 2.21 percentage points in 1991, is now ahead by 3.80 percentage points at 77.27 per cent; Tamil Nadu's literacy rate is 73.47 per cent. A remarkable feature of the improvement in literacy is the sharp increase in literacy rates in the States of Rajasthan (22.48 percentage points), Chhatisgarh (22.27) and Madhya Pradesh (19.44). The spread across major States with a population of at least 20 million each in 2001 is between Kerala at 90.92 per cent and Bihar at 47.53 per cent; the difference is still large at 43.39 percentage points but less than the difference of 52.32 percentage points in 1991 between Kerala (89.81 per cent) and Bihar (37.49 per cent).

The other heartening aspect of the literacy situation in 2001 is the reduction in the gender gap in all States and Union Territories except in the small Union Territory of Dadra and Nagar Haveli with a population of only 220,451. The biggest improvement in female literacy rates has occurred in Chhatisgarh (24.87 percentage points), Rajasthan (23.90) and Madhya Pradesh (20.93). The same is true of male literacy rates as well, if Dadra and Nagar Haveli is excluded. An idea of the general improvement in literacy across the country can be had from the following fact. Only around 27 per cent of the country's population lived in States with literacy rates of 60 per cent and above, and these States accounted only for 35.94 per cent of all literate persons in 1991. By contrast, in 2001, 72.71 per cent of the population and 78.31 per cent of all literate persons lived in States/Union Territories with literacy rates of 60 per cent and above.

However, one should not get overly euphoric about the advance in the literacy rates. Certainly, the participatory mass literacy campaigns of the 1990s, especially the early ones which had somewhat of a free run before becoming hopelessly bureau-cratised, did score significant success. Even where the mass literacy campaigns were not particularly successful in terms of literacy achievement, they did motivate non/semi-literate parents – especially the mothers – in a big way to send their children to school. Much of the increase in the overall literacy rate has to be attributed to improved enrolment and retention ratios in primary/ elementary schools. But there is a need to enter a caveat as well. Wherever mass mobilisation for literacy campaigns had taken place in the 1990s, it would have become more difficult for non-literate women to report themselves as non-literate than was the case before the campaign. In a neighbourhood milieu, where women had been enrolled as learners in significant numbers in literacy campaigns, it would have been difficult for many of them who had not acquired literacy to report themselves as non-literate. There might be a small upward bias in the reported female literacy rate, though its extent is hard to gauge.

Finally, the census figures on literacy should not lead to complacency. Nearly half the women in the country in the population aged 7 years and above are still non-literate, 50 years after the Republic came into existence, even by a rather minimal definition of literacy. Far more attention needs to be paid to elementary education, and the constitutional promise of free and compulsory education has to be redeemed at least now. That task requires political will and a reversal of the disastrous policies of liberalisation, privatisation and globalisation that abandon education to the tender mercies of the market.

VII

UNBORN DAUGHTERS : DECLINING SEX RATIO OF THE CHILD POPULATION (0-6 YEARS)

Financial Express April 3, 2001

Growing Imbalance in Child Sex Ratio

— *Mahendra K. Premi*

With a population of 1027 million (531 million males and 496 million females) as of 1 March 2001, India has completed its first census of the 21st century. This is the 14th census count in the series of census taking in India. The Provisional Population Totals released by the Census Commissioner on 26th March 2001 recorded a sex ratio (females per 1000 males) of 933, which has been an improvement of six points over the 1991 census sex ratio and is a matter of some satisfaction. A part of this improvement in sex ratio can be explained by favourable sex ratio in deaths, this being almost 110 males deaths for every 100 female deaths; another part might be the result of better enumeration of females in the 2001 census compared to the previous one.

While the improvement in the overall sex ratio is noticed in majority of states and union territories, among the major states Kerala, Uttaranchal and Uttar Pradesh have registered more than 20 points increase; and Bihar, Jharkhand, Rajasthan, Tamil Nadu and West Bengal have registered between 10 to 20 points increase. In contrast, there has been a decline in sex ratio in Gujarat and Maharashtra

on the one hand, and in Haryana, Himachal Pradesh, Punjab and Delhi on the other hand. The sex ratio among children aged 0-6, however, declined by 18 points, from 945 in 1991 to 927 in 2001. We examine here the factors responsible for the decline in child sex ratio in India.

Child Sex Ratio

The 1991 census tabulated for the first time separately sex ratio for the age group 0-6 and 7 and above. At the national level the "child sex ratio" (in population aged 0-6 years) declined from 962 in 1981 to 945 in 1991. These were the children born between March 1, 1984 and March 1,1991. A decline of 17 points in the child sex ratio in a decade was regarded as very substantial and a matter of serious concern. Data relating to the child sex ratio in respect of major states and union territory of Delhi indicated that the same declined by 38 points in Rajasthan, 33 points in Punjab, 28 points in Orissa, and 26 points in Madhya Pradesh between 1981 and 1991. There were 55 districts where this sex ratio was less than 910 females per 1,000 males (or, inversely, 1100 males per 1,000 females). Among them, ten districts – Kurukshetra, Kaithal, Jind, Hissar, Amritsar, Patiala, Faridkot, Bhind, Jaisalmer and Salem – reported the 0-6 age group sex ratio below 870 (1150 males per 1,000 females).

In the 2001 census child sex ratio has declined further by 18 points - from 945 in 1991 to 927 in 2001. This decline is found in all the states and union territories except Kerala (5 points increase), Sikkim (21 points increase), Tripura (8 points increase) and Mizoram (2 points increase). But it is a matter of very serious concern that the child sex ratio declined by 82 points to mere 793 in Punjab, by 59 points in Haryana, 54 points in Himachal Pradesh and Chandigarh, 50 points in Gujarat and Delhi, and 42 points in Uttaranchal.

Several questions have been raised from time to time with regard to the trend in overall sex ratio and particularly about the child sex ratio. For example, have the living conditions of the females in general and young girls in particular deteriorated over time? Has there been a greater undercount of females or an over count of males in the census? Has the decline in death rate continued to be favourable to males? Has the sex ratio at birth become more favourable to males in recent years? Is the practice of female infanticide and foeticide in certain parts of the country substantially responsible for the shortage of girls?

It is noteworthy that the children in the age group 0-6 were born between March 1, 1994 and 28 February 2001. During this period birth rate in the country declined from 28.7 in 1994 to 26.1 in 1999 and the death rate declined from 9.3 to 8.7.

Differential Undercount

Estimates of undercount by sex derived from the post-enumeration surveys of 1951,1971, 1981 and 1991 censuses indicate that the male-female differential in the percentage of undercount had decreased over time. Further, the undercount of females in the 0-4 and 5-9 age groups has not been very different from male undercount and cannot explain the decline in child sex ratio between 1981 and 1991. One may expect that the female undercount in child population has not deteriorated in the 2001 census.

Sex Differential in Death Rate

Sex-wise crude death rate and the sex ratio (males per 100 females) of deaths by residence (Table 1) indicates that the male mortality has been higher than female mortality during the 1980s and the 1990s. Moreover, the differential in male-female death rate has increased in favour of females. This implies that differential mortality is not a factor in explaining declining sex ratio in India.

In examining child sex ratio one should, however, concentrate on infant and child mortality. While the overall mortality differential has become favourable to females, the available data suggest that the girl child has continued to suffer more in this regard. Hence, this could partly explain the decline in child sex ratio.

Table 5.1: Crude Death Rates by Sex and Sex Ratio (males per 100 females) among Total Deaths, India, 1983-1993

Period	Death rates by sex			Male-Female difference	Number of male deaths per 100 female deaths		
	Total	Male	Female		Total	Rural	Urban
1983-87	11.7	11.6	11.8	-0.2	106.1	104.1	117.4
1984-88	11.5	11.4	11.6	-0.2	105.8	103.8	117.0
1985-89	11.0	11.0	11.0	0.0	106.7	104.8	117.6
1986-90	10.6	10.6	10.6	0.0	107.0	105.0	118.4
1987-91	10.3	10.4	10.3	0.1	108.0	106.0	119.5
1988-92	10.2	10.2	10.1	0.1	107.9	105.9	119.2
1989-93	9.8	9.9	9.7	0.2	108.6	106.3	122.3
1995-97	8.97	9.19	8.74	0.45	112.2	110.2	123.0
1996-98	8.96	9.16	8.75	0.41	111.3	109.4	121.9

Sex Ratio at Birth

In all probability, it has been the changing sex ratio at birth that has contributed most towards the observed phenomenon. This may be partly due to the newly developed practice of female foeticide.

It is noteworthy that data collected by the Office of the Registrar General on about six million births that took place during 1971-81 in hospitals, health centres, and institutions located in urban areas in various parts of the country recorded SRB of 891 female births per 1000 male births or 112 male births for every 100 female births.

The SRS based sex ratio at birth (SRB) over the 1981-90 period was 109.5 male births per 100 female births (Table 2), which is much higher than the internationally found SRB between 102 and 106. The official population projections made in 1996 used the above SRB at the national level. At the state level it has varied from 104.7 in Andhra Pradesh to 115.0 in Haryana (Table 2). All the four southern states have, however, shown conformity with the international figure. SRS data for the 1990s indicate further imbalance in SRB, it being 111 male births for every 100 female births.

Table 5.2 : SRS based Estimates of Sex Ratio at Birth for the Major States, 1981-90

India and major states	Sex ratio at birth	
	1981-90	1996-98
INDIA	**109.5**	**111.0**
Andhra Pradesh	104.7	103.2
Assam	106.4	109.1
Bihar	111.7	111.5
Gujarat	111.1	113.9
Haryana	115.0	123.3
Karnataka	107.3	105.3
Kerala	105.5	107.1
Madhya Pradesh	108.2	109.9
Maharashtra	108.5	109.4
Orissa	106.2	107.6
Punjab	113.2	122.8
Rajasthan	114.1	114.8
Tamil Nadu	104.9	104.9
Uttar Pradesh	111.6	115.0
West Bengal	105.6	105.6

Concluding Observations

Data presented in Table 1 indicate that in recent years the female death rates have become lower than the male death rates. This must have led to improvement in overall sex ratio in favour of females. SRB becoming more favourable to males would, however, influence the overall sex ratio in the opposite direction.

In contrast, the sex differential in infant mortality rate as also in child mortality rate has still not become favourable to female child. The two factors together, particularly in the latter part of the 1990s, should explain a part of decline in the child sex ratio during the 1990s.

Child sex ratio of 793 in Punjab and 820 in Haryana, especially with sex ratio at birth of 122.8 and 123.3 respectively point towards rampant practice of female foeticide along with a certain amount of infanticide in these two states. The districtwise data on child sex ratio as and when they become available will throw more light on this very important aspect.

At the moment, child sex ratio is available only at the state level. When these data become available at the district level, it would be possible to pinpoint those districts that have registered child sex ratio below 910 (or 1100 males per 1,000 females). There would be several districts showing worse sex ratio and their identification would be quite important. With the availability of data with rural-urban breakdown one should be able to identify whether the practice of female foeticide is basically an urban problem or it has reached in villages as well.

It is noteworthy that Uttar Pradesh and Uttaranchal both have registered an improvement of more than 20 points in overall sex ratio between 1991 and 2001, but the child sex ratio has declined sharply therein, especially in Uttaranchal. This requires a detailed probing to understand the factors behind this phenomenon. Further, all the states that have shown large decline in child sex ratio between 1991 and 2001 – Punjab, Haryana, Himachal Pradesh, Gujarat, Maharashtra, Chandigarh and Delhi – are basically economically well developed and have recorded a fairly high literacy rate. This is contrary to expectation; hence, one needs to examine the various issues at length.

Grassroots Vol. 1, No. 5, April 2001

Doctors and Women Collude to Abort Female Foetuses

— Harminder Kaur

Jeeda village of Bhatinda district is just like any other village of Punjab with one difference. Even after driving nearly half a kilometre into the village the girl child is conspicuous by her absence. Boisterous little boys scream and race through the bylanes. But there are no girls among them.

Little seems to have changed in Amritsar, Gurdaspur and Bhatinda districts of Punjab except the mushrooming of sex determination clinics and the great antipathy to having baby girls. A visit to several villages of Bhatinda district revealed that the upper caste families in particular do not wish to have a girl.

Adverse sex ratio has prevailed

in Bhatinda district for decades. Only the reasons for not having girls have changed. First, it was fear of sexual assault by invaders, then inheritance laws in their favour (a share in the property including shrinking agricultural land). Now dowry and the desire for small sized families have contributed to the desire for a male child. The only difference is that earlier there was female infanticide, now it is female foeticide aided by doctors who have introduced the facility of sex determination tests (SDT) in villages.

Today women repeat the slogans given by the doctors. "Better to spend Rs 1,000 now than Rs five lakhs later," as they abort the female foetus. Women are not only aware of SDTs, but approve of it. They say that when "Nagpal" – Dr GS Nagpal, who has ultrasound clinic on Mal Road in Bhatinda – introduced the "facility" a decade ago, handbills were distributed in their villages.

The clinics get a dual benefit. The sex determination test takes place between the 14th and 16th week of pregnancy. Government hospitals do not terminate pregnancies after 12 weeks. Therefore, women rely on private clinics which charge Rs 4,000-5,000 for the test as well as the medical termination of pregnancy.

Pratap Singh, sarpanch of village Gillpati, blames women: "They don't want to have girls," he says. Surjit Kaur, a dalit, of Jeeda village points out "if upper caste women go on giving birth to girls, their men remarry. Mothers-in-law call them names like dhote khuran wali (woman with white feet which means an ill omen) or as

someone responsible for the "Rs 5 lakh decree" against the family. This is the amount that will have to be spent on the marriage of the girls. Women naturally don't want such colossal expenses.

Angrez Kaur of village Gillpati says, "if the government takes strict action against those taking dowry things may change." Pratap Singh explains, earlier the expense on a girl's marriage was between Rs 2 and 3 lakhs. Now it is about Rs 15 lakhs. In Bhatinda we are still farmers and cannot get that kind of income from land these days." Balwant Kaur of village Sibia bemoans that dowry greed is growing: "The in-laws treat the new bride like a blank cheque which can be encashed any time. You may give any amount and still there is no guarantee that your daughter will be treated well. Because of these circumstances people do not want girls."

The situation is getting from bad to worse. Investigations by People revealed that earlier the first baby was accepted irrespective of whether it was a boy or girl. If the first child was a girl, when the second baby was expected the mother underwent a sex determination test (SDT). Now even if the first child is a boy the family still insists that the second too should be a male to make a jora – a pair.

This has permeated to some extent among the lower classes also but a lesser number among them resort to female foeticide. Surjit Kaur has three daughters but doesn't think they are a burden on her as she feels their wedding would cost only

Rs 2,000 to 3,000. This is slightly higher than the cost of a sex determination test – Rs 1,000.

Surjit Kaur finds girls a great asset. "We rear cattle. They handle cow dung and help in other household works." Besides, most dalit families eke out a living doing menial jobs. Both men and women work as agricultural labour. More working hands means more money. They also find the cost of the SDTs high.

Travelling through Jeeda, Gillpati, Sibia, Jhumba, Kheta villages of Bhatinda, it was the same story. An increasing number of women from upper caste families abort female foetus.

Even though, the Pre-natal Diagnostic Techniques Regulation and Prevention Act came into being in 1994 and was implemented by Punjab in 1996, little has been done for its strict implementation. As a result, ultrasonography is a flourishing business for most doctors of this district.

Bhatinda city has more than 40 ultra sound clinics. Many among them also do X-Y sperm separation and help parents to select the child of their choice. This test costs between Rs 15,000 and Rs 20,000. The registered medical practitioners help the clinics with business from rural areas.

The 1999 birth figures made available by the civil hospital, Bhatinda, show that there remains an adverse female sex ratio in every month of the year in rural and urban areas.

What is even more disturbing is that the male-female ratio of births remains near equal in the urban as well as rural areas. In 1999, the percentage of male births in rural areas was 57.4 as against 57.3 in urban areas. Education has had little influence on people's decision to terminate female foetuses.

The Indian Express, April 15, 2001

'We don't kill cats, dogs as often as female children'

— *Pamela Philipose*

Masculinity is alive and well in Haryana. You see signs of it everywhere. In the graffiti of Hrithik Roshan biceps that bloom prodigiously on walls of village gyms. Or in the old men who sit outside tea shops on battered cane chairs, sipping tea and carefully smoothening out their luxuriant moustaches.

But the ultimate symbol of masculinity, it seems, is not in any of this. It is in the sex of the child you bear. If it is male, you're okay. If you have at least two sons, it's perfect. There's even a local phrase that goes: ek beta, kaani; bina beta, andhi; do beta, sunaini - if you have one son, you are one-eyed; if you have no sons you are blind, if you have two sons, well, that's a state of blessedness.

Home truths like this have a habit of escaping the confines of spoken speech. They become common sense and find their expression in the realities of a state that was carved out of the erstwhile Punjab state in 1966.

Here's one reality that the latest census highlighted. Although Haryana has one of the fastest growing economies - its per capita domestic product, at Rs. 12,158 (1997), is just below that of Goa and Punjab - it has today the lowest female-male ratio in the country: 861 women for a 1,000 men.

What's more, over the last 10 years, it has registered the sharpest decline in the number of female children in the 0-6 age group in the country: from 861 to 820.

Only she knows the number of times local women's groups have picketed clinics, petitioned MLAs, and held statewide rallies on the issue. "Haryana, they say, is developed. But is this *vikas* (development) or *be-vikas* (non-development)? observes Sangwan, who is also a Janwadi Mahila Samiti activist.

She points out that 15 years ago there would be stickers pasted on trees saying, 'Spend Rs. 5,000 today and save Rs. 5 lakh tomorrow'. There was even a clinic in nearby Sirsa that displayed aborted female foetuses in glass jars.

Today, all this has been declared illegal. There's the officiously termed nationwide law, the Pre-natal Diagnostic Techniques (Regulation and Prevention of Misuse) Act 1994, to prove that.

The ads and the glass jars may have disappeared but they are not needed anymore. If there is one thing that is universally known, across every caste and community grouping in Haryana, it is the fact that sex determination test facilities are freely available.

Of course, now that it is illegal, the test is more discreetly conducted and is more expensive too. A young doctor explains, "When Bansi Lal had declared prohibition in Haryana, liquor was freely available, but at a premium. It's the same thing now. Earlier you could have got this test done for a few hundred rupees. Now you would have to pay something like Rs. 800 for it. They don't put anything down on paper, of course, but who can stop anyone from verbally informing someone about the sex of her unborn child?"

Kamlesh, another women's activist, believes that things have never been this bad. "Earlier there was a guilt about it. Now it is seen as a matter of choice. People say it's better to do this rather than bring unwanted girls into the world. Doctors justify it in the name of family planning.

A Rohtak-based imaging expert puts it this way. "Every day, I have to turn away at least three patients who come to me and say, "Test karna hain". He looks nervously around him and whispers, "Just across the road from me is this gentleman who is raking in cash doing this. Believe me, in places like Panipat, they offer to tell you the sex of your child after 10 weeks of pregnancy, even though it is a scientific fact that there is no discernible organ development at this stage."

He warms up to his theme, "Mark my words, the practice is so widespread that we don't kill cats and dogs as often as we destroy female children."

The Indian Express, April 16, 2001

Girls vanish, Haryana Men Hardpressed for Brides

— *Pamela Philipose*

Bringing up your daughter, so goes Haryanvi peasantspeak, is like watering a plant in your neighbour's courtyard. For women, verbal whiplashes of this kind are part of daily life.

Anyone in Haryana can reel them off: *Ladka mare nirbhag ka, ladki mare bhagyavan ki* - if your son dies you are cursed, if your daughter dies you are blessed. It seems the whole family's honour is dependent on male progeny.

Expressions such as *Jitne ladke, utne haat* - the number of sons you have is the number of hands you have - could well be throwback to the days when life was rough in this region.

Delhi-based social historian Prem Chowdhry, author of *Veiled Women - Shifting Gender Equations in Rural Haryana from 1880 to 1990*, believes the region's economy went through some upheavals during colonial rule.

"When famines were frequent, male progeny were regarded as valuable. Whether female infanticide took place or not is not certain, but clearly there was widespread femicide. Women and girls died – of neglect," she says.

The pattern persists to this day. Jagmati Sangwan, of the Janwadi Mahila Samiti, says: "Women's workload, especially in rural areas, is enormous. Changes in farm technology have added to her burden because many jobs once handled by men - such as *buggy chalana* (riding the buffalo cart) - are being done by women now."

What Sangwan finds amazing is that despite a woman's crucial role in the family and local economy, her social status is still pathetic. It's a process of devaluation that seems to be linked with property rights and inheritance practices. Several states have, in fact, tried to make laws curbing a woman's right to inherit land.

On paper, a daughter is entitled to an equal share of her father's property. In reality, any daughter who tries to assert the right is socially pilloried. *Ghar thodne ka kaam kar rahi hain* (she is breaking up the house) is the general view.

Haryana has seen no significant social movements to counter these prejudices. Rohtak's district magistrate R. K. Khullar explains: "For some reason, the state has been unfortunate with its voluntary sector. The total Literacy Movement has not had half the effect here as it has had in neighbouring Rajasthan."

So insidious has been the devaluation process that women themselves have largely internalised it. Since it is only through their sons that they gain social status, they become accomplices in devaluing their sex.

Surinder Nagpal, a Rohtak-based physician who with his wife runs a flourishing practice in the heart of Rohtak town, believes that in traditional Jat society men don't want to acknowledge they can be infertile. "It is the woman who is blamed for everything - from infertility to the inability to produce a male child. Sometimes, this is taken as a sanction to marry again."

His gynaecologist wife, Anila Nagpal, describes her average patient: "Women here are generally severely anaemic. They are nervous and won't talk about their problems, especially if they are with their mothers-in-law. They'll say something innocuous like 'I have stomach pain'. Then I'll have to ferret out information."

According to Anila, several patients tell her privately they have no problem with bearing a daughter, but their lives would be made miserable if they failed to produce a son. "If it's their second or third daughter, life can become truly impossible. I don't keep an ultrasound because the pressure to get the tests done is enormous," she says.

In fact, earlier, people would seek sex determination tests after they have had a couple of daughters. Now, they want to know the child's sex from the first pregnancy.

Many believe that such indiscriminate female foeticide will have dangerous social consequences. Reports are already trickling in about how unemployed young men in the state find it difficult to get married. From all indications, the search for brides will get tougher as time passes.

M. K. Bishnoi, senior medical officer, Rohtak's Civil Hospital, believes that brides will be unavailable in the future. "Think of a society where there are fewer women? Think of the consequences. Won't crimes increase? Won't society lose out somewhere?"

The Indian Express, April 17, 2001

As government falters, Haryana girls strike out on their own

— Pamela Philipose

Somewhere along the road from Delhi to Rohtak, one comes across unending herds of emaciated, heavily horned cattle, ambling aimlessly in a haze of dust, almost oblivious to the prods of their red-turbaned minders who dance in and out of the masses of horns and hooves.

Unlike this apparition from neighbouring drought-hit Rajasthan, Haryana appears almost prosperous. Today, its wheat has been harvested and the newly shorn fields stretch on, pockmarked with small industrial units.

But paradoxes are part of life here, as recent census data reveals. Only 77.55 per cent of households have toilets and 78 per cent are dependent on firewood and cowdung for cooking fuel. But demographers are most worried with its population that is galloping at a rate far higher than the national – 28.06 per cent compared with the national 21.34 per cent.

A study by the Rohtak-based research centre, SEARCH, four years ago showed that families here continue to have children until they have enough surviving sons. So small families have more sons and large families have more daughters. There are women who have gone through six to nine pregnancies just to bear one or two sons.

Some medical practitioners have seized upon the trend to justify female foeticide. They argue it is better than allow unwanted girls to swell the family size. But this is a perverse argument that does little to contain the burgeoning numbers.

Says Rohtak's district commissioner R. K. Khullar: "We have realised that managing family size and discouraging female foeticide have to be addressed in a holistic fashion. Mere legislation and seeking ban on sex determination tests are not enough. To this day, no one has been booked for this crime. Social engineering via legislation can't take you far."

That's why, Khullar says, Haryana has tried to follow the total reproductive health approach. "We now provide money to panchayats to transport pregnant women in rural areas to hospitals. We are trying to strengthen community health centres to handle emergencies and perform caesareans. The idea is to encourage people to have planned families,"

Incidentally, in 1994, Haryana came up with the "Apni Beti Apna Dhan" scheme which provides Rs. 500 for every infant girl born to families below the poverty line within 15 days of delivery.

An amount of Rs. 2,500 is invested in Indira Vikas Patra certificates and given to parents. At 18, if the girl is unmarried and has passed the class V exams, she is entitled to Rs. 27,000. But no one knows how effective this scheme has been. There are suspicions too that corruption has rendered it ineffectual. Yet pressure is building on state authorities to act. Even before the latest census figures came in, Chief Minister Om Prakash Chautala issued a "special message" to his compatriots.

In flowery language that extolls the virtues of motherhood, it reminded people that sex determination is illegal and both sons and daughters should be welcomed as God's gift. Today, the message hangs outside the ultrasound rooms of public hospitals as a small flag of good intention.

And the recent census data has called for stronger action. So the Haryana health department has directed all its civil surgeons to step up vigil on private clinics in their districts and stop sex determination tests. But the real hope for the future lies in women themselves. Says women's activist Jagmati Sangwan: "In our cities and smaller towns, young women now want to study and earn. They may be the first woman in the family to complete the 10th standard exams, but they want to do an employment-oriented diploma. They tell me they want to learn computers."

In the state where only 2.29 per cent of the people study up to graduation and beyond and only 0.51 per cent have technical education, these aspirations are valuable. They speak of change. The sight of teenage girls, astride bicycles, making their way through the streets echoes the change.

The Indian Express, April 17, 2001

Akal Takht to crack down on foeticide

— Dharmendra Rataul

Concern over the growing cases of female foeticide among Sikhs in Punjab has been voiced by none other than the highest temporal seat of the religion. Observing that the practice was against the Sikh Rehat Maryada, the Akal Takht said today it would issue directives on the subject.

Terming foeticide as violative of the tenets of Sikhism, the Jathedars said serious efforts should be made to restrict this practice.

"Women have always held a position of esteem in Sikh society. The practice of killing the girl child should be condemned at any cost," said Jathedar Giani Joginder Singh Vedanti. His PA, Prithipal Singh Sandhu, said the clergy would issue a formal statement on the issue on April 17. The Akal Takht would issue "instructions for Sikh society to say no to the killing of the girl child".

According to the Sikh Rehat Maryada, "No Sikh will have any type of relation with the one who kills a girl child. This principle should be enforced in the true spirit of the Gurmat to restrain the decreasing population of girls which had disturbed the sex ratio here," pointed out Vedanti.

The Indian Express, April 18, 2001
Editorial

Beyond the ban

Only by enabling women can female foeticide be prevented ?

The skewed child sex ratio, specifically in the Haryana-Punjab belt, as revealed in early census estimates, has caused widespread disquiet in both states. Since the trend clearly points to rampant female foeticide, authorities in Punjab and Haryana now plan to step up their vigilance against the misuse of sex-determination tests. In Punjab, the highest seat of Sikh religious authority, the Akal Takht, even has plans to issue instructions to Sikhs everywhere to socially boycott those who adopt such heinous practices. Such responses may have come at least two decades too late because this trend has long been manifesting itself in the region. But they are, nevertheless, welcome. Certainly, those who exercise a moral or pedagogic influence on society must raise their voices to address a problem that just doesn't seem to go away: the social devaluation of girl children.

The selective abortion of female foetuses is, of course, not unique to India. It is well known that one of the consequences of China's one child policy, first introduced in 1979, was the dramatic decline - observed some ten years later - in the number of girls born there. But this doesn't mean that India can afford to pretend that the steady decimation of its girl children is a normal feature of life. The big question facing Indian administrators is whether legislation seeking to ban the misuse of sex-determination tests can make a difference. Unfortunately not. In 1994, the Pre-natal Diagnostic Techniques (Regulation and Prevention of Misuse) Act - a national -

level legislation - came into force. To date, not a single conviction has been made under it. As reported by this newspaper recently, all that the law seems to have done is to drive the business of sex-determination tests underground. Imaging experts in Haryana pointed out that the results of ultrasound tests may not be set down on paper any more, but there is no way any government can stop a medical practitioner from revealing the sex of the foetus to those who seek such information and pay handsomely for it. Indeed, the two premier regulatory bodies of the medical community in the country - the Indian Medical Association and the Medical Council of India - had, in 1999, launched a collective all India drive against the practice and even threatened to revoke the licences of those who performed these tests. To little avail, alas, What has clearly provided a fillip to the trade is ultrasound technology, which first came into widespread use in the early nineties. Not only did it make the tests safer and more foolproof, it made their administration much easier.

This seems to suggest that while the proper regulation of ultrasound facilities, and the like, is vital, this by itself will not address the phenomenon of female foeticide. What is also required is a multi-pronged approach to safeguard and extend the rights of girls and women. These rights include the right to proper nutrition and health care, the right to at least eight years of schooling, the right not to be married at an age below the legally prescribed one and the right to

inherit an equal share of parental property. In other words, to ensure that female foetuses are not aborted, the nation must also ensure that a woman's life chances are not aborted.

The Pioneer, April 20, 2001

Jathedar's Warning to Sikhs

Female Foeticide Guilty to be Declared 'TANKHAIYA'

— Reeta Sharma
Chandigarh

Jathedar of Akal Takht Joginder Singh Vedanti declared that female foeticide was against Sikh tenets and violative of the Sikh "Rehat Maryada". He warned that any one indulging in this crime against the girl child would be declared a "tankhaiya" (guilty of religious misconduct) and would be excommunicated.

This stern message follows close on the heels of the Census-2001 provisional figures revealing sharp decline in male-female ratio in Punjab as well as Haryana, causing an imbalance in the population that portends danger singnals for the society.

Besides, the Jathedar is reported to have received innumerable complaints of many a sensitive Sikh that a large number of Sikhs are indulging in female foeticide. It was a clear writing on the wall that the Sikhs, both in rural and urban areas, were drawn towards newly-opened sex determination clinics.

The results, by and large, pushed the families to indulge in female foeticide primarily because of overwhelming "son-fixation synd-rome". In fact, The Pioneer was the first, on April 9, to have pointed out that the Sikhs were not following Sikh Rehat Maryada, when so evidenlty indulging in killing girl foetus.

There is no denying the fact that the Hindus too in Punjab –despite being under the influence of Sikhism – were denying the right of the girl child even to be born by opting for the abortion.

The Pioneer report had quoted a message from the Sikh Rehat Maryada published by the Shiromani Gurdwara Prabandhak Committee (SGPC), under the sub-title – Gurmat di rehni" (life as ordained by the teaching of the Gurus) – where it has mentioned dos and don'ts for a Sikh, including "Guru ka Sikh kanya na mare, kuri maar nal na varte" (A Guru's Sikh should neither kill a girl nor have relationship with one who kills a girl). The report had further quoted the sex ratio figures to substantiate the hypothesis of declining ratio between males and females. As per the census-2001, the sex ratio had been continuously rising from 1,911 to 1,991 showing declining trend only after 80 years.

It is shocking to note that Punjab ranks 29th amongst all States and Union Territories in the country when it comes to the sex ratio figures.

The Pioneer, April 21, 2001

Progressive Edict

The edict issued by the Jathedar of the Akal Takht against female foeticide is welcome. Religious leaders, who have great influence with their communities, must be more pro-active in pushing socially beneficial issues. The keepers of tradition must align with progressive social forces. By so doing, the religious establishment can ensure that it remains a socially relevant and progressive force. For too long, there has been a tendency among representatives of religions, to align with forces that are inimical to progress. The Catholic establishment, for instance, was instrumental in banning of Martin Scorcese's 'The Last Temptation of Christ'. Similarly, Rajiv Gandhi's Government caved in to pressure from the Muslim clergy and banned Salman Rushdie's 'Satanic Verses'. It is heartening that the Sikh clergy has alinged with progress, taking note of Census statistics showing a declining female component in male-female sex ratio in the country after 80 years. Punjab's 29th position among states and union territories in terms of an adverse female component must reflect a growing tendency in North India towards aborting female foetuses. It is incumbent on the agencies of the state to enforce the existing laws banning the use of a legitimate technology, amniocentesis, for instance, to snuffing out the life of female foetuses.

Though equality and reserva-tions for women in legislatures are much talked about, the continued killing of female foetuses indicates the orientation of the Indian mindset which is conditioned by the norms established by a patriarchal society. Patriarchy in India is still, unfortunately, trapped in the rubric of a semi-feudal social structure, which is deeply exploitative and suppressive when it comes to the assertion of the rights of women. Though the issue of empowerment of women seems to be central, in many ways, to academic and semi-academic discourses, the reality on the ground seems to stubbornly neglect the concerns of the urban elites. To some extent, this is because of the fact that the Nehruvian elite of post-Independent India has been content to perpetuate its own status and not bothered about spreading the values associated with modernity among the people at large.

But in the context of globalisation and much less restricted information flows, the killing of female foetuses cannot be suppressed for much longer. Not long ago, a study done by the noted economist and winner of the Nobel prize, Dr. Amartya Sen, had compared Kerala, China and North India, and had also shown how a balanced sex-ratio, to be achieved by state initiative that accounts for "missing woman" is somewhat misplaced. It is more important, in developing societies, to take care of and empower the women who are very much "there", and in the grip of severely exploitative situations. To be sure, there is no dearth of non-govermental organisations championing the cause of exploited woman. Unfortunately, their circle of influence is limited. At this point, the coming forward of a religious leader in the cause of unborn girls, which can go a long way towards ameliorating the lot of exploited women in our society, was long overdue. The Jathedar's move must be widely lauded.

The Tribune, April 21, 2001

Akal Takht on Girl-Child

Alarmed at the increasing imbalance in the male-female ratio, as revealed by the latest census, in the region an NGO has sought the intervention of the Punjab and Haryana High Court. The Voluntary Health Association of Punjab evidently belives that only judicial intervention can arrest the trend of the decline in the female population in Punjab, Haryana and even Himachal Pradesh. It is indeed true that the introduction of the Prenatal Diagnostic Techniques, [Regulation and Prevention of Misuse] Act, 1994, has failed in its objective of putting an end to the revolting practice of female infanticide. However, the judiciary can only express its displeasure over the tardy enforcement of the law against infanticide. It cannot play the role of an enforcement agency. It is the lack of the political will to act which is responsible for the sharp drop in the number of the females in the country. Private clinics not only in the region but elsewhere in the country continue to defy the law against conducting what in popular parlance is called sex determination test for finding out the gender of unborn baby. The female child, thereafter, is destroyed in the womb, putting in the process even the life of the luckless mother in jeopardy. However, there is now a ray of hope at least for the members of the Sikh community. In what is path-breaking initiative, the five head priests of the Akal Takht have declared the practice of killing the girl-child as "bajjar kurahit" (unpardonable sin).

What the highest spiritual seat of the Sikhs has issued is not a request but a stern directive to all the followers of the faith. Those found violating the order against infanticide would be excommunicated from the panth. The directive from the Akal Takht is likely to be taken more seriously than the threat of punishment under the provisions of the Act against sex determination tests. The five head priests deserve the gratitude of the entire nation for their positive stand on the issue. But the situation among other communities is as serious because of the centuries-old bias against women which is reflected in the sharp drop in the female population in the country. Community and religious leaders from among the Hindus and Muslims too should raise their voice against the pernicious custom of killing the girl-child.

The Times of India, April 20, 2001

India's missing women, the product of official apathy

— *Jan Swasthya Abhiyan*

The 2001 Census reveals that there has been a dramatic drop in child sex ratios (0-6 year olds) in the states of Punjab, Haryana, Delhi, Gujarat, Chandigarh and Maharashtra as compared to the 1991 Census, Punjab has an alarming ratio of 793 girls per thousand boys. These were the states where the private foetal sex determination clinics were first established and the practice of selective abortion of female foetuses become popular in the late 1970s and early '80s. Even southern states such as Karnataka, Tamil Nadu and Andhra Pradesh have shown a decline in child sex ratios. The drops in this Census are less than in the northern states as the sex determination clinics emerged in the south only a decade after they became popular in the north. The emergence and spread of the prenatal sex determination clinics are the early warning signals for the distortion of sex ratios at birth in the coming decade following selective elimination of girl foetuses.

The People's Health Assembly (PHA) held in Calcutta in November 2000 was a collective effort of 18 major networks of organisations in the country. Jan Swasthya Abhiyan, which has been launched following the PHA, organised a dialogue on the challenges of sex selective abortion (female foeticide) at Rohtak, Haryana on April 14-15, 2001. Delegates of 8 states right from Jammu & Kashmir to Tamil Nadu were involved. Women's organisa-tions, researchers, medical professio-nals, trade unionists, media representatives and NGOs participa-ted in the deliberations. This event is significant in that it involved participants who have been warning the government and the public for nearly a decade about this impending disaster. They have been highlighting the lack of ethics in the medical profession and the almost complete lack of enforcement of the 1994 national law against prenatal sex determination.

The drop in child sex ratios is a reflection of the worsening status of women in our country. Regrettably, the 1994 Prenatal Diagnostic Technologies

(Prevention and Regulation of Misuse) Act (PNDT Act) has not been implemented in these states. For instance, the National Advisory Committee has not been meeting every six months as mandated by the Act and the Appropriate Authorities in almost all the districts have not been constituted by the states as of June 2000. The National Appropriate Authority has not taken effective steps for even the registration of all ultrasound machines. Prenatal sex determination tests are a basic human rights violation. Female foeticide must be seen as one manifestation of gender violence against women. Further, efforts aggressively to implement various Acts such as the Medical Termination of Pregnancy Act, Dowry Act etc., which protect women's rights must, also be taken up. The campaign against prenatal sex determination is not part of the campaign against abortion. The right to abortion is an essential right of women. While population policy documents in the country may not be explicitly promoting sex determination, in actual reality a significant part of the decline in growth rates is caused by selective elimination of girl foetuses in parts of the country where female foeticide has received widespread legitimacy. Family welfare policies should endeavour to attain a demographic transition to lower fertility rates with gender equity. Otherwise, the current emphasis solely on population stabilisation would lead to a serious decline in child sex ratios in other parts of the country also.

Given the enormity of sex selective abortion, the following steps should be taken as a matter of official policy -

- The government should effectively implement the 1994 PNDT Act. The Appropriate Authority of the Act should urgently take steps to notify the state governments to register all ultrasound machines as today ultrasound has become the most common technology abused for sex determination.

- The government should file criminal cases immediately against medical professionals, scan operators and clinic owners who violate the PNDT Act. Particularly, those who advertise prenatal sex determination should be identified and prosecuted. Regulatory authorities such as the Medical Council of India should take action against the erring Doctors.

- The government should urge professional medical associations such as the Indian Medical Association (IMA) and other specialist medical organisations to get their members to register their ultrasound machines and monitor their use. Regrettably, even prominent IMA members such as national office bearers and even the Delhi health minister have not taken the lead in getting ultrasound machines registered.

- The government should vigorously publicise the PNDT Act, highlight the value of the girl child and sensitise society. The national population policy should explicitly state that population stabilisation should be attained without distortions in sex ratio at birth.

☀ All government programmes for the welfare of the girl child and women should be implemented vigorously to reduce and eliminate gender biases. The long-standing demands for women's organisations of equal wages for women, property rights and social security measures should be immediately enforced.

What the law say....

The Prenatal Diagnostic Techniques (Regulation and Prevention of Misuse) Act, 1994 came into force from January 1, 1996.

Main provisions:

☀ Prohibition of the misuse of prenatal diagnostic techniques for determining the sex of the foetus leading to female foeticide.

☀ Prohibition of advertisement of prenatal diagnostic techniques for determination of sex.

☀ Permission and regulation of the use of prenatal diagnostic techniques for the purpose of specific genetic abnormalities or disorders.

☀ Permitting the use of such techniques only under certain conditions by registered institutions.

☀ Under no circumstances are these techniques to be used to determine the sex of the foetus. (S.6) (This includes ultrasono-graphy)

☀ No person conducting prenatal diagnostic procedure (under S.4) shall communicate to the pregnant women concerned or her relatives the sex of the foetus by words, signs or in any other manner.

☀ An Appropriate Authority shall take note of violations.

But there are loopholes....

☀ The understanding of pre-natal sex selection being an act of violence has been given up and a narrow interpretation of the Act is being forwarded, which gives a licence to all doctors to conveniently adopt this technique without the fear of law.

☀ Under the new PGD technique, sperm can now be processed in a laboratory to separate XX and YY chromosomes, ensuring the birth of a boy. Thus, sex selection takes place pre-natally, in this instance even before conception.

☀ A Union health ministry letter of February 2, 1999, states, "The (PNDT) Act relates to testing in a pregnant woman. The question of pre-conceptual sex planning is not covered by this Act".

☀ There are wide spread advertisements by various clinics providing prenatal sex selection.

Sources of Data

CENSUS OF INDIA 2001, SERIES 1, INDIA, PROVISIONAL POPULATION TOTALS, Paper –1 of 2001.

SERIES –3, HIMACHAL PRADESH, PROVISIONAL POPULATION TOTALS, Paper – 1 of 2001.

SERIES –4, PUNJAB, PROVISIONAL POPULATION TOTALS, Paper – 1 of 2001.

SERIES –5, CHANDIGARH, PROVISIONAL POPULATION TOTALS, Paper – 1 of 2001.

SERIES –7, HARYANA, PROVISIONAL POPULATION TOTALS, Paper – 1 of 2001.

SERIES –8, DELHI, PROVISIONAL POPULATION TOTALS, Paper – 1 of 2001.

SERIES –25, GUJARAT, PROVISIONAL POPULATION TOTALS, Paper – 1 of 2001.

SERIES –28, MAHARASHTRA, PROVISIONAL POPULATION TOTALS, Paper – 1 of 2001.

ALSO

ASHISH BOSE, DEMOGRAPHIC DIVERSITY OF INDIA, 1991 CENSUS, STATE AND DISTRICT LEVEL DATA, Supplement 1998.

CENSUS OF INDIA 1991, SERIES 1, INDIA, Paper – 1 of 1994, REPORT ON POST ENUMERATION CHECK.